EDIFIED

Marissa Gail Fike

Romans 14:19 NKJV

Edified

Marissa Sail Fike

Honeybush Press

Cover design by: Called and Chosen Co.

ISBN: 9781736890301

Dear Reader,

To borrow the viewpoint of one of my characters, I don't believe it's by mere chance or happenstance that this book somehow ended up in your hands. Whether you selected it from the library bookshelves, borrowed it, found it, or simply heard it calling your name from its place in the bookstore, I believe that your choosing to take it home was a very guided decision, and that God must have something great in store for you. Whether you are just discovering the joys of God's ways or you are a seasoned believer, I hope you will see this book as God's love letter to you. There's something He wants you to know or be assured of, and when you discover it, I can't wait to hear what it is! Connect with me on Instagram @m.sail.f!

Abundant blessings,

Marissa Sail Fike

1

Grace - Tuesday

"What do you think about this one?"

My best friend, Rae, angles her phone for me to see. A sparkly diamond necklace displays proudly on the screen, forming the shape of a heart at the bottom. It's stunning and positively everything she's been looking for, except for the price tag. My eyes flick down to the hefty collection of numbers beneath the picture and my smile fades.

"Better check those digits."

Rae turns the screen back and her gaze settles on the price.

"Ooh," She winces, "Adam would kill me."

I scroll down my own screen, tapping a picture of another necklace. It looks like a cheap version of the one we were just looking at, but maybe it's worth settling on for a grand total of $12.95.

I pass my phone to Rae and she considers the image.

"I mean, it definitely looks fake," she says, "But I could sure use the several hundred dollar discount."

The barista arrives with our drinks and a brown paper bag.

"One Vienna Latte and one chai tea," She says setting them down on our table, "And *this* is my treat."

The paper bag crinkles as she sets it down in front of me. I didn't even order it, but I know what's inside.

I clutch my heart and give her the biggest smile, "Ava, you're truly the best."

She shrugs and waves me off.

Ava is my long-standing, favorite barista employed at *Aroma Mocha Café,* and I purposefully come in Tuesdays when I know she'll be working the evening shift.

I open the paper bag and allow the warm scent of cinnamon to swirl into the air, breathing it in with an unreasonable amount of pleasure.

Rae laughs at me from across the table as I pull the steaming cinnamon bun from the bag and set it down on a napkin.

"So what do you think about writing personal vows?" Rae asks, taking a sip of coffee.

I sit back in my seat, letting my treats cool down.

"I mean, personally, I think traditional vows cover all the bases, but it's totally up to you. Your wedding."

She nods, "I definitely thought about writing personal ones, but I think it might be more special if we shared our personal vows with just each other later, you know? Just pure one-on-one authenticity."

"Right," I smile, absentmindedly fiddling with the string on my tea bag.

Rae had recently gotten engaged to her boyfriend of two years, Adam Compton. Naturally, being best friends since Freshman year of high school, she asked me to be her maid of honor, which meant weekly brainstorming sessions at one of our places, or in this case, The Café. Rae's only ever had one other boyfriend

— Samuel Ross — and it was just a casual relationship during our Sophomore year. I've never seen anyone light up her world the way Adam does, though. She's never really been the type to gush over someone she liked, but these days it's not abnormal to catch her smiling into nothingness thinking about her fiancé. The man of her dreams.

"I'm really so happy for you and Adam," I smile, taking the last bite of my sacred pastry, "How'd you get so lucky, Ms. Brooks?"

Her eyes glaze over with that dreamy expression as she rests her chin on her hands, "You know, I really don't know. I've never met a guy so sweet, capable, and loyal at the same time."

As soon as she says it, her smile fades. Her eyes lock with mine and suddenly the once comforting taste of cinnamon in my mouth tastes like nothing at all.

"I'm sorry. I didn't mean to ..."

I swallow, "No, it's fine. Don't worry about it."

I try to give her a smile, but she doesn't look convinced.

"Just because Jayden wasn't loyal doesn't mean Adam isn't allowed to be," I sigh, "In fact, I would be pretty concerned if you thought he wasn't."

The abundance of bracelets gracing her wrists jingle as she reaches for my hand across the table. She doesn't say anything, and she doesn't need to. Everything that needed to be said had already been covered about a week ago when I called her crying about the break up.

She gives my hand a squeeze, "Are the pills I gave you helping?"

I nod, rubbing my temple, "I try not to take them ... but those first couple of nights, it was a necessity, you know?"

She smiles sadly, "I do."

I try to pull off a genuine smile while reaching for my phone, "Let's get back to this necklace shopping, shall we?"

She nods, "We've gotta be getting close."

* * *

Rae and I bonded for the simplest reason when we were younger, and that's that neither of us liked our actual first names. I agreed to call her by her middle name instead, and she agreed to shorten mine to Grace instead of Gracelynn. Personally, I always thought she had the most whimsical name, like something a famous country singer might have.

Lacey Rae Brooks – Soon to be Lacey Rae Compton.

The change in her last name kind of ruins the celebrity effect in my opinion, but I would never tell her that. In the same respect, she wouldn't tell me that Jayden's last name never fit right with my first name. Regardless of how many different fonts I wrote it in my notepad, Gracelynn Brielle Grayson just didn't sound right any way you slice it. It was far too much like that character in "*The Wedding Singer*" who's first name was Julia, who was marrying a man with the last name of Gulia. Julia Gulia and Gracelynn Grayson. I'd have been better off just sticking to my maiden name if Jayden and I worked out the way I always thought we would.

My mind takes every opportunity to think about what could've been between us, especially when I'm alone at home for the day. I thought for sure that September fifteenth, our fourth anniversary, would be the day he'd pull out the sparkly ring that'd seal our love forever. It'd be the ring I've had pinned to my Pinterest for years now, and always made sure to show him. I'd been anticipating it for months actually – to the point of getting my nails salon-ready the day before. That way, the hidden photographer he'd hire would capture the prettiest pictures of my hands covering my mouth in surprise, wrapping around him in an adoring squeeze, and finally, receiving the ring. The idea had been rehearsed in my head so many times, it almost felt real.

But the fact is, it *wasn't* real. Sure, I'd gotten the surprise of a lifetime ... but one that devastated my heart in a way I never thought possible. I recall the pictures of *her* vividly in my mind ... her long silken hair ... her exquisite curves.

I absentmindedly reach for Amity, my cat, and pull her onto my lap. She lets out a yowl of protest, but allows me to run my fingers through her fur as we watch the TV blankly. We're supposed to be watching some nature documentary about butterfly migrations, but my mind just wants to think about Jayden.

He shouldn't still mean as much to me as he does. *I* broke up with *him* after all. But it's hard to undo four years of your life with someone.

We had made so many plans together and shared so many dreams. I had our wedding colors picked out, we had agreed on names for children, and we had decided where we were going to live. We even had a joint savings account for our goals (which, unfortunately, I had to withdraw my portion from that very day).

I have to say, the most common misconception about breakups is that the person initiating it no longer has feelings for the other person. I was a crying, sobbing mess when I broke it off with Jayden, and even then I was hoping he would somehow procure the magic words that would fix everything and undo what he'd done. Then we could go back to being the happy couple I thought we were.

I know I did the right thing, ending the relationship. You can't have any sort of connection with someone who lies to you. But separating myself from him is still one of the hardest things I've had to do. *Everything* reminds me of him. The songs on the radio, certain places we had deemed 'our spot' — hell, even certain scents ignite my feelings for him.

My throat begins to swell, and I squeeze Amity a little too hard. She growls at me and jumps down from my lap.

I squint at her from across the room, "I could've gotten a dog, you know, but I settled for your sorry self instead."

She slowly blinks her eyes at me.

"A dog wouldn't leave me in my time of need." I add.

At that, she stands and casually strolls out of the room.

As ridiculous as I know I'm being, the swell in my throat increases in size as I stare at the TV screen, tears brimming. A cloud of colorful butterflies fills the screen, on a mission to get somewhere. They flutter in unison across an ocean, across a field, and across a highway. I point my remote at the screen and click the *off* button.

I'm wallowing and I know it. I need to do something productive to get my mind off of self-pity.

I quickly wipe my eyes and force myself off the couch. I glance around the room at the various stacks of objects that need to be sorted through.

This house used to be my Grandma Jackie's before it was mine. When she passed away a couple years ago, my mother, being her only child, inherited the house. She has allowed me to live in it for the past year rent-free, under the condition that I neaten it up and make it look new again.

Just as I'm about to get started on a stack of old dishware, my phone vibrates in my pocket. I glance down at the screen before accepting the call.

Aunt Kim.

"What's up?" I say, suppressing the crack in my voice.

"Hey girl, what are you doing?"

"Sorting through Grandma's stuff," I smile, "I'm almost done, I swear."

Kim is not really my aunt. She's actually my mom's cousin. But she and I have always been super close, and for some reason, I always used to insert the *'aunt'* status before her name when I was a baby.

She snorts, "I can't believe it's taken you almost the entire year you've been there."

I switch ears, propping the phone between my cheek and shoulder as I sort through the plates with my freed hands. "Year and a *half,* actually. And really? Are you *actually* surprised? This is Grandma's stuff we're talking about."

She laughs, "You're right. She always was kind of a hoarder."

Or a *Collector of Many Things,* as I liked to call her.

"I can't believe Corinne hasn't been out there to claim some of her mom's old stuff yet." Kim says, referring to my mother.

"Eh," I say, "Not exactly the sentimental type."

"Excuses," Kim snuffs, "The truth is simple. She doesn't have time for much of anything anymore since she got that nursing degree. Even the super important things like coming to visit her dear cousin Kimmy. How is that going for her, by the way? Have you heard?"

"I don't know honestly. I haven't really heard from her."

When *was* the last time my mom and I talked anyway? As far as I know, she's loving her new job at Oakland Medical.

"I don't really mind doing this, though," I continue, "The sorting, I mean. Organizing things has always been kind of therapeutic for me."

"Girl," she laughs, "I don't know anyone else who'd enjoy that."

I smile, although I don't see why they wouldn't. There's something blissfully rhythmic about sorting items into methodical piles and finding suitable places for them. Plus, much like my grandmother was, I'm enamored with vintage things. So while I have made the space my own by adding my personal furnishings and decorative touches, I have also opted to keep a few of her things that I found interesting.

Her old vinyl record player, for example, and her sleek vintage typewriter. I can only imagine the numerous stories and love letters that have been conjured on that thing. Finding objects like that made digging through the piles worth my while, and it certainly provided a structured distraction from my mind's malicious thoughts of love lost and time wasted.

"Well," Kim says, "I won't keep you any longer. I just wanted to check in. Make sure you're okay and all that."

The lump in my throat surfaces again. Somehow knowing someone cares enough about my wellbeing to call and check up on me makes me emotional all over again. *God knows it's more than I could expect from my mother.*

"Thanks, Aunt Kim." I clear my throat, "I'm okay."

"Alright, girlie." She says, "I love ya. Organize away!"

"Love you," I say back before tapping *'end call'.*

I sort the last dish into the 'goodbye' bin before moving on to one of the last remaining piles. It mostly consists of books upon books.

I pull my hair back into a ponytail, although a few brown tendrils escape the elastic and fall down the frame of my face. I settle on my rug in front of the first pile, crossing my legs, and breathe in the pleasant aroma of old book pages.

I expel my breath with an involuntary smile and begin working.

The process gives me a strong feel for my grandmother's taste in literature, which turns out to be a far stretch from mine. She owned multiple editions of Pride and Prejudice, and every single *classic* there had to be written. My taste is definitely more modernized, but I'm still careful to flip open the covers of each book and check for any personal notes before discarding them into the reject box. I get into a good rhythm of sorting after realizing each of these books had to be either a classic or ancient — nothing I would want to salvage for myself. I fall into the pattern of *grab - open - check - discard,* and find peace in the consistency of it.

I carry on like this for at least half an hour until my hand reaches for the next book and finds a strange cover material and heavier weight settling into my palms.

I draw my eyes to the book in question and find that instead of the typical paperback or cardboard cover, the book I've grabbed is wrapped in thin leather and sealed with string. Its pages are thinner than regular paper, bordered with gold, and almost spilling out of the book's binding. On the cover, inscribed in gold lettering, are the words: *Holy Bible.*

I gently perch the book on my lap, staring at it for a moment. I know what the Bible is. I probably even have one somewhere around here ... but for some reason, the idea of *Grandma Jackie's* Bible has my interest piqued.

I bring my fingers to the delicate string that binds the book and carefully untie it, loosening its grip slowly so none of the pages fall out. With anticipation, I gently lift open the cover, releasing an invisible cloud of dust to unfurl in the air.

My eyes settle on the first page of the Bible and my heart thuds a little louder. On the page is a neat scrawling of cursive writing, saying,

This book is for you, my sweet Jacqueline Rose. It is a parallel study bible that has both the NIV and NKJV translations side by side. Live by it. Write in in the margins. Make it your own, and you will always be blessed. Love, Mom.

The first thing I noticed was the date in the top right corner of the page: *August 2, 1983* – Grandma Jackie's 35th birthday.

I scan the page several times over before bringing my hand to the right side of the book, bending it slightly and fanning through the pages. My eyes are greeted by a wave of color.

I open the book to a random page, right in the middle. I am greeted by a rainbow of highlighted scriptures and an overwhelming amount of handwriting in the margins. The top of the page says *Psalm* and Grandma Jackie's writing points with multiple arrows at a specific text.

I bring the book closer to my face and squint to see the tiny words.

He counts the number of the stars; He calls them all by name. Great is our Lord and mighty in power; His understanding is infinite.

I flip to the next page, which is equally crowded with color and ink, and then quickly to the next and the next, without reading what any of it says.

I snap the book shut, feeling a chill suddenly shake my body.

After a moment, I gently wind the string around the book and set it down on the coffee table. I stare at it for a minute as my breathing begins to steady again, and in the spirit of cleansing both my mind and my living space, resolve to place it in the discard box.

I don't even read the copy I have around here somewhere. I don't need another one.

In its new location of discarded books, I stare at the Bible a moment longer. It looks so … out of place.

Suddenly feeling guilty, I take the Bible from the rejects and place it back on the coffee table. This book meant something serious to Grandma Jackie. Probably more than her vinyl player or her typewriter ever did, and I always try to keep the things I know were special to her.

I stand and stretch my arms, the hem of my silk pajama pants hanging loosely on my hips. I turn the light out in the living room and head to my bedroom, not bothering to pick up Amity along the way. She watches me walk past her with what I could only describe as a look of contempt.

She waits until I've shaken out my hair, flipped on the diffuser, and I'm crawling into the covers before sauntering into the bedroom and jumping up on the bed. She curls up next to me, flicking her black tail against my shoulder.

"Oh, so now you want me?" I say running my fingers through her soft fur.

She purrs loudly beside me — a peace offering for being a jerk earlier.

I smile and close my eyes to the rhythmic sounds of her purring and the soft hum of the diffuser motor … but sleep doesn't find me.

I get up to add a few extra drops of lavender to the diffuser, but still, I lie awake for hours after.

Sighing, I reach over for the bottle of pills on my side table and tip one from the container into my palm. I hate doing this. I'd rather do anything than put unnatural chemicals in my body … but desperate times call for desperate measures.

As of the last week or so, thoughts of Jayden and everything that happened between us have kept me wide awake for hours. Tonight, however, something different is lingering in my mind.

Something about the words *"His understanding is infinite"* struck me, and won't allow my mind to shut off for the night.

About ten minutes later, I feel the pill begin doing its work. My muscles noticeably relax as a state of calm washes over me. As much as I hate traditional medicine, at this moment, I am only thankful.

2

Rae - Wednesday

Morning light spills through the cracks of my bedroom's window shades, casting thin lines of sunshine onto the bed. I lay on my side with my phone propped up, switching back and forth between two different text-font options for the wedding invitations I'm designing with my '*Invidesign*' app. The room's temperature outside of the covers is cool and crisp, just the way Adam likes it, but the level of warmth underneath the covers is just right for me.

Two strong arms, emanating heat, wrap themselves around my waist and pull me into a firm, masculine chest. A smile draws up the corners of my lips as Adam kisses the back of my head and nuzzles me, making it clear he has no intention of leaving any time soon. My body fits perfectly against him, his warm breath steady against my neck, and for the hundredth time this morning, I wonder how I got so lucky.

In our new position of cuddling, I tap my phone screen back on and continue editing the invitation draft. I've decided on a text-font. Now I just need to decide on a picture for the front of the invitation. The light of my phone screen must be disturbing him because he stirs behind me.

"Baby girl." He purrs, nipping at my ear.

I smile again, loving the way his voice sounds first thing in the morning.

"What are you doing?" He asks, his voice muffled against the pillow.

I shift slightly on my back so that I can show him the invitation I've been working on, "What do you think?"

He squints against the bright light to see the image on the screen. I admire the five o'clock shadow on his chin as he examines my work.

"Very nice, honey. Great job." He concludes with a smile.

How I love those beautiful white teeth.

"Okay, so my question is, should it be *this* picture?" I say, showing him one option before sliding the next one in its place, "Or *this* one?"

"Mmm," His voice rumbles in his chest, "Either one will do fine."

I pout my lips and turn more towards him, "Come on, I want a real opinion."

He sighs slightly, opening his eyes again to view the screen.

"The first one." He says, settling back down on the pillow.

I turn the screen back towards me and take a good look at his choice, trying to visualize how the invitation might look in person. It's a picture that we took on my phone's camera when we went to the beach together last summer. I squint at the photo. It's nice and all, but it definitely looks like it was taken selfie-style, and I'm starting to think we ought to just have professional engagement pictures taken. As much as I hate taking pictures, how many couples use a basic beach-selfie as the main picture on their *wedding* invitations? Also, if the picture was taken with my phone, would the quality be grainy on a paper-invite?

"Are you sure?" I say, peeking over at him, "Because it might be better to just wait until we have some professional pictures done."

He groans in reply and tries to pull me closer again, but I can't focus, because verbalizing what I've just said made me realize how urgently I need to book a photoshoot. Not only should I have had my invitations ordered by now, but also addressed and ready to be delivered. According to my wedding timeline planner, I'm pushing it as it is by ordering them so last-minute. And if I still need to book a session with a photographer before I can even finish *designing* the invitations, the situation just got dire. Photographers around here are booked out *months* in advance, and that doesn't account for the time they'll need after the shoot to edit all the pictures.

I escape Adam's grasp, toss the covers aside, and quickly reach for my bathrobe because the crisp room temperature is freezing against my bare skin.

"Babbbeee." Adam sighs, "Where are you going?"

"I have to call a photographer and try to book a session for us *this week.*" I say.

He sits up against the headboard and gazes at me, "Honey... the picture you showed me was fine."

"No," I say, sliding on my slippers, "It looks like a selfie that we took ourselves and the quality might show up poorly on the actual invitations."

I turn on my heels, on a mission to find Adam's Yellow Pages, but he catches my wrist and gently tugs me back. I involuntarily swivel around and fall back on the bed. He holds my face in the warmth of his palms, forcing me to meet his gaze — those alluring grey-green eyes.

"Lacey Rae, you have got to relax."

His voice and the gentle touch of his fingers tucking a lock of hair behind my ear has a strong, calming effect on my body.

The right corner of his lips raise in a half-smile, "Listen, love. You have seven whole months left to make this thing happen. Seven. Whole. Months."

He kisses my right cheek, then my left, then my forehead, "I promise there is enough time."

I nod, unable to take my eyes from him. The dim morning light accentuates the lines on his stomach and chest beautifully… His skin takes a golden tone in this light.

"Come here, beautiful." He says, pulling me closer to him, "I just need some time with you this morning."

My stress slowly melts away. Pressed against his skin, there's no place I'd rather be.

3

Grace - Wednesday

I pull my hair up into a messy bun and glance at myself in the mirror. My eyes fall to the black leggings hugging my calves. A loose, purple tank top with a pale pink lotus flower on the chest outlines my figure and flows over the curves of my hips. As I flick my eyes up and down the outfit, I consider changing into some actual yoga pants instead of the leggings.

It's unreasonable for me to second guess the perfectly flattering outfit, but ever since *it* happened, my cruel mind has marveled at my insecurities.

Your thighs are too thick for leggings. You'll look like you're desperate for attention if you go out in that.

I shake my head and bring my eyes back up to my face in the mirror, pushing my black-framed glasses back into place. I'd never been self-conscious of my body before, and I'd always embraced my curves. But that was before a much thinner, much more delicate looking girl caught the eyes of the man I loved.

Rae had shaken her head in amazement when I first opened up about my problem with comparing myself to that girl.

"Are you kidding me?" She'd said, "You're a babe! Hadley is an *unnatural* level of skinny. Don't you dare go comparing yourself to her."

I cringe at the memory of her name. Rae, of course, has never actually met the girl, and had been exaggerating for my benefit. The only reason Rae and I know anything of Hadley's looks is because of the pictures I found of her on Jayden's phone.

Maybe it was immature of me to compare myself, and who knows, Hadley *might just be* unnaturally skinny, but she'd apparently been good enough for Jayden where I hadn't been, and a part of me couldn't help but wonder *why*. Where was I lacking that Hadley was not?

I meet my own hazel eyes in the mirror, analyzing them. Maybe *they* are the problem. Maybe if they were just blue like Hadley's ...

I wrinkle my nose, disgusted with my own thoughts. Why do I torture myself like this? Isn't this the reason I joined a yoga group in the first place? To love and accept my body for what it is? To give my brain an outlet to think about something other than Jayden? To explore my interest in a new hobby that *I* enjoy for *myself*, not because it has anything to do with him?

I kneel to lace up my boots. This outfit is comfortable and will do just fine. If I would have felt fine wearing it when I was dating him, I should feel confident wearing it without him. He is *not* the source of my security.

I retrieve my keys and pull on a purple hoodie with the Nike symbol on it before heading out the door. It's been so long since I've worn anything but Jayden's hoodies that exploring my own closet's selection of sweaters and fall apparel was almost like a gift from myself, which is perfect timing with the forecast predicting icy fall weather to invade Vermont within the next couple of days. For now, warm sun spills from the sky shining against my beautiful Volkswagen, to whom I've affectionately given the name Persia.

I ignite the engine and Beyonce's, *"Irreplaceable"*, filters through the speakers. I crank the volume and roll my windows down, feeling a little better already. Sunrise yoga meets twice a week and I've only been to one class so far. It was Rae's suggestion to immerse myself in some activity just for myself. She'd gone with me the first time for moral support, but I know she's too busy to ask her to come with me regularly.

When I first walked into the studio, I had expected to find a group of hip young ladies striving for body positivity and discussing their fitness. But I was surprised to discover a room full of older ladies, none of whom could be under the age of fifty, gossiping about their husbands and competing with each other on whose body hurt the most on the daily. It isn't what I'd been expecting, but it certainly turned out to be entertaining, and the actual stretching session had successfully cleared my head for the most part.

"Grace!" the instructor — Nancy, I think — greets me as I walk through the door, "I'm glad to see you back."

I press my hands together and mirror the little bow she gives me, "I'm glad to be back."

I unlaced my shoes and placed them in one of the little cubbies to the left of the door. Everyone in the building walks around barefoot as some kind of respect thing that I don't understand, but it makes for a comfortable, homey sort of atmosphere.

The studio smells of synthetic Frankincense — a little sweeter smelling than the natural oil would be — but it is pleasant, nonetheless. I grab a mat from the shelf and enter the sanctuary.

"Well, hey pretty girl!" one of the old ladies calls from her spot on the floor, "Where's your friend today?"

I smile when I realize by 'pretty girl', she means me. Maybe these leggings aren't so awful after all.

"Rae?" I say, setting my mat down next to hers, "Oh, she's busy with wedding planning this time."

"Ooooh!" Another lady — Betty, who I remember from last time — scoots her mat closer to ours, "Let's see a picture of her young man!"

I smile, opening my phone to Rae's contact photo. It's one of my favorite pictures of them together at the beach last year. Ooh's and Ahh's ensue from the older ladies, who have now formed a circle around my phone to get a glimpse of Adam.

"Well, he sure is a handsome fella, isn't he?" One of them says.

"He's a sweetheart too," I smile, "I really like them together."

"I remember I used to have a beau like him." Betty comments, "A handsome, tall blonde with the kindest smile. He turned out to be a real skank, though. I tell you what, I carved my name right onto the front of his car."

I cup a hand to my mouth to keep from laughing.

"Girl, if I were you, I'd kick up some trouble now, so you have some good stories to tell when you're an old woman like me."

A middle-aged lady with brown hair nudges Betty, "Don't tell her that. I found enough trouble when I was her age without seeking it out."

The ladies continue to swap stories amongst themselves before the session begins. My mind wanders to all of the possible things this man could have done to Betty. I'm sure she'd tell me if I asked her, but then again I'm not all that sure that I'd want to know.

Maybe he'd done something similar to what Jayden did, and if that were the case, is it possible I let him off too easy? Is it possible that my reaction had been satisfying to him, rather than place-putting? Maybe he deserved to have my name carved into his shiny new car instead of being cried on and asked over and over why he did what he did.

Or maybe I should've acted like I didn't care — as if it was no sweat off my back that his shallowness would no longer be a part of my life. Instead, I had just let him know how much he hurt me, which I'm almost certain didn't even phase him since he allowed himself to betray my trust in the first place. I couldn't just hide my pain from the guy, though. I'd spent four whole years learning how to be vulnerable with him. I thought he valued that in me, but I guess it's just a lesson learned to be more careful with my heart next time.

My phone vibrates the way it does when I have a new Facebook notification. The class hasn't started yet, so I tap the screen to life.

A sudden wave of nausea roils in my stomach with so much force, I wonder for a moment if I'll need to get up and leave class to throw up. I had not yet taken care to 'unfollow' Jayden's Facebook posts, so my phone had sounded to alert me that he had posted a picture. That picture is of him giving the camera a thumbs up, while his other hand is occupied around the waist of a tall, skinny brunette clad in business attire. The girl isn't Hadley, but still a knock-out to say the least. His caption announces that he's been promoted to a higher position at his workplace, and once again, my gut twists. Why the hell are things going so right for him? What has he done to deserve that, while I'm left feeling alone and defenseless?

I force myself to push away thoughts of him. This place is supposed to be a sanctuary for my mind.

As class begins and we cross our legs into a meditative position, I remind myself that what I'm doing is right, and I'm handling it exactly as I should. Acting out and doing something vengeful would only tell him that I'm still thinking about him and what he did, and moreover, that I'm still letting it bother me. God knows *he's* clearly moved on.

They say that silence is sometimes the loudest response you can give someone, and I'm holding on to the hope that there may be some truth to that.

4

Rae - Wednesday

I sit cross legged on the yellow patterned rug in my room — the rug that is, in theory, supposed to make me feel happy. But at this moment, I feel anything but happy.

The yellow pattern is completely concealed by thirty or so sheets of paper, all of which are flowered around me and littered with red ink. At least half of the pages have hand-drawn frowny faces glaring back at me from the upper right corners, taunting me with their implications.

On the first day of this class, the whiteboard had three different faces drawn on it: A smiley face — or at least an attempt at one — a frowny face, and a face with a simple straight line for a mouth. Beside the corresponding faces, the words *satisfactory, unsatisfactory,* and *average* were written in boxy green letters.

Mr. Algray had straightened the stack of lecture papers in his hands before standing and passing them out to their respective owners. I remember his speech at the beginning of the class: "Your work will not receive any number grades for homework." He'd said, "This is not that kind of class. Instead, we'll be using the Smiley Face system to assess your improvement and let you know where you'll need more preparation for the tests."

A snort had escaped from the girl sitting next to me, "The Smiley Face system? Really?"

She'd articulated my own thoughts. I'd honestly rather get a number grade. At least then I'd know if I'm failing by a lot or just a little, and at least then my failure wouldn't feel so personal.

It wasn't a big deal at first — the frowny faces I was receiving. I felt like between my job, the wedding and my other school subjects, *trigonometry* homework that wasn't getting graded for real *certainly* wasn't a priority. I was also certain that if I really took the time to sit down for a few hours each day to focus on the homework, I'd be getting smiley faces returned to me. So in my mind, it was okay to slack on the homework as long as I took time to understand it later on. But now, with the semester almost halfway over and my midterm coming up, I'm not so sure this was the best approach.

Mr. Algray told us that the only things we need to ace are the midterm and the final. That way, he knows we've been listening all semester. Since the homework isn't getting any grades, he's making the midterm count for forty percent of our final grade and the final exam count for fifty percent. The other ten percent is reserved for attendance and professionalism which of course, I feel fine about, but you can't pass a class with ten percent total. He warned us that the tests will be extensive, and we need to be thoroughly prepared for them, as we will not be able to bring our books or any notes in the classroom.

This is usually the part where I am comforted by my carefully written notes taken throughout the semester because I know I can depend on them for studying purposes — but because of Mr. Algray's homework system, half of my note sheets are not filled out or are marked up in his red ink with no helpful explanation as to why.

So not only do I have to reckon with the idea that this test is coming up, but also that my messy, halfway-done, and ink-littered homework notes are all I have to work with, which is stressing me out to a new level tonight.

My phone whistles cheerfully at me in the midst of it all, playing the ringtone I've set for my mom.

I tap the green 'accept' icon and bring the phone to my ear, "Hey."

"Lacey, how are you honey?"

I rub my temple with my free hand. My mother refuses to call me by anything but my first name, which she has always adored.

My eyes flit over the papers around me, "I'm … making it."

"What's wrong, honey?" She says, "You sound upset."

"No, I'm fine. Just … managing some schoolwork."

"Oh, that reminds me! I keep meaning to ask you about how your classes are going."

"They're going," I begin collecting my frowny-face papers into a stack, "nothing's changed much there."

I know what she's going to say. Even through the silence I can hear her concern.

"You probably know this already sweetheart, but your scholarship —"

"I know." I say, trying to weave a smile into my words so she'll let it go.

I've called the school once already to confirm that I must make at least a B in trigonometry this semester, and an A in everything else in order to keep my scholarship: The one and only reason I'm able to go to college, currently.

My mother is silent on the other end of the line.

"What's up, mom?" I say, starting to get the feeling that she didn't just call to rag me about school.

"I just wanted to see if you'd be coming to A&B tonight." She says.

Oh.

I quickly search my brain to think of excuses that would get me out of attending *Above and Beyond,* the women's prayer and Bible study group in town.

"Everyone misses you there," she says, taking my silence as a cue to keep convincing me, "Kaya asks how you're doing almost every week. She told me she reached out to you a couple of times, but you never replied. She wants to know if you're okay."

"Please assure them that I'm doing fine," I say, remembering the three unread messages I have from Kaya, "Just busy with wedding stuff."

"You don't want to come on out and tell them yourself?" my mother persists.

I squeeze my eyes shut. I don't know how to tell her I don't want to attend A&B *at all* anymore without breaking her heart. I used to try to go once every few weeks for her sake, but for the last five months I haven't made it out there once.

"The topic tonight is supposed to be really good," She says, "And I miss you."

Her voice breaks my heart. It's full of so much hope. Hope that I'll go to this study group and suddenly convert my life into something better than it is — something more like my sister, Livia, who got married to a Christian man at the modest age of twenty-five and blessed my parents with their first grandchild one year later.

"Alright." I cave, "I'll be there."

"Great!" She cheers, "I'll see you at five!"

As soon as we end the call, my phone pings at me with a reminder from my calendar.

Wedding Dress fitting – Tomorrow. Thursday @ 9 am.

I frown, beginning to feel overwhelmed. Not only does it feel like the demands never stop rolling in, but I have been dreading the dress fitting for so long now. I don't know if I'm ready for the type of feelings that ride along with me each and every time I try on clothes.

My mind longs for the bottle of Xanax pills I gave Grace to help her sleep, but I push the thought out of my mind. For almost a year now, I've been using them very rarely. Only on an as-needed basis, so that I am reliant on nothing.

I hear my mother's voice ringing in the back of my mind. *You are stronger than you give yourself credit for.* I use her surety as an affirmation and try to think of another way to deal with my anxiety.

With my phone still in my hand, I dial Grace.

"What's up!" She says brightly.

"I'm stressed out." I groan, falling back onto my bed.

I hear the sound of her car beeping on the end and then a door shut, "What's wrong?"

"Are you in the car?" I ask.

"Yeah, I'm pulling out of the yoga place now."

A whole new wave of guilt shadows over me. I should have gone with her. I was the one who encouraged her to join a group in the first place in efforts to help clear her mind about everything), but what good is that when I can't even remember to be there for moral support? And here I am, about to ask her to drop everything to provide that very thing for me?

"How was it?" I manage.

"It was alright," She giggles, "Betty had spicy new ex-boyfriend stories for us. But what's up? Do you need me to come over?"

I bite my lip, "Do you have time?"

"Of course I do," I can hear her smile, "I'm like, ten minutes away."

I sigh, relief washing over me. Grace is someone I can really talk to about these things. She's a great listener and is objective when she advises. Most of all, she helps me keep all of my thoughts organized. As hard as I try to use planners and follow her lead, she's definitely the one it comes naturally for.

We hang up and I try to make myself look more presentable, slipping on a few bracelets. A few minutes later, Grace walks in the door looking relaxed yet gracefully put together in her yoga attire. Her skin tone is one I've always been a little jealous of, cream colored and slightly tanned, free of any imperfections.

"Okay," I say, shooting her an accusatory glance, "Can you stop looking flawless long enough for me to have a breakdown?"

She smiles incredulously at me, "Not true, but thank you?"

I pat the couch next to me and she settles in, pulling the elastic from her hair and letting it fall loosely to her shoulders.

"Okay, spill," she says, "what's up?"

"Well," I run my fingers through my hair, "My mom is pressuring me into going to A&B again and I literally cannot tell her no, I have a stupid test coming up that I don't feel prepared for, and I just *know* I'm gonna look like an unsightly bride ... don't get me started on that."

"Whoa, whoa," She says, offering me her hair tie, which I take and tame my unruly waves with, "unsightly bride? Start there."

I sigh, "The dress fitting is tomorrow."

She purses her lips. She knows without me having to tell her how hard it'll be for me.

"I just wish that ... just for a day ... I could *only* feel good. Not like, the temporary good feelings I get after a workout, but just consistently vibrant and beautiful the whole day ..."

"Rae, you are all of those things," Grace says, "You're a beautiful girl and you'll be a stunning bride."

I shake my head, looking down at the scars on my arms — at the one on my chest that slithers out slightly above the hem of every low-cut top I wear. "When the makeup artist tried to cover them, it looked awful. I asked her to at least try because ... I'd been banking on her being able to help me close the door on this issue. But it made them more prominent in my opinion. There's no way I'm walking down the aisle like that."

Grace takes my hands, holding them so that my wrists are facing up. The loose bracelets I'd put on before she got here shift on my arm, revealing the worst of my scars — where my lower wrist meets my palms. She studies them with great care, which would be a hard limit for anyone else — but she's Grace, and we've been through everything together.

In a maternal sort of way, she caresses my hands gently with her thumbs, "You don't need the make-up, Rae. I cannot express to you how unnoticeable this is to everyone else. The only reason you focus on it so much is because it's on *your* body — you know that right?"

"You can't tell me they don't notice ..." I say, feeling unwelcome warmth brimming at my eyes.

"The lace sleeves on your dress will cover up anything you don't like, remember?" Grace says, "That's why we picked that one."

That's the only *reason we picked that one.* It's a hideous dress, really, but all the styles I liked — the ones I always imagined myself wearing — would look horrendous with lace sleeves added on.

"I don't know why you let yourself worry about this. You're getting married … you have a man who adores you … he clearly doesn't mind the scars. In fact, I believe the words he said to me when I was putting him through the wringer was that he *loves* them. Because he loves *you*."

"I know …" I look down at the couch cushion and pull a loose thread from the seams.

She studies my face thoughtfully, "You're just stressed out, Rae. That's totally valid. You have college and work and wedding planning to manage all at once."

"And now my mom …" I say, wanting to move away from this topic.

"Right," She says, allowing the subject change. "What's this about a *B&A* meeting?"

I sigh, "It's A&B, short for Above and Beyond. It's a Bible study thing my moms trying to get me to attend."

Grace seems to brighten at this, "Why don't you go?"

My gaze drifts to a place on the wall just past Grace and locks on the light switch. Suddenly, it feels like a much better focal point.

"Aren't those Bible study groups mainly just people trying to uplift each other?" She says, "That sounds like exactly the kind of encouragement you could use right now."

I shrug, "I haven't been in awhile."

A few beats pass between us.

"Like, in five months I haven't gone."

She studies me, "Why is that?"

When I don't reply, she looks at me a little more directly, "Did something happen?"

"No, no," I wave my hand, "I just..."

Feel guilty for being an insufficient Christian? Don't really feel like being one-upped in spiritual knowledge by my mom and sister, on top of everything else I have going on?

I want to say these things, but I don't. With all the obligations I have right now, I'm not going to let the guilt of supposedly living a *"sinful"* life haunt me too.

What I *do* say, is, "Would you be into the idea of coming with me?"

She smiles, taking my hand and squeezing it, "Of course. This could be good for both of us."

5

Grace - Wednesday

From the passenger seat, Rae reads off the directions to the new A&B meeting location. She added about three more wristbands to her pre-existing array before she'd leave the house with me.

Rae has good days and bad days. I've figured out that if she feels comfortable with the people she's going to see, she'll only wear one or two bands, covering what she believes to be the worst of her scars — but if we're going to see a group of people she doesn't see all that often, she layers on more and more. They look great on her, but it's always been a curious compulsion to me, seeing as though the light scarring on her upper arms is always visible no matter how many bracelets she piles on her lower. But if it makes her feel more confident and free to focus on other things, even if it's only a little extra coverage, then that's reason enough for me.

We pull into a large parking lot, but the actual building turns out to be a lot smaller than I thought it'd be. It's nothing more than one simple room with six square tables pushed together.

A few potted plants adorn the corners of the room while a coffee station and a table covered with decadent-looking treats occupy the far wall.

We arrive with only minutes to spare, so the room is already full of attendees. One of the girls in the middle of the room turns and smiles widely as her gaze falls on Rae and me. She politely excuses herself from two ladies she'd been conversing with and walks over to us. She's strikingly beautiful with light brown skin, high cheek bones, and dark-reddish curls that cascade down her shoulders and graze her elbows.

"Rae," She says, giving her a squeeze, "I'm so glad to see you."

Rae tucks a lock of hair behind her ear and smiles when the girl pulls away, "You too, Kaya."

"And who is your friend?" Kaya turns towards me with a smile.

"This is Grace." Rae says.

"Hi," I extend my hand, "Nice to meet you!"

She wraps her arms around me instead and squeezes tight, "So happy to meet you, Grace! It's amazing how many new sisters we've gained recently."

"Looks like it," Rae says, glancing around the room, "You all must have doubled in size since I was here last."

"We are blessed," Kaya agrees, scanning the room as well.

An alarm beeps from Kaya's watch.

"Oh, I guess it's time to start up already," She says, glancing down at the time and switching off the sound, "Stick around after the study if you can! I'd love to catch up."

Rae nods, "For sure."

As Kaya heads towards the tables, I turn to Rae, "So you don't know that many people here then?"

"I actually do," she says. "There's just a lot of new people too."

"Okay," I smile encouragingly, "So who do you know?"

"Well, Kaya's our leader, and ..." Her eyes lock on something across the room, "There's my mom. And my sister."

I follow her gaze across the room to see Livia, gorgeous and oddly autonomous without her little boy cradled on her hip, standing next to a very enthusiastic Mrs. Brooks, who beckons us over with both hands.

I chuckle and take Rae's arm, leading her over to her family. Mrs. Brooks embraces us with bear hugs and tells us how happy she is that all *three* of her daughters are here — naturally including me in with her blood relations.

"Good evening, ladies," Kaya says, straightening her stack of papers on the table.

We all take our seats.

Mrs. Brooks and Livia lay their Bibles out on the table in front of them, and I briefly feel awkward for not having brought one. What was I thinking, going to a *Bible* study with no *Bible.* But then, Livia gently slides hers across the table and looks between Rae and me.

Can you share? She mouths.

I smile at her and accept her offering as she and her mom scoot closer to share Mrs. Brooks' copy.

"To all the familiar faces I'm seeing around these tables," Kaya says, smiling, "It's *so* good to be back in session. And to any new sisters we may have joining us for the first time tonight, welcome to Above and Beyond,"

I catch myself eyeing up the drink station, wishing I poured myself a coffee before it started.

"We all have different reasons for being here tonight," she continues, "Some of us are simply looking for fellowship among believers ... some of us are seeking out hope ... and some of you probably saw the advertisement banner at Aroma Mocha last week and thought, why not? May as well go for laughs if nothing else,"

This elicits a few chuckles around the tables, including from Rae.

"But whatever the case may be, something brought you here this very night, and I like to think it was a very guided decision. I don't believe any of you are here by chance; I believe there's something we all need to hear *desperately,* for numerous different reasons depending on each individual. Best of all, with so many minds in this room, all representing vaults of different experiences, lessons learned, and shared trials, you might not take away the same thing from the presentation as the women sitting next to you. That's why it's important for us to do *more* than just meet, preach, and leave. We are here to share with one another, to laugh together, to uplift each other in prayer, and to love each other as sisters in Christ."

A few 'amens' chorus around each table.

"Our varying life challenges, the common ground we've found by being here tonight, and most of all our *passion* for God's way of life ... these are the things that connect us as a family,"

Up until now, I'd been immersed in what she was saying. All the way up until I recognized one of the faces that had voiced a passionate '*amen*'.

I stare at it, squinting slightly, trying to make sense of what I'm seeing. The girl plays with her hair, twirling strands of bleached blonde between her manicured fingers as Kaya speaks. Two icy-blue eyes flit across her notebook paper as she jots down a few sentences. Her figure is slighter than mine, but certainly *not* unnaturally skinny as Rae had suggested.

I tuck my hands under the table to hide the fact that they have paled and are shaking ever so slightly. My throat suddenly feels dry and irritated. Kaya is prattling off A&B's code of conduct, but it sounds fuzzy in my ears.

I can feel Rae staring at me from my right. She follows my gaze to the culprit, breathing a sharp intake of air when she processes who she's seeing, and grabs my freezing hand. Even as my body reacts so negatively to seeing *her* in person, I can't tear my eyes away. I drink in the sight of her with thirsty eyes, while analyzing each detail of her. I can't help but wonder, why *her?*

Her lashes flick from her notes and her eyes meet mine. My heart is instantly filled with fight or flight emotions. Everything in me petitions to avert my gaze from hers, but I can't, and my lips refuse to move from a straight line. I'm flooded with visuals of what she must look like through Jayden's eyes. What was his reaction when he first saw her? When those cold blue eyes held his gaze? When he first took her to bed …?

Then she *smiles* at me and returns her gaze to her notes.

I take my hand from Rae's and dig my nails into my chair. That *sly* little *homewrecker.*

Rae passes me a folded piece of paper, which I open with shaky hands.

Do we need to leave?

I flip the paper over and steady my hand long enough to write the word *No,* and slide it back to her.

She looks at me carefully, and then quietly crumples the paper and stuffs it in her bag.

I'm definitely seething, but I'm not going anywhere. I came here for Rae, and because I hoped the meeting could give me more insight to Grandma Jackie's Bible. When Rae asked me to come with her to a Bible study of all things, it felt like fate that just one day beforehand, I had come across my grandmother's majestic old Bible. It felt like this night … being here … was meant to be a special, story-book kind of event that was meant just for me. And I refuse to let *Hadley* take anything else from me than she already has. Leaving would be like another victory for her, and just like getting vengeance on Jayden at this point, it would show her that I still give a damn.

"So per tradition," Kaya's voice filters in through my thoughts, "We will go ahead and start the session off with a little ice breaker."

She passes around sheets of blank paper.

"I want you to write down your name and something fun about yourself, then fold your paper into an airplane. From there, everybody get up out of your seats and throw your airplane. For about thirty seconds, go around the room, pick up any airplane that's been thrown and throw it again, so that all the papers get good and mixed up. After the thirty seconds, everyone select an airplane and take your seats. One by one we'll read what the person has written on the paper. Whoever's name you have, they will say how long they've been attending with us, and it'll be their turn to read next."

My jaw tightens when I receive my paper, a plethora of possible 'fun facts' coming to mind.

My name is Grace Rains, and I hate cheaters. My name is Grace Rains, and I know what you did. My name is Grace Rains, and you better watch your back.

I take a minute to breathe and steady my temper before trying again.

My name is Gracelynn Brielle Rains, but I go by Grace.

I know that Rae wrote the same thing about her name for her fun fact, because it was always our go-to icebreaker fact all through high school when every English and Performing Arts teacher insisted upon 'fun, interactive introductions'.

We fold our paper airplanes and throw them around for thirty seconds, steering clear of Hadley's line of direction. I lose track of mine within the first ten seconds between the forty or so women circulating around the room. Some people didn't know how to make paper airplanes, so they simply throw around crumpled up wads.

We all sit down after the time is up and begin to go around the tables with our papers. Kaya kicks off the reading, and several girls take their turn after her, but I can hardly focus. My mind feels blurry from trying to process what's happening.

"I got Hadley Harris," The sound of her name snaps me back into the present as a young pregnant woman takes her turn, "and she wrote that she enjoys singing in the shower."

You've got to be kidding me. Singing in the shower? Go on, Hadley, tell everyone what you *really* enjoy doing in your spare time. Let's all take this perfect opportunity to get honest.

Hadley smiles, raising her hand, "That's me!"

I smirk. Her voice is higher pitch than mine or Rae's. It instantly irritates me.

"I've been regularly attending A&B meets for about four months now I guess, and it truly has been one of the best decisions I've ever made." she says.

How interesting that she started attending regularly just one month after Rae stopped. What is she even doing, going to a *Bible* study? Doesn't the Bible have some pretty clear scriptures about cheating?

"Okay," She unfolds her airplane and clears her throat, "I got Gracelynn Brielle Rains — Ooh, that's a pretty name — and her fun fact is that she goes by just Grace."

I swallow. What are the odds that she would get *my* paper, of all the forty that were floating around the room? Was she trying to be facetious when she called my name pretty? Or by her personal insertion of the word *just* right before 'Grace'?

I realize everyone is staring at me, waiting for me to say something. I stare down at my airplane which has been decorated on the outside with a dark, swirling design. I start to open it and then remember I have to say how long I've been attending.

"Oh, this is my first time at an A&B meeting."

A round of clapping passes through all five tables, and I smile politely, "I got Zoe Catrina, and she loves photography and art."

A girl with a dark-colored pixie cut stands. Her arms are covered in ink, she wears black, winged eyeliner, and a delicate necklace with a polaroid camera charm. She tells us that this is her sixth time in attendance.

The cycle continues on like this until the last person has been introduced.

Soon the ice breaker is over and Kaya gets on with her presentation. I don't hear most of it — only bits and pieces of background noise. I'm too exhausted from the extremely coincidental run-in this evening and from the forced interaction between us that has ensued.

After about thirty minutes, I hear Kaya's personable voice concluding the message, "If you take nothing else from this night, let it be one of the Lord's most gracious promises to us: *'I will do whatever you ask in my name, so that the Father may be glorified in the Son. You may ask me for anything in my name, and I will do it.'"*

She closes her Bible, "Please feel free to stick around for awhile. Have some food and some fellowship, and thank you for coming out tonight."

The women begin filling the room with chatter. Rae scuffs her chair against the floor, "Ready to go?"

"Yep." I say, following suit.

We leave the building without any goodbyes and enter my car in silence. Both of us just sit there a moment letting everything sink in.

"I am never going back there," I breathe.

Rae shakes her head, "I don't blame you."

6

Rae - Thursday

I usually drive with the radio on, but today en route to the dress fitting, I have too much to think about.

I never got to see, or even talk to Adam yesterday, and after everything that happened at A&B, I have the overwhelming urge to call him and give him an update. Something about the patient way he listens to me as I sort through my thoughts always helps me gain a better grip on things.

He picks up after just a few rings.

"Hey, beautiful."

I smile, "Hey."

"I missed talking to you last night," He says.

"I missed it too, but I knew you had an early morning today. I didn't want to wake you when I got back from A&B."

"So how did it go? Do you feel better about the whole thing?"

I know he means about appeasing my mom once and for all.

"Well," I grimace, "I basically made a bee-line out of the building. Didn't pause to say goodbye to mom or Livia, or even catch up with Kaya, as she specifically asked."

"That bad, huh?"

I shake my head, "Not the message — no. Just the company."

"Hm," He says, "What do you mean?"

I grimace again, "You know the girl Jayden cheated on Grace with?"

"Not personally, no."

"Well, she was there."

"Ohhh," He says, "Was Grace?"

"Yes …" I lament, "Thanks to me. I asked her to come with me."

"Damnnn." I can hear his smile, "What kind of friend are you, anyway?"

"I didn't know," I frown, "I feel really bad about it."

"Don't feel bad, baby girl. You haven't been there in ages. There's no way you could've known, and I'm sure Grace isn't holding that against you."

"I know," I say, "But like, I also didn't come across super friendly to Kaya or my family by leaving so quickly, you know?"

He laughs, "You're overthinking this, I promise. Who's Kaya again?"

"The leader." I say.

She hadn't made a big deal of my presence, but had still managed to make me feel welcome. She didn't mention anything regarding my absence or how long it's been, only her genuine happiness in seeing me again. It was actually me who had called myself out on how long it's been since I last came to a meet when I mentioned how much the group had grown since then.

I'd said, 'You all must have doubled in size since I was here last.'

You all.

As though I'm not even a true member of the group, but some sort of outsider looking in. Kaya hadn't missed a beat, though. She simply smiled and smoothly carried the conversation.

Adam shifts on the other line, "I'm gonna have to let you go, babe. Second period is about to start back up and I'm supposed to be lesson-planning."

"Oh," I say, "Sorry to hold you up. I just ... this is all I could think about during my trig class this morning," *when I really needed to be paying attention to the lesson.* "I just needed to like, info-dump on someone, you know? Process everything."

"Of course," He says, "And I fully expect a more thorough update when I come by after work. Sound good?"

I smile, "Sounds good."

We hang up and I'm almost to the bridal boutique.

At a stop-light, I open the messages on my phone, scrolling past the recent ones from my mother asking if I'm okay, and finally read the texts from Kaya over the past few months.

From: Kaya (A&B)

Sent: 5/25/19

Time: 9:04 am

"Hey, girl! Just wanted to say we missed you last week. Your mom said you weren't feeling good - can I bring anything by for you?"

From: Kaya (A&B)

Sent: 6/2/19

Time: 10:14 am

"Congratulations on your engagement!!!! May God bless both you and Adam throughout your union. I'm SO happy for you!"

From: Kaya (A&B)

Sent: 8/11/19

Time: 6:01

"Love you, Rae. Hope you are doing wonderful. Keeping you in my prayers <3 Hugs!"

The light turns green and I set my phone down as a little more guilt piles itself on my shoulders. I had ignored these thoughtful messages so long. But I mostly feel guilty because my mother was right: The message last night *had* been good.

I found myself enjoying Kaya's words and the spirit of the group, but part of me still feels like I don't belong there. Like I'm less worthy than the rest of the attendees to claim what they call 'grace', and it's the very feeling I've been trying to avoid the entire time I've been absent.

It used to seem like every time I'd go to an A&B meeting, it was mostly these women talking about how they can better themselves spiritually, which is totally cool and everything, but it was the *things* they suggested that made me feel lesser than them. They'd suggest things like visiting orphans and widows more often together, which is usually something you do when you're really scraping for things to improve on. It's not what you're thinking about when you're where I am — at the bottom of the improvement scale, still focusing hard on issues like keeping my language pure and my hands off of Adam ... which I suck at. Or, dare I say it, *not* hating certain aspects of my body, which is supposedly *'God's own creation'*. The truth is, the part of my body that I hate is *not* His creation or even slightly His doing. It's mine. It's all mine.

* * *

I pull into the boutique parking lot and park in a spot labeled: Reserved for VIPs and Our Brides to Be!

Despite everything going on, I still can't help but smile every time I get to enjoy my status as a bride — every time someone admires my ring or says, "congratulations!" when I buy something bridal.

I walk into the store which is bustling with groups of women and stylists pulling various gowns for their clients to try on. Hanging from the hooks on a dressing room in the corner is my dress — an unsightly thing with far too much fabric.

My stylist is propped on a chair in front of my dressing room's runway, checking things off on her clipboard.

"Good morning, lovely lady!" She says with enthusiasm.

"Hey," I say as she squeezes me into a hug.

If I could describe Sonya in one word, it would be "bubbly". She's a voluptuous woman in all the right areas, but dressed like a professional in her lady suit. She's probably the most energetic and optimistic woman I know, but I'm sure that's just how someone who works off commission has to be in order to talk a bride into deciding on a dress.

"Do you need anything before we get started? Bathroom? Hot tea?"

I smile, "I don't think so, thanks."

"Alright then!" She says, unhanging the dress, "Let's slip this baby on!"

A few minutes later, I'm standing in front of the runway mirrors, tugging on the sleeves. The neckline of the dress goes up high enough to cover my chest scar and the sleeves fall loosely down my arms, which is not something I wanted, but I worry that trying to alter the delicate lace will rip it somehow or completely ruin the pattern. The worst part of the dress is the skirt, which ruffles all the way down to the floor, instead of gracefully outlining my hips gliding down.

"So," Sonya says with anticipation, "How do you feel?"

I flick my eyes down the length of the dress. It's hideous, really. Makes me feel anything but bridal.

"It's very ... Victorian." I swallow.

She fluffs out the bottom for me to see the skirt in all its ruffled glory, "Are we having second thoughts?"

I scan the dress again, searching for any redeemable qualities. I know I picked this one because it covers everything, but I should still feel beautiful on my wedding day, and this dress doesn't do it for me.

"Could I maybe still ..." I bite my lip, "try another one? Is it too late?"

She smiles, "Honey, it's never too late!"

Of course it's not. I am every commission stylist's dream. The bride who literally buys a dress only to find she hates it the next time she tries it on for sizing and opts to buy yet another dress.

"Ridiculous," I whisper to myself, shaking my head when I send her away with a description of my dream dress.

Moments later she comes back with a strapless, mermaid-style gown with a sweetheart neckline. My lips moisten slightly as I take in the site of it — the stunning details in the beading. It's everything I've ever wanted.

She unbuttons the back of my Victorian dress and helps me slip into the modern one — a design that she told me just hit the market.

I step out of the dressing room and onto the runway, convincing myself to walk all the way down before I look in the mirror. I feel strangely underdressed without any bracelets on my wrists; but at the same time, it's also kind of liberating. Like my traditional shackles have been shed.

When I reach the end of the aisle, I glance up at the mirror. For a moment, my eyes widen with joy. The dress fits my curves like a glove. It would need no alterations at all.

But then …

I notice how the fluorescent white lights of the dressing area bring notice to the light-colored marks on my bare arms and I look away. I don't even want to see how much the scar on my chest pokes out through the top of this dress, which is lower cut by a lot.

"You are glowing!" Sonya beams.

I wrap my arms around my waist, staring at the floor.

To the left of the runway, a little girl in a flower girl dress stops and looks up at me. She doesn't say anything, but her lips part slightly.

I'm so uncomfortable, I don't know what to do with myself. I feel like a spotlight's been placed on me, revealing every insecurity I have. The idea of me having to deal either with this feeling on my wedding day, or the feeling of being in a hideous dress is enough to draw tears to my eyes.

"I have to go," I say, turning on my heels and walking right back into the dressing room.

I dress quickly in my regular clothes and rehang both dresses before stepping out.

"I'm sorry," I say to Sonya, "I should have known better than to come without my maid of honor. I'm too indecisive."

She laughs, "Aren't we all, hun. That's alright. When would you like to reschedule the fitting?"

"Um," I say, rubbing my temples, "Can I get back with you on that? I need my … day planner."

Day planner. Sonya and I both know I use my phone calendar for everything.

"No problem," She brushes it off, "We'll see you next time!"

When I get out to the car, the tears really start to come. I turn the key and drive straight home, not bothering to burden anyone with a phone call.

It wouldn't be so bad if I didn't have to wear white. In the summertime, I feel comfortable wearing tank tops and casual clothes — but never white — because white enunciates the light color of each scar I have like glaring beacons of my flaws. Hanging out with my closest friends and family at a grill out is another story than my wedding day, when every girl dreams of looking flawless.

When I reach home, I go straight to my bedroom and lay flat on my bed.

I stay there long after my tears dry.

***

I was four years old when it happened, and yet I remember it so vividly. My mother was always the ideal homemaker. She stayed home with us from the time we were babies until we were old enough to go to elementary school. Before that, she homeschooled us, and she taught us a plethora of useful domestic skills. How to bake, sew, garden, and more, but a personal favorite hobby of hers was candle making, and it was something she never let us help her with.

"Not until you're older," She'd say, "It's too dangerous."

One day, the fresh scent of oranges and lemon came wafting up the stairs into my bedroom where I was supposed to be taking a nap. It was the undeniable aroma of my mother's favorite candle scent, which she called "Citrus Sunshine." I heard her start the microwave — a sign that she was only melting a small batch of wax — and proceed to the guest bathroom. I listened for her to turn the handle on the shower and waited for the muted sound of her singing to rise up through the vents into my room before executing the idea that had been forming in my mind: I would show my mother how grown-up I am. Grown-up enough for her to start letting me help her make candles. But mama never showered for more than five minutes or so, which meant I'd have to be fast.

I crept down the steps, sneaking past the guest bathroom.

If she knew what I was doing, she'd probably try to stop me. But I didn't want her to. I knew I was old enough to do this, and she'd be so proud if she saw I've made a candle all by myself.

I grabbed a mason jar from the cupboard under the sink and began positioning the wick. I remember thinking that part was difficult — getting the wick to stay perfectly centered. It took way more time than I hoped it would.

The microwave beeped to a stop in perfect unison with my mother turning the handle to the shower off. Panic set in.

She'd be mad if she saw me doing this. Not proud at all. For me to secure the reaction I wanted, I'd have to hurry and finish up.

I rushed over to the microwave, completely silent in my sock feet. I balanced on my tiptoes, pulled open the microwave and reached for the container of melted wax. It was still halfway in the microwave, halfway out, when my bare fingers realized the searing-hot temperature of the container and retracted, lightning fast. The container tipped out of the microwave and came crashing down to the floor.

I jumped back, but the boiling wax shot up at me in a splatter. Droplet-shaped bits of wax seared into my arms, erupting my skin in the strangest sensation — one I almost mistook for a freezing cold temperature. One bit of burning wax had latched onto my chest and dripped down my stomach beneath my shirt. That's the one that felt painful immediately.

My eyes welled with tears, streaming down my face as my arms and chest began to sting, but I did not cry audibly until my mother burst out of the bathroom, her hair dripping wet down her yanked-on clothes.

"Lacey!" She cried, rushing over to me.

She kneeled and immediately threw off my shirt, scanning my chest and then my arms. Saying nothing over the sound of my crying, she took my hand and rushed us into the bathroom, where she plopped me in the tub and ran cool water over my chest and arms.

It felt like torture, freezing and burning all at once. If she stopped running the water, I couldn't get relief from the burning, but if she kept the water running, I was subjected to being freezing cold. I couldn't decide which was worse.

I stayed in the tub while my mother made phone calls — first to a doctor and then to my father. We didn't end up going to a doctor though. When it was time for me to come out of the tub, my mother simply gave me ibuprofen, a glass of water, and several cold compresses to hold where it hurt the most. I watched, sitting at the kitchen table, sniffling as she scrubbed at the floor where the hot wax had dried. It looked terribly difficult to scrape off the tile.

She didn't make me help her clean. She didn't say a word. Nothing along the lines of "What did you do?", or "This is why I told you not to try this", and now that I'm older, I think that's because she felt guilty.

At the time, she simply studied my burns every once in awhile and insisted we go to the doctor the next day to make sure we were doing everything right. It was then that the doctor told me there would be scarring, but that I was 'not to worry, dear, they will be very light'.

But they weren't light. Not to me.

It wasn't a big deal at first. When the pain finally subsided, the new little marks on my skin didn't make me feel all that much different. But when it came time for me to start going to middle school, that was a different story entirely. Other kids would point at my arms and ask me what happened to them. Bullying was not tolerated at the school, but the kids still found a way to make me feel as singled out and different as possible. I noticed when someone looked my way a little too long (but not at my face), and I took it a little too personally that all the other girls seemed to get picked to go to the dance with a boy before I did. When I reached eighth grade, the people who appeared to love me for the marks on my arms were the girls who had marks of their own. Theirs were different from mine, though. Their marks were self-given ... cuts they made into their flesh to relieve the tension of life when it became all too much to bear. They told me that my marks make me strong. That they are proof of my badassery, and my ability to move on in life even when it sucks. So eventually, following suit, I too began to make more little marks into my skin.

I hated myself for it. Every time I did it, I knew I was making myself look even more like the reject my peers took me for. But there was also a certain release to it ... a certain high that it gave me. It made me feel in control of what happened to my body, and therefore in control of my life. It gave me a different type of pain to focus on; Physical instead of mental.

When my mother found out that the wrist covers I began wearing around the house weren't to cover the burn scars, but to cover self-inflicted harm, she immediately pulled me from the school I was going to and cut me off from my friends. She enrolled me in an expensive school for the pompous — At least that's what all of us at Rose Valley thought — and scheduled me to talk with a doctor every other week, who prescribed me the Xanax.

At first, I resented my mom for it, but then at my new school, I met Grace. She loved me in the same way that my old friends had, but she didn't encourage any bad habits. Instead, she liberated new, positive ones like working out together and trying new and inventive fruit smoothies every time we hung out. She invested in me, and I invested in her, and now, she's the greatest friend I have.

But the sad part is, I don't even think my burn scars would be that bad anymore. The ones that really stand out are the ones pooled beneath my palm. The ones I gave myself.

I can try my best to forget the memories and the pain I felt, but I can never erase the scars. They're something I'll have to carry with me forever. A constant visual of my inability to cope.

* * *

I hear the front door open and shut, releasing me from the memories of my childhood. It must be evening time now.

A few minutes later, Adam appears in the doorway of my bedroom. His appearance brightens my mood immediately and I feel myself smiling.

"Oh my …" He says, pausing at the door with a hand to his heart, "Is that girl really mine?"

I smile and pat the bed next to me.

"Hold on," he says, searching his pockets and retrieving his phone, "I've got to capture this stunning goddess that somehow ended up on my bed."

I snort, rolling my eyes, "Flatterer,"

"Maybe," He says, taking an actual picture.

"And I'm pretty sure this is my bed." I add.

He saunters over to me, taking my face in his hands, "Not just yours. Not for long." He kisses me sweetly.

I lift my chin, returning his embrace.

"How was your day?"

"Perfect now." He says, "How was yours?"

I smile, but don't say anything as he kisses down my neck.

At my silence, he stops and looks at me, "All good?"

I purse my lips and shake my head.

"What's wrong?" He says, shifting me into his arms.

"I had the dress fitting today." I say.

"Yeah? That's awesome. How'd it go?"

"Not good," I say half-heartedly.

"Not good?" He echoes, "Well that's not okay."

I shake my head again.

A few beats pass between us.

"Don't you like your dress?" He smiles hopefully.

I run a hand through my hair, "I actually hate it."

He patiently waits for me to continue as he lightly runs his fingers down my shoulder to my wrists. He knows what I'm getting at. It's a conversation we've had so many times.

"The sleeves look stupid," I say, "The whole thing is just ugly. I can see how it might look good on some other bride … just not me."

"Well," He says, kissing my wrists, "You're the only bride that matters here, baby girl."

I look into his eyes which hold my face attentively.

"If you're worried about these," He says, trailing up my other arm, "I love them."

He shifts on top of me and pulls up my shirt, "especially this one."

He kisses the long line of the scar from my stomach to my chest, "If you looked any other way than this, you wouldn't be my Rae."

I smile, looking away from him, but he gently pulls my face back to his. I helplessly fall in love with his gaze for the hundredth time.

Adam has always been my soul mate. I love everything about him, and he loves everything about me. Even the things that I don't. I can only imagine how deeply my insecurities would have swallowed me by now, if not for him.

He kisses me slowly, passionately.

I hook my fingers around the bottom of his shirt and pull it upward, over his head. It's in this moment that my insecurities fade into nothing.

7

Grace - Friday

I hear the doorbell ring its cheery tune, pulling my attention away from the project I'm working on — an herbal lotion requested of me by one of the ladies at sunrise yoga. I glance at my watch, which reads 3:46 in the afternoon. Who could that be?

The doorbell sounds again.

I lift a purring Amity from my lap and set her down on the floor. She trails me to the front door, where I am greeted by a middle-aged looking woman with tight, honey blond curls and name tag from *Swift Thrifting* that says, *"Hi, my name is Marla!"*

I smile at her, "Hi, can I help you?"

"You must be Grace. Sorry I'm so late! This is the right address, isn't it? *Hyssop 'N' Sage?*" She says, referencing the name of my home business.

I must've scheduled an appointment for her that I forgot to write down somewhere.

"Oh, yes, it is. And I should be offering *my* apologies. I completely forgot I had anyone scheduled for today." I open the door a little wider for her to step in.

I almost add, *'You would not believe what I've been through lately.'* but then I think better of it. No reason to blend my personal life with my work.

She laughs a hearty laugh that makes Amity run, "Honey, trust me. I understand busy. Don't give it another thought."

I lead her into the sunroom, which is not only my favorite room in the house, but also the room where I meet with all of my clients. I feel a small sense of pride as I draw the shades and the room becomes one entirely of windows. Sunlight spills through the glass, highlighting my plants and salt lamps. I gesture to the couch which is adorned with brightly colored pillows.

"Please," I say, "have a seat and make yourself at home. Can I get you anything? Coffee or tea?"

She settles in, grabbing a mandala pillow and smoothing it with her hands, "Tea please, *anything* that'll help with this headache."

I smile, heading over to the coffee station I have set up against the wall. Although I only drink coffee on rare occasions, I always want it as an option for my clients.

"So tell me again a little about what you're going through." I say, selecting a few loose-leaf teas and mixing them into a steeper, "Your headaches don't seem to be caffeine related, do they?"

I listen attentively as she explains the severity of her migraines and how often she has them. When I finish steeping her tea, I pour it into a mug and offer it to her along with a bowl of sugar cubes.

"They're just awful," She concludes, taking the mug, "and I've tried just about everything I can think of to get rid of them."

I shake my head, "I'm sorry you're having to deal with that."

"Me too," she takes a sip, "I'm not even able to play with my grandkids anymore."

I nod, "Well, I think I might have just the thing."

"Yeah?" She says, raising a brow.

I nod again, "For your specific case, I'd like to try a tincture of lemon balm, feverfew, and peppermint, mixed with a little bit of bourbon. I think I may even have a bottle of that blend already made up around here somewhere, so if you'd like to give it a try, I could send you home with a sample today."

"That sounds wonderful," She says, rubbing her temple.

"I'll go get it for you," I smile, "just stay right here and relax."

She manages a smile and nods.

I stand and venture over to the medicine cabinet in my bathroom.

While rummaging around the over packed cabinet for the appropriate bottle, a cardboard box falls from the shelf, bouncing off my shoulder and onto the floor. I locate the little glass vial in the corner of the shelf, retrieve it, and close the cupboard. Setting the vial on the counter, I stoop down to pick up the fallen box, which turned out to be a pack of tampons. I go to open the cupboard once more, but I stop short of returning the box, taking a moment to eye it skeptically.

I slowly set the box down on the counter and begin to silently count, ticking off the numbers with my fingers.

Twenty-seven days ago. If my calculations are correct, I should be starting my period tomorrow.

Perfect. Nothing to worry about.

But as I place the box back in the cupboard, my head begins to spin with unpleasant recollections. Now that I'm really thinking about it, I have felt… *off*… lately.

This morning, I felt so tired I could barely get myself out of bed, which is unusual for me. I also haven't had much of an appetite lately, and then there was that strange bout of nausea during sunrise yoga ...

But that was just because of Jayden's picture, I reason.

Still, I pause. All of my studies in homeopathic medicine have turned my mind into a natural symptom-connector, and a typical diagnosis I would assign to someone experiencing nausea in the morning, lethargy, and a decreased appetite would be ... pregnancy.

My head begins to throb, while making connections left and right. Possible symptoms of pregnancy begin to highlight themselves like little beacons in my mind, refusing to be ignored.

I hear Marla set her mug down coffee table and shake my head, hoping to clear it.

These could easily be symptoms of depression too. God knows I deserve a little depressive allowance after last night's disaster, which I've tried to suppress to the depths of my mind all day today. After all, my period isn't even late yet. This is something I can put off worrying about until tomorrow, when I don't have a client waiting on me.

***

I've waited patiently. I woke up this morning with a determined attitude and spent the day flipping through my holistic textbooks, searching for ways to speed along the process. I had a bowlful of pineapple, sat directly in the sunlight, performed countless squats, and even went so far as to make a formidable tea concoction of turmeric, cinnamon, and parsley. According to the textbook, all of these things are effective methods for inducing a period, but by the time midnight rolls around the corner, I slowly realize it won't be coming. Not today.

Along with that realization comes a flood of additional unwelcome questions. I gently close the book I'm reading and set it on the dresser with shaky hands.

What will I do if it never comes? The baby couldn't be anyone's other than Jayden's.

I try to think back. When is the last time we even had sex? It must've have been about three weeks ago, give or take. What measures had we taken to be careful?

My brain is mush. I can't remember all of this on my own. Would it be out of line to let him in on this possible concern?

I pick my phone up off the side table, tap the 'contacts' icon, and scroll down to his name, which I must have forgotten to change from *'My Love'*. The words smack me in the face.

I take a slow, steadying breath, and edit them to display his first name instead. My finger hovers over the 'type a message box'.

The cursor blinks expectantly at me.

I squeeze my eyes shut and shake my head. *Way too soon.*

This doesn't mean anything. I could just simply be late. Periods aren't always on time. But if I'm not just late ... and this *is* real ... would telling him do me any good? Would the idea of us having a family be enough to remind him of the good thing we had — the plans we made — and apologize? Do I even *want* him to?

Not telling him things has been the hardest. He was my confidante for so long. My go-to, even when it came down to telling him minute parts of my day. Realizing I could no longer laugh with anyone about our inside jokes, or that I had no one to tell about the awesome fruit smoothie combination I'd discovered for breakfast, or the shirt I saw in the store that would be just *perfect* for him, totally sucked, and made me feel desolate. But it paled in comparison to realizing I couldn't find comfort in him about this. Is this something I'll have to deal with alone?

I've only ever had one other pregnancy scare, and I was with him. We were nineteen, and I told him immediately. He held me in his arms and told me it would be okay — That this was the risk we knew we were taking, and if it came down to it, he couldn't wait to start a family with me.

Maybe it was a young boy talking, but it brought me so much comfort to be in his arms and to hear his promises. The next day we'd gone out and bought Plan-B. He was with me when I took it, holding my hand, and kissing my face. I remember being amazed at how tiny the actual pill was, but it'd been effective. Now, of course, in my current situation, it was far too late for emergency contraceptives.

I've been on birth control ever since the first scare, but his assurance and promises of undying love were enough to make me a little careless with it. I tried to remember to take it every day, but sometimes I'd accidentally skip or take the pill a few hours off from the time I took it the day before.

Again, his voice echoes in my mind of the night he told me that we'd figure it out *together*, because it was me and him against the world. And in this moment, I want nothing more than to soak in that kind of comfort, but when I pull out my phone a second time to message him, a horrible image crosses my mind:

His phone going off, lighting up the darkness of his room at approximately 12:07 am. He reaches over to grab it from his bedside table — the wooden one I bought for him — to read what looks like a desperate cry from me, as *Hadley* buries her face into his chest.

I furrow my brow, and squeeze my eyes shut again. A hot tear escapes them this time and rolls quickly down my cheek.

Would he leave her for me? Hell, of course he wouldn't... he practically left *me* for *her*. Being pregnant wouldn't make any difference in that situation. I really am completely alone in this, and on top of that, my pride is hurt for what feels like the hundredth time this week. Hurt because of what he did, and hurt because despite it, I've still considered trying to make us work.

I lean my head back against the headboard and shudder, an indelicate sob escaping my chest.

The gentle sound of Kaya's voice reverberates in my mind as she flipped through the pages of her Bible, "If you take nothing else from this night, let it be one of the Lord's most gracious promises to us: *'I will do whatever you ask in my name, so that the Father may be glorified in the Son."*

The words held a hollow meaning to me until now. I'd let my mind gloss over them the first time she read them, in a hurry to flee the scene.

Now, I simply let the tears fall as I bow my head, feeling powerless. I don't move from where I am. There is no kneeling at my bedside as I'm sure is proper. I simply remain still as three short words desperately escape from my heart to my lips.

"God," I whisper, having lost my voice to the tears, "Help me."

8

Rae - Saturday

Adam and I decide to have brunch at our favorite pizzeria. He had insisted on taking me out for a treat today, leaving me with the anticipation of having "big news" to share.

I sit across the table from him, waiting expectantly.

He takes a leisurely sip of water.

"Well?" I say.

"Well what?" He smiles.

"What's the big news? What are we celebrating?"

"Oh, that," He waves his hand passively, trying to appear nonchalant, "It's nothing really."

I narrow my eyes and widen my smile.

He stretches his arms behind his head, "Just that I finally got that raise at work. That's all."

My mouth drops into an open smile, "Are you serious?"

He gives into an ear-to-ear grin, "Dead serious."

"Adam!" I cheer, reaching across the table for a kiss, "That's incredible!"

"One step closer to an extravagant honeymoon." He says as I pull away.

My heart warms. I've always dreamed of going to Italy and staying in the colorful village of Burano. Adam has devoted himself to making that dream a reality for me.

"I'm so glad your contributions to the school are finally getting recognized." I say, "You know, by someone who isn't a sex-crazed teenage girl."

This makes him laugh.

Adam is the heart throb of the school — sexier than a teacher has any right to be, and all the high school girls drool over him.

"What about you?" He says, folding his hands on the table and leaning in, "I didn't bring you here just to talk about me. Tell me what's been going on with you."

I shake my head and take a sip of my water, "I don't know where to begin."

He gazes at me attentively, "Something on your mind?"

That's an understatement. I could tell him about the frowny-faced homework I've been receiving from my trig class, but I think I'd rather just suffer alone on this one than let him know how much of a lost cause I am in his area of expertise. Adam is a math *teacher* ... He would never understand. Or worse, he might try to *help* me.

Instead, I opt to tell him about the text I got this morning. Maybe he can help me decide what to do.

"Kaya texted me today." I say.

He raises an eyebrow, "Above and Beyond lady?"

"Yes. She invited me to a last-minute get-together tonight."

A baby shower, to be exact, for a girl named Macie, who I take to be the pregnant girl who kicked off our icebreaker the other night.

"Are you gonna go?" He says, nodding to the waitress as she sets down a piping hot tray of pizza and an alfredo pasta bowl.

"I don't know yet," I say, "I kind of feel like I should. You know, make-up for my hasty dash the other night. But don't you think that'd be kind of a betrayal to Grace to go to another A&B event?

He shrugs, "Why would it be?"

"Because Hadley will probably be there …"

His brows pinch, like he's trying to remember who she is.

"Jayden's lover," I offer.

Recognition dawns on his face. I take a bite of pasta as he chews thoughtfully,

"I mean, do you *want* to go?"

I wince, "Kinda … mom will probably be there. I sort of owe her an explanation for last night."

"But you can call your mom anytime," He says. "Don't think about if you *need* to go. I'm asking if you *want* to. Last I heard, you were avoiding A&B like the plague, and you only went the other day because of your mom."

I consider this before concluding, "I think I want to go."

"Okay," Adam says, "Why?"

I sigh, "Because the whole vibe of the group is just … different. There's a lot of new faces there now, and they're genuinely nice, caring people. Especially Kaya."

Adam nods, "Then you should go."

"But Grace … and Hadley …"

"Grace doesn't need to know everything, babe. I'm not saying to go and then rub it in her face that you're hanging out with these people. Just keep it low-key. Enjoy yourself. It's not like you promised her you'd never go again."

I pull a slice of pizza onto my plate. He *is* right... Grace is the only one who said she wasn't going back. And it's not like I'm going to hang out *with* Hadley. We probably won't even *talk* the entire time I'm there, because what reason would there be for it?

"It's up to you," He concludes. "I'm not going to tell you what to do, but your *mom* goes to this group, for heaven's sake. I'm pretty sure Grace would understand."

***

"In a quarter mile, turn left onto Rose Valley Boulevard." My GPS sing-songs through the speakers of the car.

It was a constant debate for me during the hours leading up to the shower. To go, or not to go. I'm still debating on whether or not coming here was the right decision as I pull into the driveway of Kaya's home.

It's a humble little brick dwelling with a garden area out front and a white picket fence. I check myself in the mirror and apply another layer of my favorite coconut lip balm before going in.

When I knock on the door, I hear a dog barking from the inside. Kaya opens it, looking relaxed and gorgeous, as an adorable, fast-moving ball of fluff mauls my legs.

"Alright, Coco, that's enough," Kaya says, picking up the little beagle puppy.

He licks her profusely, ears flopping joyfully.

I can't help but smile, "He's adorable!"

"Thanks! Adopted him about three months back"

He wriggles free from her grasp and runs off into the living room, and Kaya welcomes me in. Her house always smells like the most decadent coffee. Now in her early thirties, she never married, but she still loves to entertain and is easily the most hospitable person I know.

"Is mom here?" I ask.

"Came and left, I'm afraid." Kaya says, "She had an appointment I believe is what she said. Come on this way though. Everyone's kind of pooled in the common area."

As I step into the living room, I realize that almost everyone who was present at A&B is here and then some — those who I assume to be Macie's family. I place my present for her on the gift table and take a seat on the couch by the girl from opening night with the inked arms.

She's looking down at the screen of a professional-looking camera and flipping through still-frames.

"Zoe, right?" I say.

She looks up at me and smiles, "Oh, hey! I've been meaning to talk to you."

This surprises me, "You have?"

"Yeah," She says, showing me the screen of her camera,

"About this."

Her screen displays a picture of Grace and I talking to Kaya before the Bible study. Kaya is in mid-sentence, her hands animating whatever she is saying in the photo, and Grace and I are listening attentively.

"Kaya asked me to take some candid pictures of opening night for the A&B website," She says, "I wanted to make sure you were okay with me posting it. Most of the other ones I got weren't nearly as photogenic as this. Someone is always yawning or blinking."

I laugh, "I had no idea you were even taking pictures."

"If you have a good candid photographer, you never will," She winks.

"Let me see it again," I say, reaching for the camera.

I try not to let it bother me that the scars on my right arm are visible in the photo, but it still does a little bit. Grace looks gorgeous as always, so I know she won't mind.

"You two would make really good models," Zoe says, "You look so athletic and sheen, and your friend has these cute, yet whimsical bohemian vibes."

Athletic and sheen? Is that what people see? I glance back at Grace, agreeing wholly with Zoe's compliment for her. Sometimes I can't understand why someone as beautiful as Grace would compare herself to anyone.

"You should tell her that," I smile, avoiding a reply that could lead to more talk about how I look, "That would make her day."

I flip through the other pictures on the camera and quickly see what Zoe means about the other candid shots, but there are also some really good intentional ones of opening night. There's one that is a surface-high view of a table and three sets of hands. One set is obviously older, withered and adorned with rings, while the other two are younger — nails painted and more bracelets than rings. There are Bibles and notebooks splayed before them along with cups of coffee. The older pair of hands rest folded on her Bible, one younger pair cups around her coffee mug, and the other pair writes notes with a blue pen.

"Wow, I really like this one," I say, "You've got some talent."

"Thanks," she smiles, "I needed some more material for my photography blog."

That's when something occurs to me.

"So you book sessions for pay?" I ask.

"Sure, whenever there's a need." She says.

I brighten, "My fiancé and I never took any official engagement pictures. Now that we're designing the invites, we're kind of wishing that we had. Would you be into booking a session sometime soon?"

"Totally!" Zoe says, "I'm usually pretty booked this time of year. You know — fall leaves in Vermont and all that — but I'm pretty sure I had a cancelation for the tenth if you want that slot. Let me send you the link to my blog."

Relief floods me. *Five days from now.* One less thing I have to take care of.

Zoe and I exchange phone numbers and we nail down next Thursday for the photoshoot. Then someone calls her name from across the room and we part ways.

I feel a light tap on my shoulder and turn around, surprised by the perfectly 'done-up' face smiling back at me. Her lashes are definitely fake.

"Hi!" Hadley says sweetly, "I think you're the only one I haven't *officially* met yet. You said your name was Lacey, right?"

I don't correct her. Let her use the name that shows up only on my legal documents.

I clear my throat, "And you're Hadley Harris."

"I am!" She laughs, "I wish I were that good with names and faces."

I'm not sure what to do. I hadn't planned on talking to her at all, and somehow here we are. Should I continue a civil conversation, or confront her somehow since she voluntarily placed herself in my path? I could pull out a picture of Grace and Jayden together and say something snarky, like, *"Do you recognize* these *faces?"*

Back in high school, I wouldn't have even hesitated to put a mean girl in her place. But for some reason, this is harder than all those times. Hadley is being so damn *nice* to me, and for the life of me, I can't figure out why.

When I don't say anything, she continues.

"I couldn't help but overhear what you and Zoe were talking about a minute ago. Something about posing for wedding announcement pictures? I just wanted to say congratulations!"

I'm taken aback.

"Thank you,"

She takes my curt replies as if I have something more to say. She widens her lip-glossed smile at me expectantly.

"He's really something special." I say, for lack of knowing what she wants from me.

"Tell me about him," She says brightly, shifting her weight.

Okay ... I guess we're doing this now.

"Well," I say, "He's probably the most attractive man I've ever seen. He's got these greenish-grey eyes and he wears glasses when he reads. He makes all his female students do a double take."

"So he's a teacher?" She smiles.

"He is," I say, "He's super intelligent and classy, but also smooth and very thoughtful."

She sighs wistfully, "He sounds wonderful."

"He is." I say again, smiling.

That's when I realize she's set this conversation up perfectly for me.

"What about you?" I say, "Are you seeing anyone?"

Her cheeks flush and she looks down, but her smile doesn't falter.

"I am," She says, "Well, sort of."

"Sort of?" I say, as pleasantly as I can muster.

"He and I used to only see each other once in awhile because of his work schedule, but lately we've been getting to see each other more and more, and it's just been lovely. We gel really well together, I think." She says.

I nod, my heart squeezing inside, "Do you have any pictures of him? So I can get a visual?"

She pulls out her phone, stares at it for a split second with the screen off before rolling her eyes, "Shoot, I forgot about this new phone. I have yet to transfer all my pics. His name is Jayden, though."

At this moment, a light bulb goes off in my head.

"Wait a second," I snap my fingers, feigning an expression of recognition, "Jayden Grayson?"

She brightens, "Yeah! How'd you know?"

"I think I know him," I say, pulling out my phone.

Way too well after countless double dates with him and Grace. But Hadley's description isn't what bothers me. It's that I'm beginning to get the feeling that she has no idea about Grace, or that Grace and I have, in fact, seen her nudes on Jayden's phone.

I pull up his Facebook page, which is covered in pictures of him and Grace. I tap his profile picture — the one of just him looking all classic bad boy with his leather jacket and perfectly done hair — and the photos of he and Grace disappear from the screen.

I turn the screen towards her, and her smile widens, "Yes! Yes, that's him."

She takes my phone and squints at it, "I don't think I've seen that one of him before. He looks so suave."

I laugh, keeping my tone light, "Girl, it's on his Facebook page."

Her brows pinch together as she hands it back to me, "That's ... strange."

"Why's that?" I pocket the phone.

"He told me he didn't have a Facebook anymore ..."

I bite my lower lip, "Really? That is ... strange."

"Alright," Kaya announces, "We're gonna go ahead and kick off some games!"

9

Grace - Sunday

Stress is one of the human body's most cunning tricksters. It can send aching pains to your head, chest, and stomach. It can steal your energy *and* your sleep from you. It can cause you to become obsessive over small matters; and in some cases, it can prolong the start of a highly anticipated period.

I glance down at my shopping list and put a check mark next to 'Guavas'. *Fresh Note* is the only store I could think of that would have them. I go through the produce section, filling my cart with strawberries, bell peppers, kiwis, oranges, and a papaya for good measure.

I head to the juice aisle next and select a container of orange juice and a pricey pre-blended smoothie drink called VitaC Boost. As I make my way over to the checkout line, I stop in the pharmaceutical section and drop a container of vitamin C capsules in my cart.

"For Immunity Health!" The label boasts.

I frown. I *wish that was all I needed.*

As I'm turning from the vitamin section, a row of bright pink boxes catch my eye.

"Ninety-nine percent accurate!" They say, *"Fast results!"*

I stare down at my cart, which is hued with a selection of orange, yellow and green things.

I'm pretty sure you're supposed to wait a whole week after your missed period before taking a pregnancy test for truly accurate results ... Otherwise, the test could spew false readings. I shake my head and start toward the checkout line. My vitamin-C rich groceries will induce my period. This is only a scare and nothing more.

I pick up a new, brightly-colored yoga mat and plop it on my cart along the way, just as a way to prove it to myself that I'm not that worried.

* * *

My cell phone vibrates in my pocket as I am cutting up some fresh bell peppers to snack on. Since the only people who ever call me anymore are Kim, Rae, and (on rare occasions) my mother, I accept the call without looking to see who it is.

"Hello?"

"Grace, it's me!"

Rae.

"I haven't heard from you since A&B. Just wanted to make sure you're doing okay?"

"Hey," I say, popping a pepper in my mouth, "I'm doing great."

I try to put some pep into my tone to make it sound convincing. I promised myself I wouldn't tell anyone about the scare, because telling people makes it feel more real. Of course, believing that it could be real will bring on more stress, and the more I stress out, the longer my period will prolong its arrival, because stress is a bitch and a trickster. Therefore, I am not stressed. I am at peace. I am Zen.

Rae clears her throat, "So um, I need to tell you something."

I take a seat with my bowl of peppers, ready to listen.

"Shoot."

There's some sort of shuffling on the other end, followed by more silence. After a minute, she sighs, "Okay, so I hope this doesn't upset you, but I went to another A&B thing ..."

I stop mid-chew, taking a moment to fully download what Rae just said. She went *back?*

"I thought they only meet once a week," I say.

"Well, it wasn't a meet," she says, "It was a baby shower get-together at Kaya's for Macie — remember Macie?"

"Yes," I briefly recall the pregnant woman who read off Hadley's name, "I remember her."

Silence.

"Well, that part doesn't really matter, I guess. I have to tell you something that happened *at* the shower. With ... Hadley. I talked to her."

My heart thuds loudly and I stop chewing my peppers completely. Rae's been *talking* to her?

"Hear me out," She says, "I didn't go up to her. She came up to *me.* She was being all ... nice, which I didn't understand at first, but ..."

I feel a momentary wave of betrayal in my heart. It's a feeling I've come to associate with Jayden's name and what *he* did, so for it to be directed at *Rae,* my best friend, because of something *she* did? I'm just not sure I can handle that right now. What reason could she have had for going back there, when I had to *convince* her to go to A&B in the first place?

"This isn't coming out right." Rae says, "Basically, I have a theory."

I swallow back my hurt feelings and force myself to listen. My best friend since freshman year wouldn't just *befriend* someone who hurt me the way Hadley did… and the only reason my mind is allowing the fear (that Rae, too, would hurt me) to infiltrate my contentment is because Jayden hurt my trust in people. Even people I've loved for years.

"Grace," Rae says, snapping my attention to her voice, "Are you still there?"

"Yes," I say, "What's your theory?"

She sighs, "I don't think Hadley knows. About you and Jayden."

That catches me off guard.

"What…? What makes you say that?"

"Because… If she knows who you are, and saw *me* with you at A&B, don't you think she would avoid talking to me, or bringing up the subject of men? Yet at the baby shower, she had no problem telling me about the guy that she's with."

I sigh, exasperated and a little angry, "Yeah, Rae. It's called being a bitch."

"No … Grace. For real," She says, "That's not the only reason I'm saying all this. I pulled up his profile picture on Facebook, right?"

I release a loud groan, "I know, Rae. I saw this morning. Why are you rubbing salt on my wounds right now?"

"What?" she says, "What do you mean?"

Jayden had deleted all pictures of us together from his Facebook early this morning and had even made his and Hadley's friendship Facebook-official. I guess that was his way of saying he's over it. If only I could send him the same kind of messages instead of stalking his Facebook profile first thing in the morning like the pathetic soul that I am.

"I think ... you should just talk to her about it," Rae says, "Come back and make the judgment call for yourself."

I rub my temples. I want to scream that I don't care. That Hadley is none of my concern and neither is Jayden.

But I do care ...

"What if he does this to more girls, Grace? If Hadley is just an ignorant player in one of his games, isn't it our obligation to tell her what's going on?"

I remain silent. The fury that is suddenly gurgling up to the surface of my chest is one that is foreign and unrecognizable to me.

I have *no* obligation to do *anything.*

"Wouldn't you have rather found out in a gentler way than you did?" Rae adds, "Something other than discovering it for the first time all on your own?"

Learning about your boyfriend's infidelity through a total stranger is hardly gentler than just figuring it out for yourself. At least finding out for yourself allows you to maintain some level of dignity.

I can feel the stress of this conversation weighing in on my body. The very idea that I'm stressing out stresses me out more, because I'm trying so desperately to avoid the prolonging of my period.

"I really can't talk about this," I say, the weight of needing to purge the stress growing heavier with each passing second.

"Grace, please don't be ma — "

I end the call abruptly.

At first, I'm surprised that I did it. The sudden termination of Rae's words is satisfying, yet guilt-inspiring. I've never hung up the phone on someone before. Especially not my best friend. Should I call back and apologize?

I shake my head. *Not until I get a good grip on this situation.*

I try to breathe a few, deep breaths, but it isn't long before my mind begins to torture me.

Will I lose *all* my friends to this breakup? Are Jayden and his *mistress* going to slowly strip me of everything I have left? I imagine them as bloodthirsty leeches — seeking out an unfortunate soul to suck the life from until there is nothing left of the victim — Only taking and never giving anything back.

'*Wrong*'. My mind maliciously retorts, switching subjects from one torturous idea to another. It forces me to consider the image of a potential fetus deep inside my belly — small, harmless, and only slightly formed. I can't say Jayden never gave me anything when he gave me *this* nightmarish problem.

I curse at how real I'm allowing this pregnancy concern to feel. That's the exact *opposite* of what I should be doing. Why is this so damn hard?

* * *

When evening comes, I can't take it anymore. I open my laptop and pull up Facebook, letting curiosity control my actions.

I type "Hadley Harris" into the search bar and select the one that has two mutual friends — Jayden Grayson and Kaya Tarelle. Her profile picture is of her holding a puppy; a still frame of her laughing as it licks her face. I squint as I scroll down to her relationship status.

Single.

She doesn't appear to post much, but she sure does get tagged in a lot of things. I click on her photos and scroll through them, searching out Jayden's face, but it doesn't appear. In fact, she doesn't have pictures with any men on here. Only groups of girls doing various activities. I recognize Kaya in one of the pictures, but the rest of the faces are strangers to me.

I realize that stalking her like this is no use. It won't tell me any real information.

With my heat subsiding, I begin to feel worse and worse about hanging up the phone like I did. It's not like I have boatloads of friends lining up outside my door. I really only have one true friend right now. Why did I feel like I had the freedom to treat her so carelessly?

I look around my living room, which is dark now without sunshine streaming through the connected sunroom. My furniture needs dusting, along with the ancient Book sitting on top of my coffee table. Amity is nowhere to be seen, and now, without even Rae by my side, I truly feel alone.

10

Rae - Monday

I stand behind the cash register of my job at *SportsTop,* sincerely wondering if I can do anything right anymore. When I was a little girl, I felt like a pro at plenty of things. I could paint the prettiest rocks in my recycle-art class, bust the best moves in dance lessons, and my jump roping skills were unmatched in gym class. I had plenty of unique skills back then, and seemingly so much more flavor to my personality. But now, at the ripe age of twenty-one, I can't even maintain basic friendships. And by 'basic', I mean a friendship that has never felt anything but totally natural.

When Grace hung up on me yesterday, I waited by my phone for a few minutes, certain she would call me back. Whenever one of us accidentally hung up on the other in the past, we always called back right away with some sort of reasonable explanation, like the phone service is spotty or something. But when the clock on my phone showcased ten whole minutes since the call was dropped, I realized she wasn't calling back. That I'd royally screwed up this time, and that she was actually mad at me.

I had debated all day whether or not I should tell Grace about going to the baby shower. Had it not been for my run-in with Hadley, I may have kept it a secret. But I decided that this was just too big of a thing to keep from her.

A sigh from the woman next in line interrupts my thoughts as she places various sports equipment on my counter. I plaster on a smile long enough to go through the motions of checking her out, surprised with my ability to act like nothing's wrong.

Most days I love my job — helping people find the athletic gear they need — but today I just want to go home or to the gym. Either sanctuary will do.

There are three more hours left in my shift and no one in the line, so to keep my hands busy, I begin running a vacuum over the floor. With the sound of the vacuum cleaner evenly humming in my ears, I begin to drift back to my conversation with Grace.

If I'm being honest, telling her about Hadley was the right thing to do, even if I'm sorry to have upset her. At the same time, though, I should've picked up on what was going through her mind the moment she used the word 'bitch' to describe another girl. Grace can be feisty when she wants to be, but ultimately, she is the essence of her name: graceful. She believes wholeheartedly in achieving self-respect and having respect for others. She chooses her words carefully before she says them. She is thoughtful and collected, and like Zoe said, whimsical. She doesn't just throw around words like that when she's okay, and that's something I should know by now.

I turn off the vacuum because the store is surprisingly bustling now, at least for our town's standards. Gevali is a close-knit community tucked between our state's capital, Montpelier, and the happening city of Burlington. There's only one store of every kind, so the faces I see in the shop are usually familiar. Today, however, a surprising amount of tourists buzz around the store. No doubt they're here to stock up on their hiking gear and see the beautiful autumn maples that Vermont is famous for.

I make my way back to the register, and to my surprise, a familiar face steps up to the counter.

"Hey, stranger," Kaya says, placing a blue, retractable dog leash on my counter.

"Hey!" I smile back, genuinely glad to see her.

"Long time, no see, right?" She winks.

"For real," I say, scanning the tag, "You doing okay?"

"I'm doing wonderful," she says, "and how about yourself?"

"I'm hanging in there." I say.

"Is that you, Kaya?" A voice says from behind her.

She turns to see who said her name.

"Marj, hey!" Kaya says, wrapping her arms around the older lady behind her in line.

The old lady — Marj — takes Kaya's smooth hands into her wrinkled ones, displaying an expression of pure concern.

"I am so sorry to hear about your diagnosis," she says, "Richard and I haven't stopped praying since we heard the news."

Diagnosis?

Kaya just smiles and squeezes Marj's hands, "Thank you so much. Please let Richard know how much I appreciate you both."

Marj shakes her head, clearly distraught, "I just don't understand how you maintain such a positive attitude, my dear. And for someone so young."

"Ah, can't take all the credit there. I couldn't do it without my helper," Kaya winks, "You know that."

At this, Marj smiles, "Oh, don't I know that. You're a good girl, Kaya."

An impatient tourist behind the two clears their throat unnaturally loud.

Kaya looks up at them and smiles before turning back to the counter.

"I'm sorry," She says, retrieving a credit card from her pocket, "I'm holding up the line aren't I?"

"It's okay," I say, accepting her card and sparing her my sales speech.

As I hand her the bag, I look at her a little closer. She doesn't look any different … She seems to be her vibrant, normal self.

She thanks me and proceeds out the door, still with pep in her step.

The old lady steps up to the counter, holding a pair of children's sneakers in her hands.

"Did you find everything okay?" I ask her out of habit.

"Oh, just fine, dear." She replies, "Shopping for my grandbaby, of course."

I nod as I bag her item, mustering a smile. "I didn't mean to eavesdrop, but I know Kaya too. She's a close family friend. You mentioned something about … a diagnosis?"

Marj winces, looking deeply saddened, "That's right. The poor girl."

"I hadn't heard about it." I frown, handing her the shopping bag.

"I remember the acronym …" Marj says, contemplating as she heads for the door, "E … E.W.S.? Or something like that?"

***

When my shift is over, I pull out my phone and google E.W.S.

My eyes widen when I see that it stands for Ewing's Sarcoma — a form of cancer in a person's bones or tissue; one that is common for children but rare for adults.

She must have been diagnosed before I started coming back to A&B, but why didn't mom tell me? Did she think I wouldn't care about someone who's been a family friend for years? Did she think I wouldn't pray about it, so there's no real point in telling me?

Would *you pray about it?*

The thought hits me out of nowhere, and suddenly I feel defensive. *Of course I would.* Absolutely. Never mind the fact that I haven't said a real prayer in a long time.

Kaya is a person deserving of prayers. You'd never know anything is wrong just by watching her. When I asked her how she was doing, she'd said she was wonderful. I've never seen her without a smile on her face, and she is always so caring towards others. It makes me wonder *how.* How can somebody who's been diagnosed with *cancer* be so sunny and loving instead of resentful and downtrodden?

Kaya had said something about this when Marj asked the same question. Her reply had been, *"I couldn't do it without my helper."*

What did she mean by her helper? Is she seeing someone new who eases the blow of such a diagnosis?

The thought warms my heart. Either way, she has me intrigued.

Who is this helper, and how are they bringing her so much joy, that cancer is just a mere detail in her mind? Moreover, how can I get some of him or her in *my* life too?

11

Grace - Monday

Loneliness can be strangely productive. I haven't booked any clients the past couple of days, so instead I've busied myself with sorting through and donating the last of Grandma Jackie's things, reading some of my favorite self-help novels, and making products for my business. In total, I've made four lotions, six soaps, three medicinal tinctures, and eight candles — a product I've learned to love making because Rae's mom taught me how in Junior year of high school. If I'm honest, Mrs. Brooks is really the one who ignited my passion for holistic medicine and making all-natural goods. She encouraged me to pursue my certifications in aromatherapy and herbalism, which kicked off my home-based business. My actual mother and I have different beliefs about medicine, her being a nurse and all, but Rae's mom was always an advocate of me pursuing my passion for homeopathic living.

These thoughts make me miss Mrs. Brooks. They make me miss Rae. I never did call her back to apologize and I feel bad for it, but I'm also still a little mad at her for everything. She really didn't have any right to dabble in this part of my life, in which I'm still licking my wounds. I've resolved that I need to take some time for myself — to cleanse and renew. Hence, the indulgence in self-help books and intense clean-out session of my house, which is tidied to perfection and finally rid of the last of Grandma Jackie's books. All but one.

I've been ignoring the Bible for no rational reason, which has felt more childish than liberating. It's almost as though I'm scared of what it might tell me I'm doing wrong ... like the reason my life sucks right now is all because of me, and it's nothing more than a direct result of my own ways.

I glance around my living room which appears bright and airy since I've drawn back the window shades. I've purged the room so deeply, there's not a single thing left to clean. A single ray of sunshine beams directly on the Book, illuminating its gold-rimmed pages.

I sigh in resignation. With no more products to make, nothing more to clean, and certainly not anyone to talk to, I saunter over to the book and pick it up.

The weight of it shifts in my hands, unassumingly.

I settle into my favorite chair next to the window and begin untying the strings that bind the book. I open the cover just a sliver before closing it back up.

Maybe I should pray or something first ... isn't that what Kaya said last week?

I recall her briefly mentioning that when you read the Bible, it should be a conversation rather than a one-sided lecture session. We can ask questions and make requests in our prayers, and the Bible, in theory, is supposed to be what God says back.

I shift to where I am sitting on my knees in my chair, placing the Bible gently in my lap. The one other time I said a prayer, I was laying down ... sobbing ... and it was only three words long.

I feel like this time it should be more formal somehow, as kind of a peace offering for the last time, but I really don't know what a formal prayer should sound like.

I straighten my back and close my eyes, folding my hands lightly in my lap.

The house is utterly silent and I feel silly, but I shake my head and try to get into some sort of prayerful state of mind.

"Praise," Kaya had said, *"Always begin your prayers with acknowledging the Majesty of your Creator. Pray in recognition of who He is, who YOU are, and offer your thanks for His goodness."*

I instantly recall the scripture in Psalm I read when first opening Grandma Jackie's Bible, and having located a good starting point, I begin forming the words in my mind before I say them.

"Lord," I whisper, not wanting to use my full voice, "You are great and mighty in power. So much so that your understanding is infinite."

I smile because I feel like that was a good start. I think if my future daughter or son said that to me I'd probably start listening.

"I just want to say that ..."

That what...?

I pause, thinking for a moment. What am I trying to accomplish with this? What is it that I need to say? Moreover, what exactly do I need to *hear?*

"I just wanted to say that I'm sorry the last time we talked was the first time ever, and that it was so brief, and possibly demanding of me." *Pause.* "I just felt ... hopeless."

I realize I'm not making myself sound too impressive and clear my throat.

"Anyway, I hope that you will guide my reading right now — that you will guide me to exactly what it is that you want to tell me…"

Pause.

"In a merciful way." I add before saying amen.

Okay. Round two.

I position the book on my lap and open up the front cover, smiling at the note from my great grandmother to Grandma Jackie. No divine force seems to be telling my fingers which page to flip to, so I close my eyes and flip to a random page toward the beginning. The title is called Deuteronomy, and there is one scripture in chapter 31 that Grandma Jackie has swirled around again and again with her pen so that it is mercilessly circled. In the margins next to it, she's written, "You are not alone - Vs. 8."

At this, my breath catches slightly, and I go on to read it:

The Lord Himself goes before you and will be with you. He will never leave nor forsake you. Do not be afraid. Do not be discouraged.

After this scripture in small letters, Grandma Jackie wrote, *"Joshua 1:9."*

Joshua is another book of the Bible, isn't it?

I flip back to the front where the index is. Sure enough — Joshua is in the table of contents. I flip to the coordinating page number until I get to the right place. Also circled with Grandma's pen, the scripture says,

Have I not commanded you? Be strong and courageous. Do not be afraid; do not be discouraged, for the Lord your God will be with you wherever you go.

I bite my lip, wondering if it was purely coincidental that the first thing I flipped to applied to my situation perfectly, and that I was then pointed in the direction of another scripture saying almost the exact same thing as the first one. It's almost as if the repetitiveness were done intentionally — like the first time reading the words was to convey the message, but the second time was for emphasis.

Maybe this is what You wanted me to hear?

Then my heart falls a little bit. Not out of discouragement, but humility. I've been avoiding this book ever since I decided to keep it, all because I thought it would brutally tear me apart, decision by decision. But if my prayer was heard, and God really did guide my reading, He led me to a gentle scripture instead. One that didn't condemn me, like I'd been afraid of, but one that simply said, "I am here for you. I am with you. Please don't be discouraged."

I gently close the book and set it on the coffee table with care. Is it *purely* coincidental that I read that scripture in the midst of being at an all-time-low for loneliness? Is it by happenstance that I somehow feel worlds of comfort after reading it?

* * *

Okay, so it hasn't been the best day.

I slip on my fuzzy, fingerless gloves and quickly stuff my hands into my coat pockets.

But I know exactly what can make it better.

Glancing up at the neon *do not walk* sign, I silently will it to change faster as the icy breeze carries the warmth of fresh baked pastries from across the street.

My mouth waters as I imagine the steaming hot plate of cinnamon buns waiting for me inside Aroma Mocha Café — the one delicious baked good I know of that has day-altering capabilities. It is their signature dish, and makes all other cinnamon buns taste like a disgrace to the pastry family.

My reason for needing such reinforcements?

I'm a full day late now ... and I don't have anyone to talk to about it since Rae and I still aren't talking. When I tried calling Aunt Kim, it went straight to voicemail. Then, like clockwork, a call from my mother lit up the phone screen in my hand. I still don't know what her original intent had been for calling me ... just that I was desperate and ended up spilling the beans. Her reaction had been what I should've guessed: She never liked that Jayden boy in the first place. I don't know if she meant it for me to feel better, but I ended up feeling way worse.

So, I resulted to braving the cold weather to do the very thing I should not be doing: stress eat.

Just when I think the wintery cold air is going to freeze me into an ice block, the pedestrian light changes to green and I make a hasty procession across the street walk.

I hurry over to the door and give it a tug, causing the little greeting bell to chime on the inside. I step into the warmth of the building and wipe the snow from my boots. The aroma of greasy baked goods fills my senses and triggers an involuntary smile on my face. *Finally.*

I can melt away all the pain and cares from today with the taste of sugary goodness.

The line is long, but I am content to wait. It gives me time to check up on all the notifications that've been blowing up my phone for the past two hours.

I scroll mindlessly through hundreds of new emails, most of which are from online stores trying to coax me into buying some sort of merchandise. *"Special deals, Just for YOU!"*, they prod me with the same generic email they send out to every previous customer they can find in their records, *"You've been chosen. Congratulations!"*, *"Sign up now for DISCOUNT."*

I sigh quietly, snapping my phone shut, "No thank you."

The line has moved up significantly, leaving only two people ahead of me. *Thank you, Aroma Mocha service.*

I eye the cinnamon buns longingly as they silently promise me a better day. There are six whole ones left in the display case, fresh from the oven like always and dripping with a thin layer of icing. I might have to spoil myself and order two this time.

The person in the front of the line finishes prattling off their order and the man in front of me moves up to the counter. He is a spikey-haired brunette with a tall, athletic build.

"I'll just have a coffee … tall, black, and … hmm, let's see."

His voice is deep and silky, but in a subtle sort of way. He carefully surveys the display case of decadent treats.

"Ah, yes. Let's have a few of those." He says, his finger pointing to the cinnamon buns.

"Good choice," The red-lipped cashier says, unlocking the glass, "How many you need, hun?"

The boy waves his hand dismissively, "Ah, just throw them all in there."

The cashier's eyebrows raise and she smiles, "Now there's a man who knows how to order!"

Her long red fingernails aid her in gripping the brown paper bag as she loads in every last one of my feel-better snacks. Every. Last. One.

I watch the entire exchange with parted lips and an incredulous expression. Did he really just order *six* cinnamon buns?

"Is that for here or to go?" The cashier singsongs, batting her eyelashes profusely.

"Let's take it for here," He says, paying no mind to her affections. Or perhaps he is just oblivious to them.

"Alright, sir, your total is $23.85." She says, handing him a plate to enjoy his pastries on.

He slides his card across the desk and she scans it, giving him one last flirtatious smile before wishing him a good day.

My lips are still parted with disbelief, and there's a good chance my eyes are slightly narrowed when the cashier called for next in line.

"What can I get for you?" She says to me, causing me to snap out of my disgust. I move up, but my eyes remain on the now empty plate of cinnamon buns. Only a few, sad crumbles remain. My mind goes so far as to consider purchasing them. Maybe if I bunch them all up together, they'll equal a fourth of the size of an actual cinnamon bun.

Who am I kidding? I obviously need a whole one for its magic to work. *Hell,* after this day I need *two* whole ones.

"Can I help you, hun?" Red lip lady repeats, tapping her matching fingernails on the desk.

"Is there any chance you'll be making any more of those today?" I ask, pointing to the empty plate.

"Oh, I'm afraid not, honey. We're gonna be closing the shop early today because of the weather, so we're just trying to sell out of what we've already made."

"Oh …" I say quietly.

I feel my eyes brim with warmth. Am I really going to cry over some glorified cinnamon rolls? No, I need to get it together. I can't let the events of today pile up and lead to a public embarrassment.

I smile weakly, passing her my card, "I'll just have an Americano. Short — with extra cream please."

"Alrighty, I'll have that right out for you if you'd like to take a seat." she says, gesturing towards the seating area.

I move out of line, and the first thing I see is the joy-robbing pastry-thief, taking a seat at one of the high stools against the window and settling in with his bag of mouth-watering treats.

Oh, hell no.

I consider up and leaving, but I already paid for my coffee and had nothing to show for it yet. Sighing, I realize I'll have to put on my big girl britches and endure the wait in the same room of the Grinch who stole my hope for a better day.

I begrudgingly choose the farthest seat away from him, which unfortunately isn't that far. The Café is ever bustling with hungry customers, hoping to escape the cold for awhile, forcing me to select a high table … also against the window … only a few tables down.

I pretend to scroll through my phone, but secretly peek at him from beneath my lashes. He's flipping through a newspaper, wearing a deceitful expression of innocence as he chews.

It's one thing to buy that many buns if you're eating them with a group of friends, but he sits all by himself, taking a leisurely sip of coffee.

"Here you go, doll." The waitress girl says, setting my Americano on the table.

I smile in thanks and wrap my fingers around the steaming cup. I'd originally intended to leave as soon as she brought it out, but instead I watch the spiky haired boy flip to the next page in his newspaper, an idea brewing in my mind.

I'm not even that hungry, but my stomach rumbles out of pure lust for the piping hot cinnamon buns piled on his plate. Maybe I could just …

No. I'm not seriously considering going up to him and offering to buy one from him … am I?

Okay … so what if I am? Who needs *six cinnamon buns* for heaven's sake!

I lift my coffee up to my face, leaning forward slightly on my elbows while I consider my options.

His face really is beautifully sculpted … he has the classic square jawline that girls rave about, nicely shaped eyebrows, and those eyes … I squint to discern their color. Earlier they'd looked to be a dark hue of brown — almost ebony, but now, in the light, I can see that they'd become a brighter shade. More of a rich, chestnut brown.

It's at that moment his eyes flick up at me from the newspaper, causing me to panic and take a quick, involuntary sip of burning hot coffee. It scalds my throat all the way down and I stifle a choke.

I whip out my phone and begin scrolling frantically in efforts to cover up the fact that I'd been staring. Maybe I'd reacted quick enough for him not to notice.

That was my hope anyway, but — no such luck. When I steal another glance at him, his eyes are still set on me, but this time, he wears a side grin. He definitely saw.

Shoot.

I have to do it now … the cinnamon bun bartering. As much as I want to just hide my face and leave, I already made it awkward. I may as well get something out of it.

I grip my coffee and take a deep breath.

Come on, Grace, don't be a wuss. Rae would do it …

Thinking of my friend who is fearless when she wants to be, I scoot my stool back and march right up to the guy's table. The only thing that stands between me and my precious pastries is *him.*

He stares at me with the same bemused expression as he folds his newspaper and sets it down on the table in front of him.

"Hi," I say curtly.

He takes a leisurely sip of his coffee, "May I help you?"

His voice is not unwelcoming. If anything, it's curious.

Feeling victorious at his intrigue, I settle in on the seat across from him, surprising even myself.

"Yes." I say, "I…"

At this moment, I hate being somewhat short. My legs don't reach the bottom rung of the elevated stool, and I'm forced to either curl them up to the top rung or leave them swinging where they fall, which definitely ruins my badass vibe.

"I was just gonna say…"

He eyes me intently, clearing his throat a little, as if to say '*yes?*'

I wish he would just quit looking at me so I could get my words out. His deep brown eyes bore into mine, making it impossible to continue.

Just then, a young woman enters the Café and walks right up to our table, choking the words from my throat.

She has long silken hair that fades from a rich ebony color into a caramel brown at the tips. She's beautifully dressed in cute white skinnies and a colorful floral top. She wears beads upon beads of matching jewelry, and as she arrives at our table, she kisses the charming pastry-stealing man curtly on the cheek.

"Liam, hey," She says before turning to me, "Who's this?"

He smiles at her and shrugs, looking inquisitively at me.

Oh my word. I have probably just caused this poor man a world of unnecessary strife with his girlfriend. I think of Jayden and Hadley, and all the questions I had for Jayden when I suspected the cheating. I instantly think to ease the situation for the man. For *Liam.*

"I'm so sorry," I say mostly to the girl as I stumble out of my seat, "I just came over here to buy one of his cinnamon rolls from him because they're all I've wanted all day. But he got here before me and bought every last one of them, and I was so incredulous that someone would *do* something like that, because who seriously buys six cinnamon buns? So I…"

I realize they're staring at me and close my mouth.

"Anyway, I'm sorry." I gather my purse, my coffee, and my jacket from the seat and I push my glasses back into place before making a swift exit out of the building.

12

Rae - Monday

I type, erase, and retype the text. I know I should say something … but *what?* Kaya never told me about the diagnosis herself, so maybe she wouldn't even want me to know. At the same time, she is always there for everyone else … Maybe she needs someone to be there for *her* for a change.

While I was avoiding A&B for five months, she made sure to text me multiple times to make sure I was okay and let me know she was thinking of me, unmoved by the fact that I never replied once.

To my knowledge, Kaya doesn't have a soul mate who keeps her uplifted like I have with Adam, unless this 'helper' she referred to is a potential suitor — one that she's keeping on the down low for whatever reason.

These ideas are all the more reason to text her. If she doesn't have a man, she deserves *someone* looking out for her. And if she *does,* who is the mystery figure that managed to capture Kaya's heart after all these years?

I finally decide on what to say and hit send before I can change my mind.

Sent: 10/07/19

Time: 3:04 pm

"Kaya,

I was so sorry to learn of your diagnoses this morning... words just aren't enough. Is there anything I can do for you?

Xoxo, Rae."

I feel slightly guilty seeing her three ignored messages against my *one* measly text. She honestly has every right to ignore my efforts the way I did hers ... but just minutes later, my phone pings.

From: Kaya (A&B)

Sent: 10/07/19

Time: 3:06 pm

"Yes :) Come over! I am planting a garden today."

Oh.

Okay then. That's not what I was expecting. Especially since it's been snowing for a good portion of the day. But at the same time, I find myself deeply appreciating that she gave me a real answer. She could have sent an impersonal, copy/pasted "Thank you for your concern, but I'm alright" type of message. The kind that is customary for people to send in her circumstances. But she didn't do that. She *took me up* on my offer.

I'm so grateful for her down-to-earth reply that I actually get in my car and drive over to 305 Rose Valley Boulevard.

Despite the light patter of snow we've had, none of it stuck to the ground as originally predicted. The sun is even beginning to peek out from behind the frosty clouds. The grass glistens in the sunlight as it's rays find small droplets of snow.

"We might have an autumn in Vermont after all, huh?" Kaya says from the porch.

She's wearing a straw sunhat, carrying a gardening spade in one gloved hand and two medium-sized packets in the other.

I meet her halfway and squeeze my arms around her. I don't know what else to do. Should I apologize again about her situation, or would she rather not dwell on the subject?

She squeezes me back as well as she can, with her arms full. When I release her, she smiles.

Wordlessly, she hands me the spade and nods to a patch of freshly turned up soil by the porch. I follow her over and kneel in the grass as she does. Icy little droplets of snow soak through the denim fabric at my knees, causing me to shiver. Kaya seems unfazed.

She still wears her smile of pure delight and straightens her hat, "You dig, I'll plant?"

I nod, "Sure."

The grass sparkles with dew all around us as we work.

"Interesting timing for planting a garden," I say after a minute.

She sits back on her heels, eyeing the seeds in her palm.

"These are called Early Scilla, and the other ones are called Snowdrops. You're supposed to plant them in the fall, and they'll bloom sometime around late winter or early spring."

She resumes dropping them in the holes I make. "Winter tends to be so colorless and dreary; I just want to see some color popping up through the snow this year."

I smile, "That'll be beautiful,"

"Mm-hmm," She hums, "Ever since I got diagnosed with Ewing's, I've tried to adapt a mindset of not waiting to do the things I enjoy most."

I frown. I had been pronouncing it *E-wings,* but Kaya had said it like *YOO-ings.* Silence passes between us as I try to think of what to say, but these kinds of conversations have never been a strength of mine. I try to think of what Grace might say if she were in my position. Addressing emotional subjects has always been natural for her.

"How bad is it?" I say, wishing I had my best friend's way with words.

"Well," Kaya says, "I am very lucky, because the cancer has not metastasized to my lungs or my bones. It's localized in my arm right now."

I wince, "Is that painful?"

"Sometimes," She says, "But it could be a lot worse."

My brows pinch together, "How are you doing through all this, Kaya? Really ... like, I want to know. This has got to be affecting your quality of life."

She smiles, "I mean, yeah. My life has kind of become a blur of blood tests, IV's and Chemo. But on the bright side, my knowledge of doctor jargon has been *greatly* enhanced. I now understand big words like 'malignancy'."

At this, my hands seem to lose their will to dig and I find myself staring at her instead. She drops each seed in the holes that I've made with an expression of pure contentment.

She turns and looks back at me with a smile, "What?"

I decide right here and now to be real with her, just as she's been with me.

"Kaya … You have such a positive attitude about everything, and I just … I don't understand it. I want to understand … to know how you stay so joyful …"

She sits back on her heels again, sealing the packet of seeds.

"Well believe me, some days are better than others," She says, "But you know … I have my helper, and He says to 'count it all joy'."

Just like that, I have my answer. By her helper, she had meant something spiritual. Of course she had. She's Kaya.

She stands, pulling off her gardening gloves and tucking them into her belt. She offers me a hand to help me up and I take it.

"Come with me," she says.

* * *

I follow Kaya into her house.

Coco greets us with boundless energy, tail wagging, and ears perked.

Kaya scoops him up, rubbing his ears as she leads us to the living room. The fireplace is lit, giving the room a warm glow of comfort.

As Kaya goes over to a shelf in the corner, Coco wriggles out of her arms and settles on a puppy bed by the fireplace.

The shelf she searches appears to be full of knick-knacks and photo albums. She selects a small, thin book tucked between the albums and joins me. A notebook, I realize, as she holds it to her chest.

"I want to share something really meaningful with you," She says.

I smile, "Please."

She looks down at the notebook, running a hand over the cover affectionately. "This book has been a source of comfort to me for a long time now. It documents some … pretty rough times in my life."

For the first time ever, she's not smiling.

"You see, about twelve years back, I hit an all-time-low in my life. My boyfriend had a problem with substance abuse, and refused to give it up no matter how willing I was to work with him on it. So I broke up with him, and it was more painful at the time than I realize it ever should've been. On top of that, the financial burdens seemed never-ending, and I was struggling. So when I received the call that my parents had been in a car crash, and neither one survived …" she shakes her head, "I fell into the darkest depression I've ever known."

I open my mouth to say something and close it again. I am caught off guard by so many different things, I don't know where to begin. I had no idea that Kaya's parents died, or on a less extreme note, that she ever dated anyone, although I probably should have assumed as much with her being years older than I am.

"I closed out a lot of people after all that." She says, "My days seemed like a blur of hopeless efforts, and I didn't want to speak to anyone. But keeping your emotions caged up after something like that can only last so long before you just … burst."

She stares down at the notebook, "This book contains those bursts. The first half of it is nothing but angry, messy words, casting blame, frustrations, and everything else."

"But then …" She opens the cover and flips to a page in the middle, "it morphs into something else. Something much more progressive."

She hands the journal to me and nods her approval for me to look at the page she's opened it to. Written in small, ornate script are the words,

Come to me, all you who are weary and burdened, and I will give you rest. - Matthew 11:28-30.

I look back up at her and she shakes her head.

"I was so tired, Rae. So defeated and upset, and I felt like no one *really* understood. Not like I needed them to, anyway. Then, in the midst of everything, along came this scripture, which popped up in a silly Facebook ad believe it or not. One thing was certain ... I needed a break from all of my emotions — some sort of rest — and here it was being offered to me so freely, if I chose to accept it."

I stare down at the scripture a moment longer before gently passing it back to her. "So ... what happened?"

She flips the page, "I wrote the scripture down so that I would remember it, and from then on out, I resolved to turn my venting into prayers. That's what the rest of the journal consists of. Pouring my heart out to God, asking questions, relieving myself of the burdens. And slowly but surely, wouldn't you know it, I *did* begin feeling a little better each time. It was better feeling like I was talking to *someone* rather than a blank page ... someone who didn't interrupt me. Someone who might actually be able to *do* something about the situation."

She sets the journal down and faces me, "My joy comes from the Lord now. No one can steal that from me, because it's mine. I *claim* the joy and the peace and the rest being offered to me through the Holy Spirit."

I think of my scars and the joy they've been threatening to rob me of on my wedding day. I think of the pressure I always feel to be better than I am ... to be more than my best. It's not that I'm comparing my struggles with hers, because I know they're not equal ... but I still find myself wishing I could have the joy and peace she's talking about.

I stare down at my clasped hands, "How do you claim it? You say it like it's just a readily available resource for anyone who wants it."

She smiles, "It is available to all those who *love* God. Whether the person has an inborn love for him or has had to struggle a little first like I did. It doesn't matter how they got to the point of loving him or if it took a long time – it just matters that they eventually do.

"And loving God," I say, staring at my palms, "Requires you to live a saintly life."

She studies me for a moment.

"You're not expected to be perfect overnight, Rae. No human being can be perfect all the time. What God is looking for is someone who is trying their *best.* He wants to see that we have a willing heart. One that is working on becoming something better than just a fleshly human being."

When I don't say anything, she continues.

"God loves giving to his children. He wants to delight us with blessings. Don't you think a Being that knows your heart inside-out, because he crafted it himself, understanding every little crook and crevice, will know when you're trying your best and reward that?"

A flicker of something lights up in my chest. Hope, maybe?

"So there you have it," Kaya says, leaning back, "You know my secrets."

Her expression switches to one of intrigue, "But that can't have been your reason for reaching out to me."

I smile, "That makes me sound so meddling,"

"But you're not a meddling person," she says thoughtfully. "You're a person who is interested in self-betterment. It's why you want to be a physical trainer, because you believe in working to become the best version of yourself."

I'm flattered by the compliment. It's almost been full year ago now that I told her what I was going to college for, and she remembered.

"My gut tells me that the reason you're here," She continues, "and the reason you were specifically curious about my 'helper', is because you wouldn't mind having one yourself."

I'm taken aback by her intuition. Is my overwhelm that obvious? I think of my test coming up, wedding planning, finding the perfect dress, upsetting Grace, and all the pressure from my mom to attend A&B. I think of my scars and the shame I feel for doing the one thing that makes me feel better about them.

The sad part is, I'm usually *not* an easily overwhelmed person. I'm not an overthinker. I don't wallow in guilt. But ever since I started to ignore my gut feelings about what's right and wrong … started to hide certain lifestyle choices from my mom and sister … I haven't felt like myself at all. So here and now, I admit to myself that Kaya is right. When I heard her mention a 'helper' — one that keeps her so damn positive through something as devastating as cancer — I *did* want in on that. That *is* why I'm here.

"It's just that …" I say, "I haven't been through nearly as much as you have, and yet, you handle yourself so much better than I do. I just … want to have that same sort of peaceful, joyful way about myself that you seem to have, so I'm not so easily overwhelmed by things that are way smaller in comparison."

Kaya raises a hand, "Now don't go thinking I'm perfect. Remember what I said about messy, angry words," She taps her journal. "There are still days that I lose sight of what's important. I break down and scream and cry just like you do."

I smile, but I can't meet her eyes.

Her voice softens, "I'm not going to dig into your personal life, Rae, so consider this as more of a rhetorical question. I know your family, and I know you're a smart girl. With that being said, I have a feeling you already know these things I'm telling you about God's love and about doing your best. You already know what you need to do to obtain what you're looking for … so, my question is, what is it that's holding you back? What particular roadblock is in your way from taking what's yours in the Spirit?"

I consider the question, even though I know the answer. I remember my decision to be real with her, and just like that, my walls break down like a crashing dam.

"Can I just … be really honest with you?"

She smiles, "I encourage it."

I open my mouth and close it again, trying to find the right words.

"By my family's standards, I'm not living a 'saintly' life. I'm like the black sheep compared to my sister …"

Her expression is attentive, "Do you mind if I ask what you mean?"

"Well, Livia's married, she goes to A&B every week, and she's just the perfect child. Ever since she was little, she listened to what she was taught and never strayed from it."

"As opposed to … you?"

"Well, not exactly. It's just like … I'm not going to pretend that I don't ever get jealous, or that I have a perfect attitude about everything, or that Adam's never spent the night with me before, you know? He does. Often."

"Ah," she nods, "I'm with you."

"And I know where the Bible points out that's wrong … but … if I'm being completely open and honest with you, I really don't *want* to make any changes in that direction. With Adam, I mean.

And I know that makes me sound terrible, but it's the truth. I know there are a lot of other things I would need to work on in order to be on my mom and sister's level, but…"

I fade off when I realize I'm word-vomiting. When she's sure I'm not going to continue, she speaks.

"Well, first of all, I don't think that makes you sound terrible, I think it makes you sound human. Which," she smiles, "Point to anyone of us who isn't human."

I smile.

"Second of all, you should never judge your spiritual progress by another person's 'level'. Your progress is completely between you and God and no one else, so try not to think of it that way. Especially if it's discouraging you from trying to grow."

"Well," I keep my eyes low, "I wish it were as easy as just *deciding* to not do it anymore, but for me … it's not. I feel like … like I need Adam."

She patiently waits for me to continue.

I sigh, "He just … makes me feel like the most beautiful girl in the world. And most days, I don't need any help with feeling that way. But like you said, some days are better than others, and on the bad days, I feel literally terrible until I get the reassurance I need from him … like I'm the most unattractive person in the world."

Kaya frowns, "Why would you ever feel that way, Rae? You're a beautiful girl *all* the time."

I shake my head, swallowing the lump in my throat, "Because of these stupid scars."

She softens, eyes falling to my arms.

"Oh, Rae… body image is something we all struggle with."

"But, until I get over it, I don't think my relationship with God will ever be where I want it to be. Not until I stop I needing something sinful from Adam to have a positive body image, and … I don't see myself ever getting over that."

She squeezes my hand and smiles, "That's not true, Rae. I think you can and you *will.* Come to think of it, I think I have a few scriptures for you that really might help with this process." She rips a piece of paper from her notebook and jots down *Psalm 139:13-16, Psalm 32:5, 1st Peter 3:3-4,* and *Luke 16:15.*

"Be sure you read them in order," She says, passing it to me. "I want you to do it sometime when you're alone, though. It should be a special and personal moment between just you and God. Maybe you could even journal your thoughts about what He's telling you. Do you think you could commit to that for me?"

I pocket the paper and nod, "I mean, definitely. If you think it'll help."

She takes my hand and squeezes, "I really do. In fact, I can already see God doing some wonderful things through you with all this."

I smile, feeling the lump in throat get bigger.

She gets up, returning the book back to its place on the shelf, "When I was going through that dry spell in my relationship with God because I was so distracted with anger, something important happened … and once I realized it, it was a game changer."

I turn towards her as she sits back down.

"I realized I could no longer tell the difference between God's voice Satan's voice in my life … because whenever I would hear that little voice in my head that said, *'God's too disappointed in how you've been acting to still be here with you. You're frustrating to Him. He doesn't want to be around you right now. Fix yourself first, then ask God to come back,'* … I believed it. I genuinely thought God himself was making those thoughts known to me ... setting his expectations clearly before me. And unfortunately, I didn't measure up."

I consider how many times I've heard that voice in my head ... *'How dare you call yourself a Christian when you're actively sleeping with Adam, even while knowing better. How dare you ask God for anything. You're dirty. Fix yourself, then come back.'*

"Slowly, I realized that any thoughts I have that are pulling me *away* from God, are not *from* God. When God speaks, it's only ever in a way that pulls us closer to him. So if your thoughts are discouraging you from working on your relationship with him, you can pretty much guess who those are coming from, because God will never do that. And He *certainly* wouldn't tell you to fix yourself on your own before seeking Him out, because God wants nothing more than to be apart of that process with you. How are you supposed to 'fix yourself' spiritually without His help?"

I nod, soaking up each point.

"It's never about being perfect before you approach him," she says, "That's an impossible expectation. It's not about making your prayers sound impressive or super formal. It's about being honest and real. He knows who you are, and doesn't expect you to be someone else around Him. He's not gonna turn you away. He just wants His daughter to reach out and talk to Him. He wants to listen and reply to you – to move visibly in your life."

I feel tears glistening in my eyes. When did I forget all this? Why have I let Satan trick me for so long?

She smiles compassionately, "I think we should pray about all this before you head out. Would that be okay?"

I nod, wiping a tear from my cheek, "I'd love that."

She takes both of my hands as we bow our heads.

"Lord, we come before you now thanking you for your beautiful daughter, Rae. I pray that you will shower your loving kindness over her, that she might feel your presence and grace in her life. I ask that you will guide her throughout her endeavors to welcome you into her life and help her to have the courage to pursue your way. I pray that she will have a truly edifying experience with you as she reads the scriptures we wrote down and the many others that you will lead her to. Help her to distinguish your voice from the devil's from here on out. Lord, we ask these things in Jesus' name, Amen."

"Amen," I follow, feeling uplifted despite my tears.

I reach over and wrap her in a hug. "Thank you so much for talking to me about all this, Kaya. I didn't realize how much I needed it."

She squeezes me back, "I'm here anytime you need me. Just like I know I can come to you."

"Yes, of course," I smile, "And I'm so sorry. I really didn't mean to make this all about me. I meant to just come spend time with you and see if you needed anything."

"Just you coming to see me made me feel worlds better," She smiles back, "The Lord has a funny way of bringing us right where we need to be. Right when we need it."

"He really does," I agree as we walk toward the door.

We hug one last time before I open it.

"And Rae?" She says.

"Hmm?"

"Just ... take baby steps. Because if you try to fix everything all at once, even *with* God's help, you will get discouraged. That's too much to focus on at a time. Just pick one thing to really grab a hold of right now and focus only on it until you feel good about it."

"I will," I say, smiling, "And I'm sorry again to hear about everything you're going through. I'll … pray for you."

And I mean it.

John 14:15-17: *If you love me, you will keep my commandments. And I will ask the Father, and he will give you another* ***Helper****, to be with you forever, even the Spirit of truth, whom the world cannot receive, because it neither sees him nor knows him. You know him, for* ***he dwells with you and will be in you****.*

13

Grace - Tuesday

I bounce lightly on the pads of my feet in front of the bedroom mirror, sizing up my midsection. I wonder if it's just my imagination making me *feel* heavier. Do mothers ever feel the weight of their baby this early on, or is any idea of that just a mind trick?

I pinch the skin of my tummy and eye it skeptically. I don't seem to have gained any weight.

Amity slinks into the room, making the door squeak. It takes my attention from my belly and reminds me of what I came in here to do in the first place. I grab my cell phone from its charger and tap out the number I've come to know by heart.

"Grace!" She says by the second ring.

"Rae." I smile, filling with warmth at her voice. "Listen — I wanted to say I'm sorry for hanging up on you the other day. That was not cool, and this is so overdue. I'm just sick of not talking to you."

She laughs, "Me too. I've missed you. And I really am sorry if I upset you. I didn't mean to."

I wave my hand, "Please. I've just been extra ... emotional lately. I'm not sure what's wrong with me."

I rest my palm on my tummy, fully aware of the lie I just told. I know exactly what my problem is.

"Hey," She says, "Don't worry about it. You've clearly had a lot on your mind."

If only you knew ... I want to say.

"I wasn't mad at you," I explain instead, "I was mad at *her.* I feel like she's trying to whittle her way into all of my relationships."

"I can understand that ..." She trails off, "But that does remind me of something I wanted to add on to that conversation. If you don't mind, that is."

Amity had darted out of the room by now, so I grab a tissue box from my bedside table just to have something to hold, "By all means."

"Well," Rae says, "I will admit — at first I was totally confused about your reaction when I brought Jayden's Facebook. I had no idea what you meant by 'you saw this morning'. So after we got off the phone, I took a look for myself, and Grace ... you totally misunderstood me. I wasn't trying to rub it in that he'd taken down your photos or anything. I was trying to tell you that Jayden had been telling Hadley he didn't even have a Facebook. When I pulled up his page the night before, all of your pictures together were still on there, and he and Hadley weren't even Facebook friends."

I frown as I process this, "Wait ... what?"

"Yes!" She exclaims, "So the only thing I can reason is that after the baby shower, maybe Hadley went home and called him out? Like '*Why are you lying to me about not having Facebook?*' So then he deleted your photos with him and 'friended' her to keep you a secret from her?"

My fingers idly rip at a tissue, anger rising in my chest, "That *cheat*."

"Right? *That's* why I was saying I think you should talk to her, Grace ... I really don't think she knows. That's what I was calling to tell you, but I got all jumbled up because I could tell you weren't happy with me. None of it came out right."

I lean against the wall, processing everything. Maybe I *should* talk to her.

"At least think about it." Rae says, "I obviously care about *you* more than anyone in this situation."

I smile, "Thanks, Rae."

A few beats pass, and I find myself wishing we could talk in person. Then I remember it's Tuesday. Our usual wedding-planning day.

"Are we still on for coffee today?" I say, leaning back against the wall, "Five o'clock tonight after work? I have a lot to tell you."

"Of course!" She says, "I'll admit that I totally forgot, but I'll get all my planners together."

"Great," I say, "Talk to you then."

We hang up and I slide my back down the wall, curling into a ball that cradles my face with my knees.

* * *

The familiar little bell on the doorknob sounds as I walk through the Café door. The sun was back out in Vermont this morning, illuminating the many brilliant colors of our famous maples, but now that it has dipped away, the evening weather is shivery again.

I find Rae seated at our usual table and hug her from behind before taking my seat across from her.

"Hey you," she smiles.

Man, I've missed her.

Ava comes up and takes our order. I get my usual chai tea and Rae gets her coffee, but when Ava returns, that's not all she's carrying.

Just as she did last time, she places a glorious smelling, grease-stained brown paper bag in front of me.

My mood instantly brightens. "Ava, I swear, you are the greatest barista in the *world*."

She purses her lips, shrugging, "It's not from me this time, but I'll take it."

I smile gratefully at Rae, "Damn you, you know I don't need all these extra carbs."

She holds up her hands, "It's not from me either."

I eye the bag skeptically, "Not ... from you?"

Ava smiles knowingly, and waltzes from our table into the kitchen.

Rae watches me intently as I open the bag and take out a yellow note. In sharp, small writing that slants slightly to the left is one simple word:

Sorry.

The word is followed by a phone number, which brings heat to my cheeks.

"What?" Rae says, "Who's it from?"

I pass her the note and set the cinnamon roll on my napkin.

Her eyes flit back and forth from the apology to the phone number.

"Um, okay, *what?*" She says, "This isn't Jayden's writing, is it?"

I shake my head, smiling through the bite of the pastry I just took.

She squints her eyes at me. "Explain. What happened within the past *two* days?"

I feel the corners of my eyes crinkle, "You're gonna laugh when I tell you what this is all about."

I relay the whole story to her, much to her amusement.

"You went *up* to him?" She whoops, "And tried to *buy* one of his cinnamon rolls?"

"I mean, yeah," I laugh, "Is that so bad? I told you I've been feeling a little irrational lately."

"Dang girl," She shakes her head, amused, "I can't leave you alone for a couple of days."

I snort, waving the note, "So long story short, I failed in actually obtaining one of his rolls, so now I guess this is sort of his apology. For being greedy."

Rae brings the coffee mug to her lips. "So, are you gonna call him?" she says, taking a sip.

"Pfft. No. Probably not. I mean, not with the chance of him having a girlfriend."

Rae nods, "Good call. Very smart. Especially with everything being so fresh still ..."

She's referring to Jayden again, for the second time tonight. A topic which I'm beginning to feel burnt-out on. But I know I can't avoid talking about him with her, perhaps any time between now and the next eighteen years, considering my circumstances.

"So," I begin, "I'm not really sure how to go about saying this, or if I even should just yet, but ... My period should've been here by now."

She almost spits her coffee.

I wince.

I wait for her to swallow and compose herself. She leans forward in her chair, whispering, "You're late?"

I frown, hating both the sound and the secrecy of the words. "I am."

She stares at me, still wide-eyed and full of concern, "*How* late?"

"Pretty darn," I say, taking a regretful bite of my roll. "Four days."

Neither the vitamin C tablets, nor my workout routines, nor my special period-inducing foods have encouraged even the smallest cramp in my tummy. She and I both know that being late is not a regular thing for me. I've been on a pretty set schedule from the time I was a young teen.

"Are you gonna tell him?" She says, asking the million-dollar question.

I pinch the bridge of my nose with my fingers, hoping to relieve the migraine I feel coming on. I try to crush the fact that migraines are a pregnancy thing with the equally valid fact that they are also a stress thing.

"Not yet," I say, "Not until I know for sure."

We sit in silence, contemplating the obvious predicament.

"You know you have to stop taking the Xanax, right?" She says.

"Yeah, I already have," I say, reaching in my purse and producing the bottle. "I've definitely felt the effects too. Sleep is just no longer a thing for me."

Her face twists in sympathy, "I'm sorry."

I hand it over, "Me too."

"Wait, wait, you said you're four days late, right? And you still don't know for sure? Why haven't you taken a test yet?"

"I've been waiting for the seven-day-late mark." I shrug, "Isn't it supposed to be more accurate that way?"

"Mm, I'm pretty sure you could take one now. The test I took that one time advertised being able to read accurate results six days *before* your missed period. Why don't we just get you one today while we're together? What would you have to lose?"

"Money," I smile.

She rolls her eyes, "If you're pregnant, you're gonna be spending a lot more than ten dollars on a pregnancy test in the next few years. Plus, I want to be there for you. I am emotionally invested in this now."

I sigh, "I guess today is as good a day as any."

We sit in silence for a few moments, taking everything in. That's when I realize that the entire conversation so far has been about me, and that's the exact opposite of what we're supposed to be doing: planning the wedding.

"I feel like I set us off track," I say, mustering a smile, "Let's talk about wedding stuff. What's the status?"

Rae sits back in her chair, "I'm pretty much up to par with my planning. Your life is way more interesting right now."

I smile, shaking my head, "So you found a photographer then? Last I knew, that was the problem at hand."

Rae looks slightly uncomfortable as she sips her coffee, "Yep. I did."

"Well?" I say, "Who'd ya get?"

Rae looks hesitant, "Do you remember Zoe?"

I nod, smiling so that she knows it's okay to talk about A&B stuff, "I was wondering if it might be her."

Zoe had posted a picture of Rae and I on the A&B blog a few days ago. Never mind that I'd been stalking the site for information on Hadley when I discovered it. The bottom line is I was shocked to see my face on the website of a group I visited *once,* especially with the headline being "*Family* of the Faith".

The truth is, ever since my impromptu Bible study yesterday, I've felt inspired to give A&B a second chance. When I read those words — *Do not be afraid; do not be discouraged,* I feel the compelling need to hear more of these affirmations. I feel as though God, who I've never really spent much time thinking about before, was speaking to me personally at that moment.

"Do you want to do something fun?" I say, out of the blue.

"Get a pregnancy test?" Rae says, raising a brow.

I laugh, "Well, yes, but something before that."

"Always," Rae smiles, "What do you have in mind?"

I scoot my chair back and hoist my bag over my shoulder. "Let's go to the bookstore."

* * *

I didn't have to drag her this time like I usually would.

Bookstores have always been more my thing than Rae's. I love everything to do with reading, from the smell of the pages to the crisp sound they make as you turn them. There are plenty of genres I know would suit Rae too — *How to Buff Your Bod in Ten Days,* for example — but whereas I would love to lose myself in the thoughtfulness of someone's how-to book, she's always been more of a YouTube-tutorial kind of gal. That's why I hadn't expected her to light up like she did at the idea of going to the bookstore.

I have one single goal for the night, and that is to find myself the perfect Bible. One that I can fill with my own mark-ups and highlights, and one that I can read without worrying about the sacred pages of my grandmother's writing falling out.

When we arrive at the store, to my surprise, Rae goes off on her own, actively seeking something out.

I take the opportunity to go over to the Bible section and take a leisurely scan of my options, but I am all too overwhelmed. Who knew there are so many different *translations?*

After walking the aisle several times and thumbing through various options, I finally settle on an NIV Bible with a simple, soft blue cover. I shift the weight of the book in my hands. It feels right to me. Its pages are gilded the way Grandma Jackie's are, and when I open the cover, I find plenty of room to write in the margins on either side of the text.

With a silent nod, I select a pack of highlighters that supposedly won't bleed through the particularly thin pages of my new book and head to the front desk. I'm making it official. I'm choosing to invest.

Rae meets me at the counter with a checkout bag of her own.

I eye her, placing my hand to my chest, "Rae? Buying a *book*? I'm shocked."

She laughs, nodding at my Bible, "You're one to talk,"

I wave her off, "I figured we couldn't keep showing up at A&B without Bibles of our own."

"Excuse me, I *have* —" She starts and then pauses, "Wait, what?"

I hand the cashier my credit card.

"You wanna go back?" She says with disbelief.

I shrug, "I'm thinking about giving it another shot."

"But … Hadley …"

"I know. Believe me, innocent or not, no part of me wants to see that girl. But … if I go, it'll be for reasons much bigger than how I feel about Hadley."

* * *

The car's headlights shine on another vehicle in the lot as we turn.

"Is Adam here?" I say as Rae pulls into her driveway.

From the bookstore, she had invited me to her house to take the pregnancy test. Apparently, she had one left over from a three-pack she once bought, and offered for me to just take that one instead of buying another.

"Uh, looks like it," Rae says, shifting her car into park, "Don't worry though, he won't bother us."

I shrink down in my seat, filling my cheeks with air.

She laughs, "I mean it. Most nights he comes over, he grades papers while I study. We just coexist."

I sigh, unbuckling my seatbelt.

Not that I don't love Adam, but he's like a brother to me at this point. The idea of taking a pregnancy test anywhere near him makes me slightly uncomfortable.

I hang back as Rae goes in first.

"Adam!" She says with sheer delight.

I join her inside as Adam kisses his bride-to-be.

"Hey, beautiful."

He looks past her and notices me, opening his arms wide.

"Hey, Adam," I say, giving him a squeeze.

"You have some papers to grade, babe?" Rae interjects.

Adam runs a hand through his hair, "Quite a bit actually. Why?"

"Grace and I are gonna have some girl time real quick," She smiles.

He throws up a hand, "Well don't let me get in the way. Girl time away, you two."

Rae loops her arm around mine and leads us to her primary bathroom. She rummages around in her drawer before producing a small, white package.

The plastic crinkles in my hands as she hands it to me. I look it over, suddenly feeling like a child.

"Um..." I mutter, "where are the instructions?"

Rae smirks, "On the box ... which I threw away forever ago. Have you never taken a pregnancy test before?"

I nudge her, "Don't make fun of me. I've only had that one other pregnancy scare, and I got my period before it ever came time to worry about taking one."

"Oh," She says, "Well, don't worry about it too much. They're pretty much self-explanatory. You just make sure the end part gets fully immersed and then wait a few minutes before checking the screen."

"Hmm," I say, eyeing the test, "Okay."

She nods reassuringly at me and leaves me alone with the test. I stare at it a moment longer before unwrapping it from the foil. My chest feels jumpy, both excited to finally hear the answer and dreading what it might be.

I follow the instructions that Rae gave me and place the test on the counter.

I take out my phone and try to busy myself for the next few minutes, but I find myself peeking at the test every few seconds to see if the window is showing anything yet.

Slowly, a single line becomes visible and I pick up the test for a closer look. I hold my breath, praying another line doesn't appear in the next few seconds.

It doesn't.

Relief floods through my whole body and my throat chokes back a sob. Tears stream down my face as I feel a heavy weight lifted off my shoulders.

Negative. The pregnancy test is negative.

There's a light knock on the door, then it opens a tentative crack. When Rae sees me, she hurries over to look at the test. Her face softens as she smiles.

I bury my face in my hands and she wraps her arms around me.

"See? Nothing to worry about."

I feel lighter with every tear that leaves me. It's like they'd all been pent-up inside me weighing me down.

"I can't even tell you how I feel right now," I manage, "Maybe I can finally put this all behind me. Maybe I can finally get over Jayden."

She nods, squeezing my shoulders, "I think you owe yourself that much."

14

Rae - Tuesday

When Adam and Grace leave for the night, I settle into my favorite spot on my yellow rug and begin emptying the contents of my bookstore bag: a pack of colored pens (the kind that glide smoothly like a quill), and a notebook. Its cover is fashioned to look like brown cork, and the word *Progress* splays across the front in gold lettering.

Honest spiritual notes begin with a welcoming keeper of your thoughts, right?

I slide my Bible out from its place under my bed. My parents got for me when I turned eight, and having received it at such a young age, the cover is appropriately a powdery pink color. I used to detest the fact that they chose to engrave my full name on the bottom right corner of the book — *Lacey Rae Brooks,* instead of just Rae — but as always, my mother insisted that it was a perfectly lovely name. Delicate and dignified all at once.

Despite the Bible's unbecoming features, I'd never dream of buying a new one in its place. Daddy wrote his name personally in the front, and with him being in the Marines, I hold everything I have of him dear to my heart.

He and my mother used to encourage us — my sister and I — to play a game with them around the dinner table where we challenged each other to see who could remember the most books of the Bible in order, and whoever won always got an extra helping of dessert. It's because of this game that when I crack open the Bible, flipping over to Luke 16 is like second nature to me. I take a deep breath before delving into my study.

Okay, Lord. This is our time together. I am doing what Kaya suggested ... what we prayed about. Help me to see what you want me to see.

The hair on my neck stands on edge as I scan down the page for verse 15.

You are the ones who justify yourselves in the eyes of others, but God knows your hearts. What people value highly is detestable in God's sight.

I write the scripture down and stare at it on my notebook page. It slowly becomes clear why Kaya had given me this one to ponder first, as it almost immediately redirects my mind to ask the question, *what do people value?* Moreover, what do *I* value?

The first page in my notebook comes alive with color as I write down everything bouncing around my mind:

Some things that people value: 1) Money. 2) Popularity. 3) Beauty/ Looks.

I circle number three several times to remind myself of the focal point for this study – that my particular insecurity would fall under the beauty category. I write,

God is saying that people tend to put way too much value on these common, earthly things, and as a result lose sight of what is really important to him: Where our hearts are.

I take a moment to think about where *my* heart has been and begin to feel guilty. My heart has been on enjoying my life with Adam. Using him as a remedy for my insecurities. It has been on intentionally ignoring what I've always been taught the Bible says about premarital sex, because of familiar it has become to me. Swallowing hard, I write these things down, and pause before reading any more.

Lord, I am so sorry. I know what I am doing is wrong ... and I'm finally coming before you to acknowledge it. I've been ignoring this for a long time, and I'm sorry. I don't know how to overcome this, or how to make the knowledge of your love alone enough to feel secure. I feel so in need of reassurance from others. No ... reassurance from Adam. Please give me strength. Help me to feel like your love is enough.

Somewhere in the middle of my prayer, tears had started to form. One drops on my notebook page, blurring the purple ink I'd been writing with.

I flip to the next scripture Kaya referred me to: Psalm 32:5,

Then I acknowledged my sin to you and did not cover up my iniquity. I said, "I will confess my transgressions to the Lord." And you forgave the guilt of my sin.

Through blurred vision and damp cheeks, I smile. I can see why Kaya told me to read them in order now. This active conversation between me and God ... His response to my prayer ... means everything to me. In my mind, there was a special emphasis on those final words: '*You forgave the guilt of my sin.*' I mentally recount the many moments of guilt I've felt lately – how burdensome it's felt. But here He is, freely offering to take it all away. This feeling of having a clean slate and the ability to start fresh inspires me anew, but there's still this issue of God's love being enough for me ... of it being *all* I need to feel secure. I flip to the next chapter on my list: Psalm 139:13-16.

For you created my inmost being; you knit me together in my mother's womb. I praise you because I am fearfully and wonderfully made; your works are wonderful, I know that full well. My frame was not hidden from you when I was made in the secret place, when I was woven together in the depths of the earth. Your eyes saw my unformed body; all the days ordained for me were written in your book before one of them came to be.

This scripture fills me with warmth, the way a good cup of coffee does. It's as though the first scripture had been God giving it to me straight, and this scripture is Him embracing me ... wiping the tears from my face.

Not only do I write down the scripture in my notebook, but I also highlight verse 15 in my Bible. God just gave me the most beautiful visual of what *"the secret place"* might look like: I imagine a place untouchable by man, deep in the earth's core. It's dark all around, save for one little spotlight shining down on a creation platform. There on the platform, I see myself standing before God, exactly the way I look today. He adds His finishing touches on me — the natural waves in my blonde hair, the dark flecks in my blue eyes, the light shade of my skin. He tucks a lock of hair behind my ear and smiles approvingly, saying, "This is good."

My heart warms as I look over my body. With this visual, everything about me feels intentional. Like I *am* exactly the way I should be, and that perhaps my most personal moment with God was when he created me ... the moment just before he breathed life into my lungs and set me free in the world.

Motivated by the experiences that followed reading the last two scriptures, I eagerly flip to the last scripture on my paper from Kaya: 1st Peter 3:3-4.

Your beauty should not come from outward adornment, such as elaborate hairstyles and the wearing of gold jewelry or fine clothes. Rather, it should be that of your inner self, the unfading beauty of a gentle and quiet spirit, which is of great worth in God's sight.

I nod to myself, jotting down the scripture. I love everything about verse three, and how a person's *heart* and inner self is emphasized throughout each scripture I've read so far, but unlike the first two scriptures, my Bible has a section of commentary on verse four. It says,

A quiet and gentle spirit is a surrendered spirit — one that is Christ-like and chooses God over and over again. This is, of course, something we should all strive for. But in context, Peter is speaking to Christian wives who are married to unbelievers. In having a gentle and quiet spirit (or one that is Christ-like), they may win over their husbands through their good examples and Christ-like spirit.

I ponder this and how Adam might react when I propose being abstinent until the wedding, which is just over seven long months away. Though my spirit is not generally quiet, I certainly feel as though it's more "surrendered" than it was before ... and if that's what it takes to spiritually win over your husband, or in my case, fiancé, at least I've taken the first step.

Before I close the book, I flip over to a set of scriptures my parents had me memorize when I was little ... the one that will solidify my reasons for doing this: Galatians 5:19 -23.

"The acts of the flesh are obvious: sexual immorality, impurity and debauchery; idolatry and witchcraft; hatred, discord, jealousy, fits of rage, selfish ambition, dissensions, factions and envy; drunkenness, or-

gies, and the like ... But the fruit of the Spirit is love, joy, peace, forbearance, kindness, goodness, faithfulness, gentleness and self-control. Against such things there is no law."

Taking a deep, steadying breath, I underline each fruit of the spirit, and circle one particular fruit of the flesh several times: sexual immorality. I also jot it down in my journal before closing the book and exhaling deeply.

Alright, Lord ... I hear you. I'm gonna need your help, but ... Let's do this.

15

Grace - Wednesday

"So what do you think I should do?" I say, holding the phone to my ear, "I honestly really want to go back to A&B tonight, but when I think about Hadley being there, I want to throw up."

My stomach churns in response. I swallow to keep down the nausea.

"Why are you letting her have that much power over you?" Aunt Kim says, "If you want to go, just go. Make her feel like none of this bothers you. Take the upper hand from her."

"Well, I don't think 'taking the upper hand' is the point anymore." I say, thinking back to what Rae said yesterday, "I'm starting to genuinely think Rae is right about Hadley's innocence in all this."

"Mmm, so what *is* the point then?"

I sigh, "It's not so much that I don't want to see her because I think she's a snake. It's because seeing her just … hurts. Imagining her with him …"

"Oh honey," Aunt Kim hums, "I know it does."

I swallow hard, "But I still feel really moved to go to A&B. It's like I'm fighting with myself. I want to avoid Hadley and save myself the pain, but I equally want set-in-stone answers that I feel like only she can give me."

"Well," Aunt Kim says, "I want to preface this with saying I don't think you should do anything if you don't feel emotionally ready for the answers. Hadley will be dropping some pretty heavy topics on you, and pregnancy or no pregnancy, this is all still really fresh."

I've asked myself this question many times: Am I desensitized enough to Jayden's affair? To the point of being able to hear what Jayden did with Hadley behind my back, and what it is that she has that I don't have, all while keeping a straight face? I'd like to say that I am — desensitized to it, I mean — but it's impossible to know for sure what I'll feel in the moment. I might feel empowered by the knowledge, or I might break all over again.

"But?" I say.

"If you *do* decide to talk to her," Aunt Kim continues, "I think it would be an excellent way to regain some control of the situation — Maybe even gain some closure." *Without having to beg Jayden for answers like a helpless wreck, swallowed by emotions that he no longer deserves to see.*

"So you *do* think I should go?" I say, "And talk to her too?"

"I'm not going to tell you what to do," Aunt Kim lovingly responds, "But if that's what you decide to do, I *don't* think A&B is the place to do it."

I nod, "I agree with that. And I also think it's going to take a lot of self-control on my part to come at this from exactly the right angle. Even though I'm pretty sure she's unaware of what happened, part of me still so badly wants to lash out when I see her."

"Right ... you don't want this to come across like an interrogation," She says. "Just try not to think of it like a confrontation. Go into it with an open mind. Try to hear what she has to say. But most of all, go into it with *confidence.* Just think, if Jayden had known from the get-go his girlfriend would be having margaritas with his mistress in the near future, he might have thought twice about being unfaithful, am I right?"

I smile at that, "No doubt."

I hear some background chatter getting louder through the speaker, "I'm gonna have to let you go girlie. It's almost my turn in the checkout line. I sure do love you, though, and I hope everything goes according to plan. Text me, okay?"

"Of course," I say, sending her love before ending the call.

* * *

I spend the rest of my morning curled up on the couch, mapping out how the conversation will go: I'll go up to Hadley and be friendly. I'll find common ground with her by discussing something irrelevant to the situation — a shared hobby we have or something — and from there I'll invite her to get a drink with me later in the evening. I'll even let her pick the place. Once there, I'll drop the heavy topics when the moment is right.

As foolproof of a plan as it feels like, I still feel like I need more time to mentally prepare. So I get out my notebook and begin writing down the exact questions I want to ask Hadley. I scribble out anything that evokes unnecessary feelings of heartache or emptiness, narrowing it down to a few key questions.

Satisfied with my conclusion, I scan the list one more time before shoving it in my purse. I take a deep breath and grab my keys off the coffee table, but I stop in my tracks as another wave of nausea rolls through my stomach.

I drop the keys and make a dash for the bathroom, barely making it in time. I heave the contents of my stomach into the toilet bowl.

***

Something about the car ride to A&B had drained my confidence in my idea. Talking to Hadley seemed like a good plan all day until now. Now that it's time to take action.

My brain floods with possibilities: What if Hadley refuses to meet with me? If Rae and I are wrong, and Hadley knows *exactly* who I am, she may very well reject me.

Nonsense – I remind myself. Everything points to Hadley being innocent.

Her answers will be tainted ... My mind hisses ... *You'll only gain* her *version of the story.* If *she feels like telling you.*

I frown, arguing with myself that hearing some sort of the truth is better than none at all.

As I push open the building's door, I quickly become aware of how packed it is tonight. Even more so than last week.

I recognize Kaya on the other end of the room greeting and laughing with members, but the path to get to her is too crowded. I spot Rae sitting in the same place as last time with her mom and sister. She waves me over. Livia smiles kindly at me and Mrs. Brooks gives me a kiss on the cheek before I take my seat by Rae, who has a little pink Bible and even a notebook in her lap. I set my new Bible on the table, feeling a bit proud that it has my name on it.

I check the time on my phone, which shows I have a few minutes to spare until the session starts. I glance around the room, trying to locate Hadley, but I don't see her yet. I wring my hands in anticipation.

"Hey," Rae pokes me, "You okay?"

I frown, taking a moment to fill her in on my plan.

At first, she seems receptive. Proud even. But as she watches me, her smile softens.

"You know, if you're feeling unsure about all this, maybe you should just give it awhile. Take some time to pray about it. Or maybe even talk to Kaya about it ... She's great about offering perspective."

I nod, considering it.

Kaya takes her seat among the tables. The session is about to start, and I see plenty of new faces, but none of them are Hadley's. I frown, scanning the crowd one more time.

As everyone finds their seats, I notice a silver platter on Kaya's table with a domed lid. She grabs our attention by tapping the lid. It makes a light, tinny sound.

"Ladies," She says, smiling, "Tonight, I am presenting you with a rare delicacy."

She places her fingers on the handle, "Something that will satisfy each and every one of your appetites with just one little taste."

I sit a little straighter in my chair.

"Tonight, I present you *with ...*"

She pauses with a flourish before lifting the lid.

Sitting on the platter, she has revealed what looks to be nothing other than a can of yellow paint.

This elicits some chuckles from the group.

"You laugh now," She says, "But just wait until you take a bite. It's truly delicious."

Half of us look at Kaya like she's off her rocker, but she says it with such conviction that we keep listening anyway.

"Believe it or not," She smiles knowingly, "This can of paint is actually edible. It has been scientifically engineered to be eaten, and testers have reported it to be mind-blowingly good. One tester commented that it changed their *life,* which may be a little extreme, but really now," She gently pushes the tray forward, "You just have to try it."

We all stare at her with curiosity, no one making a move to try the mysterious edible paint. She waits patiently, glancing around at us.

"So tell me this," She says finally, "Why are none of you, in fact, eating the yellow paint?"

At our silence, she adds, "Really. You can answer. It's not meant to be rhetorical."

Livia sits forward, "Um, because you can't consume turpentine?"

Kaya counters, "Why not?"

"Because it's poison." Livia replies.

"Ah," Kaya nods, standing up from her seat and slowly pacing the room, "So you're saying deep down in your gut, you know that eating paint is poisonous. Lethal, even."

We nod in agreement, wondering where she is going with this.

"But I tried to get you to eat it anyway," She says, pausing, "I even threw some interesting ideas at you that made it seem at least partially sensible to try the paint, and I'm willing to bet that if you had been fasting for twelve days prior to this meeting, having had no food at all during that time, my convincing might have been just enough to make you try a taste."

She walks back over to the paint can and covers it with the lid, "Ladies, I want you to understand that that is how Satan works." She pushes the tray aside. "Deep down, we get gut feelings about sin. We know when something isn't right, even if it's just a tiny inkling. Yet, Satan carefully picks moments when we are weak to tempt us into doing something sinful. Whatever form of trickery he has to use in order to get you to give in to sin, he will use, even if it means lying to your face to make it seem desirable. Notice how I conjured up several carefully crafted lies to get you to try the paint? So, say you *are* starving, and say I *am* successful in convincing you to take a bite. It doesn't matter what I said to get you to do it. Maybe I told you the paint tastes like its color: The most luscious, juicy pineapple. Or maybe I told you that consuming it would make all your troubles go away. Whatever the case, what happens when you *do* eat the paint?"

She pauses, encouraging interaction.

"You die." One girl supplies.

"Exactly," Kaya points in her direction, "You die. And why is that? What am I getting at here?"

Mrs. Brooks looks up from her note taking, "Because sin kills. Just as consuming paint kills, so does filling your body with sin, even if it's a slow, subtle death."

Kaya points, "Yes, Laurie, thank you. And Satan has a way of making sin appear attractive to us. In the same way that God knows your heart inside out, so does Satan — but *he* uses that intimate knowledge to target your weaknesses. To get us to give in to temporary pleasures that'll deprive us of eternal life. Because in reality, he would do *anything* and *everything* to keep us from obtaining it."

She stops pacing, "How does it feel to have an enemy like that?"

My heart thuds as I consider her words.

She flexes her hands in and out of balled fists. "If you're familiar with this feeling, the feeling of being tempted at your weakest moments, you're in good company. Because Jesus was *also* tempted in this way. I want us to turn over to Matthew 4 in our Bibles and read verses: 1-11."

I sneak a glance over at Rae's Bible to see how far into the book she is flipping and begin flipping through my own to find the right place. Everyone else gets there before I do, and Kaya begins reading it out loud, so I try to listen as I continue to flip.

"Then Jesus was led by the Spirit into the wilderness to be tempted by the devil." Kaya reads, *"After fasting forty days and forty nights, he was hungry."*

Damn. I can't even go a few hours without food.

"The tempter came to him and said, 'if you are the Son of God, tell these stones to become bread.' Jesus answered, 'It is written: Man shall not live on bread alone, but on every word that comes from the mouth of God.'"

Kaya pauses, "Now, I will note that Jesus has some really strong replies here. He quotes right from the word of God to shove off the devil. However, his replies are not what I want us to focus on this time. We'll save that for a future session. Right now, I want you to notice the *persistence* of the devil, and he *himself* quotes scripture."

I finally found Matthew 4 in my own Bible and am following along with her as she reads.

"Then the devil took him to the holy city and had him stand on the highest point of the temple. 'If you are the Son of God,' he said, 'throw yourself down. For it is written: He will command his angels concerning you, and they will lift you up in their hands, so that you will not

strike your foot against a stone.' Jesus answered him, 'It is also written: Do not put the Lord your God to the test.' Again, the devil took him to a very high mountain and showed him all the kingdoms of the world and their splendor. *'All this I will give you,' he said, 'if you bow down and worship me.' Jesus said to him, 'Away from me, Satan! For it is written: Worship the Lord your God, and serve him only.' Then the devil left him, and angels came and attended him."*

She closes her Bible and sets it gently on the table, "I want us to take note that no matter *how many times* Jesus pushed Satan off, the devil came back and tried again, unfazed by the first rejection." She shakes her head slowly, "The devil is patient. Which is a very scary concept, because patience is not a trait that we typically associate with him. But sisters, I want you to be as skeptical of him and his tricks as you were of me when I was trying to get you to eat the paint. I want you to be as *strong* at pushing him off as Jesus was, *even* in His weak state. Is that even achievable, do you think?" She challenges.

A few people nod, while a few shake their heads.

"It *is,"* Kaya presses her index and thumb together for emphasis, "And let me tell you why. Philippians 4:13 reads, *'I can do all things through* Christ *who strengthens me."*

The room is silent.

"*All* things, ladies. That's a pretty broad spectrum. But we *need* a relationship with Him in order for it to work. Because let me tell you, the only thing powerful enough to fight off a relentless *enemy* of divine nature, is a relentless and divine *God* who is fighting for you."

Her tone is quieter when she next speaks, "So how do we obtain this critical relationship with God and Jesus Christ?"

She flips to a bookmarked page in her Bible.

"The answer lies in James 4:8. Turn with me there if you would."

I remember the index in the front of my Bible and consult that before turning to James, which turns out to be much more efficient than peeking over at Rae's Bible.

"Come near to God" Kaya reads, *"and he will come near to you. Wash your hands, you sinners, and purify your hearts, you double-minded."* Not only this – not only will God draw near to us if we draw near to him, but in verse 7, the word says, *'Resist the devil, and he will flee from you.'"*

An 'Amen' escapes one of the women and I smile down at my Bible. The passion of this group is not only joy-inspiring, but infectious.

Kaya smiles, "I want to circle back to the thought we started out with about the paint. Does anyone know why I specifically chose yellow paint to illustrate this idea about sin? Why didn't I just choose something like, say, a plate of really rich looking brownies, or perhaps, a check made out for a large sum of money?"

Zoe raises her hand in the air and Kaya laughs.

"I knew you art majors would be way ahead of me. Go ahead, Zoe."

"It was a play off the Vincent Van Gogh theory."

Kaya nods, "It was. For those of you who don't know, the story goes that Van Gogh thought yellow was such a happy color, that if he ate some yellow paint, it would get all the happiness inside of him."

This gets a few laughs.

I notice in my peripheral that Rae is doodling a picture of a yellow paint can next to a handwritten list that contains a lot of official looking words. One of them is 'sexual immorality', and it is circled numerous times. I peak over at my friend who has never spoken much about religion, but she seems thoroughly invested in her doodle.

"So, I want to leave you all with this," Kaya says, "If you allow yourself to consume something as poisonous and as lethal as sin, all because Satan has successfully convinced you that it will bring you some level of happiness, remember that any happiness that comes from taking part in sin is *temporary,* and it leads to death. It is not worth losing your salvation over. *True* happiness comes from God's blessings for you, and happiness from God is eternal. Remember that just as Satan attacks you personally, God *blesses* you personally, in ways that are specifically crafted to bring *you* joy. Draw near to him, and he will draw near to you. Resist the devil and purify yourselves. Be *liberated.* I promise, it is well worth your time, and well worth anything you feel moved to give up."

Everyone begins folding their Bibles and I realize the session has ended.

I also realize I haven't gotten my chance to talk to Hadley since she never showed up.

I lean over to Rae and whisper, "Do you think Kaya has her number? Hadley's?"

Rae nods, "I bet she does. Do you want me to go with you to ask?"

I lock my eyes on Kaya and swallow, "Sure."

We get up and walk over to her, but there's a crowd around her I have to snake through. They're all saying things like, "That was a wonderful message", "Very creative!", "We're praying for you", and "Hang in there." I'm not sure why they would be saying the latter of the four, but when I finally reach her she smiles at me and pulls me into a bear hug.

"Grace, I'm glad you came tonight! It's good to see you again."

I smile back at her, "You too, Kaya. We had a really good turn out tonight."

Kaya glances around, "I know right? I'm so thrilled!"

As Rae approaches, she smiles wide and holds out her arms. Kaya wraps herself in them, swaying as she squeezes.

"Great message," Rae says, "I really felt that one."

Kaya smiles, "You inspired me to give it."

I find myself shocked at what a stark difference this is between the last time I'd seen Kaya and Rae together. Rae had been just as eager to slip away from A&B as I'd been, but now she appears comfortable and even happy.

"How have you been since we last talked?" She says, "Did you get a chance to study?"

Rae nods, smiling in earnest, "I find it kinda funny how I know where all the books of the Bible are, but very little about what's in them it seems. How had I never heard those things before?"

Kaya nods knowingly, "Because '*the word of God is alive and active*'. It's always the same yet it always changes."

Rae raises a brow, "Isn't that a scripture too?"

Kaya nods, "The first part. Hebrews 4:12."

Rae smiles, "So hey, listen, I was hoping I could grab a member's phone number from you real quick."

Kaya pulls out her phone, "Sure! Who do you need?"

"Hadley Harris?"

Kaya waves her hand, "Oh yeah, of course I got my girl Hadley."

I'm a little taken aback by Kaya's fondness.

Rae types the numbers into her phone and I stand there numbly, trying to concoct a new plan. One that involves texting Hadley instead of a casual conversation.

Kaya looks over at me and visibly softens, "Hey, is everything alright?"

I snap out of my thought process and smile, "Oh, yeah, of course."

Kaya looks over me thoughtfully, "You sure? You look a little tired. Are you doing okay?"

Just her asking almost brings tears to my eyes. The simple act of someone really caring.

"I just ... have a lot going on."

She nods attentively and then glances around the room before jerking her head to an empty corner. She leads and I follow her. Once there, she turns to face me with a soft smile.

"So tell me. What's up?"

Where to begin? What should I tell this extremely compassionate, almost-stranger?

"There's just someone I need to talk to ... about something really personal ... and I'm just struggling with even the thought of it. I don't really want to, but I do at the same time."

She nods, "Okay, I won't press. How can we pray about this?"

I'm relieved that she doesn't ask for details, but I'm also at a loss for words.

"Well ... I'm not entirely sure. I feel really unsure about the whole situation."

"I understand," She smiles, "Let me ask this one thing. Has this person done something against you? Is that what you need to talk to them about?"

I nod, impressed.

"There's an awesome Bible verse about this you know. It's in Matthew 18, and it says *'If your brother sins against you, go and tell him his fault, between you and him alone. If he listens to you, you have gained your brother.*"

"Really?" I say, "I've never heard that."

She nods, "So the one thing you shouldn't feel unsure about is taking that step and having the conversation. You're doing the right thing."

Her words bring warmth to me. I suddenly feel reassured of my plan.

"I think I know what we need to pray for," She smiles, "Will you join me?"

I nod, bowing my head with hers.

"Great God in Heaven, Grace and I come before you now, thanking you for the work you're doing in her life. Thank you for leading her to the Godly conclusion that she should approach her brother or sister in Christ about what it is they've done to hurt her. I pray now that the conversation they have is spirit-led. That both of your children involved have the heart to listen to one another and speak lovingly and peacefully about the subject they're discussing. Please bless that the outcome of this conversation is another brother or sister gained, rather than lost. Give your beautiful daughter Grace the right mindset and the right words to say what needs to be said. We thank you for all of these things, Lord, and we ask it in Jesus name, Amen."

"Amen," I echo.

She squeezes my shoulder and smiles, "I'm proud of you."

I smile, not only feeling far more sure of myself than before, but grateful that despite my previous word to never come back here, God brought me to A&B this night.

***

I hadn't given her a name in my phone. Her contact remains nothing but a collection of numbers. As petty as the decision was to leave her name blank, it somehow made the whole operation easier for me.

I hit 'send' on my carefully drafted text and set my phone down as I tuck myself into bed.

To: Unknown Number

Sent: 10/09/19

Time: 8:12 pm

"Hey, Hadley, It's Grace from A&B. I don't know if you remember me, but we met unofficially on the first day. I think you even got my paper airplane for the icebreaker, ha ha. Anyway, I was just wondering if you might want to grab a drink with me sometime this week?"

____

I'd agonized over the simple text. My first draft was not only cheesy, but a total lie. I'd concocted two paragraphs explaining that my goal with joining A&B was to get to know some awesome girls who share the faith, and I thought it'd be "super fun" to hang out together sometime this week. With a scoff, I erased the whole thing. I tried again, writing a more cryptic message the second time. I had gone back and forth between typing, "There's something you should know," at the end of the text, or "I need to tell you something". In the end, I erased that last sentence altogether, and just sent the text as it was before I killed myself thinking about it.

I don't expect her to answer right away, but to my surprise, my phone pings a few minutes later:

From: Unknown Number

Sent: 10/09/19

Time: 8:16 pm

"Hey, Grace! I do remember you :) And sure, that sounds good to me! When are you thinking?"

—————

I read the text over a few times. Her willingness to meet should be a good sign … right?

I consider my schedule before texting her back. I know my workday tomorrow is booked with clients. It'd have to be on Friday — the day after tomorrow.

To: Unknown Number

Sent: 10/09/19

Time: 8:21 pm

"I'm thinking Friday around 11 am? It's 5 o'clock somewhere, right? Lol."

—————

Three minutes later -

From: Unknown Number

Sent: 10/09/19

Time: 8:24 pm

"Bahaha I like your thinking. Sure, I'll be there! What place?"

—————

To: Unknown Number

Sent: 10/09/19

Time: 8:26 pm

"You pick :)"

—————

From: Unknown Number

Sent: 10/09/19

Time: 8:30 pm

"Vanelos?"

To: Unknown Number

Sent: 10/09/19

Time: 8:32 pm

"Perfect! Vanelos at 11. See you then!"

From: Unknown Number

Sent: 10/09/19

Time: 8:35 pm

"Can't wait!!!"

I set my phone down with a shaking hand, grateful to have gotten the conversation out of the way.

I try to close my eyes and get some sleep, but my mind torments me with all the possible scenarios that could take place at Vanelos. I need to get my mind on something else. Anything else. Which is how I find myself daydreaming about Liam.

I think about the note he wrote me along with the cinnamon bun, and how it's currently pinned to my bulletin board.

I should have thrown it away by now, honestly, but I guess the whole thing was just sort of flattering. I've been so critical of my appearance and my body ever since the breakup, which is something that is foreign to my usual self. In a way, the note sort of served as proof to myself that I still have it. That I still have game, and that a man will go to great lengths to get my attention.

It feels good for a moment, but then the feeling turns sour. I *do* understand why he wrote "sorry". He wrote it because he selfishly bought *all six* of the remaining cinnamon buns, which should definitely not be allowed. But what I *don't* understand is why he included his phone number on the note when he obviously has a girlfriend.

I think of the classy girl who came up to our table.

I ought to call him just to give him a piece of my mind. It should be common girl code to put a man in his place when he flirts with you while dating someone else.

I scoff. What a world it would be if every girl abided by that code.

16

Rae - Wednesday

I twist my key in the lock of my front door before I remember that there's no need. Adam should be waiting inside.

He texted me during A&B saying he was coming over with a surprise, so I had to remind him of where I was. He replied that it was okay, and he'd be waiting for me. I smile with anticipation and turn the door knob.

There aren't any lights on in the foyer, but the kitchen light is on around the corner, and I can hear the faint sound of soft jazz playing. I kick off my shoes and follow the sound.

My eyes fall on a lush bouquet of sunflowers — my favorite — arranged in a vase on the table.

I stop to admire them, feeling the corners of my eyes crinkle with a smile, when Adam appears around the corner. He holds a bottle of wine in one hand and two glasses in the other, and *wow,* does he look sexy.

He wears a white button-up with the top two buttons undone and his sleeves rolled halfway up his rippled forearms. His face is dusted with the hint of a 5 o'clock shadow and his beautiful white teeth glow when he sees me.

He sets the glasses down, not taking his eyes off of me, and scoops me up in one quick motion. A laugh bubbles out of my chest as he squeezes me tight, and I am happy I chose to wear my new yellow dress to A&B tonight so that I match his finesse.

He kisses me, long and sweet, my stomach fluttering with each movement of his jaw against my fingertips. When he pulls away, I almost feel dizzy.

"Hey gorgeous," he says.

I tuck a strand of hair behind my ear, "Hey."

I take a few steps back, taking it all in. He's taken the liberty of lighting candles and placing at least two on every surface — the table, the window sill, the server, and the shelf on the wall.

"Surprise," He smiles.

I laugh, pressing myself back into his chest, "What did I do to deserve all this?"

"Are you kidding?" He says, "A woman like you deserves this every night. My only regret is not having the time to do it more often."

I smile and nuzzle into him, "Only 'cause you're working so hard for us. To take me to *Italy* no less. How can I complain?"

Adam breaks every rule in the book when it comes to how attractive a teacher is allowed to be. He smiles and pulls my hand into the kitchen.

"I was going to make salmon and asparagus to add to the surprise, but ..." He says, extending the last word, "you got here sooner than I thought you would."

I turn to him and smile. The words to explain how much I love him just don't exist.

He picks me up and I wrap my legs around his waist. He sets me gently on the counter and I breathe in the scent of him as he trails his hands down my back. He always smells like warm spices — like cloves with a hint of cedar.

My stomach swirls with excitement as I think of the night ahead of me.

But then …

Then I remember.

The two words I circled over and over in my notebook. The way those two words apply to my night. The yellow paint.

I squeeze my eyes shut as he trails kisses up my neck, not wanting to do what my gut is telling me to.

I brush his cheeks lightly with my fingertips, bringing his face to mine. I smile at him, my body aching for his touch, and I force out the words as pleasantly as I can muster, "Honey, can I talk to you about something real quick?"

"Of course, love." He says, wearing a curious expression.

I glance to the dining room, "Could we maybe go sit down?"

He eyes me carefully, "Yes?"

I hop down from the counter and we take our seats at the dining room table. Maybe I've already made too big of a deal out of this. Maybe I should just say "Psych," and let him keep doing his thing.

"You're not pregnant, are you?" He says before I can form any words.

"What?" I laugh, "No, that's not what this is."

His shoulders relax, "I saw the test wrapper in our trash can …"

I can't help but smile at his obvious relief, "Not for me, love."

Recognition dawns on his face, "Ohhh, for …?"

I nod, "But that's not what I want to talk about."

His whole posture softens, "Thank God. What's this about then?"

"Well …" I say.

I really don't know how I'm going to go about suggesting this, but there's never been anything I couldn't talk to Adam about, so I take a deep breath and just begin. "I've more or less kind of set a goal for myself."

He shifts in his chair, listening attentively.

"I've been reading a little bit," I fidget with my wristbands, "and I was just wondering … do you ever think that maybe we spend *too* much time being intimate?"

He smiles at me, mischievously, "No baby girl. I can honestly say that has never *once* crossed my mind."

My cheeks heat as I try to tamp down my desire.

"But don't you think the idea of waiting until your wedding night is kind of romantic and sweet?"

Adam glances around the candlelit room, "Am I not being romantic enough for you?"

"No, no," I say, holding up my hands, "It's not that at all. It's just that … well, I think maybe it might be kind of nice if we waited until we're married."

"Yeah?" His face doesn't fall into an expression of disappointment. He doesn't look angry with me or surprised, he simply appears thoughtful. He doesn't take his eyes from mine for a moment. "Why do you think that?"

I bite my tongue for a moment, sending up a quick prayer.

Lord, give me the right words.

I sigh and reach over for the bag I took to A&B. In it lies my notebook, with all of my Bible study notes on sexual immorality, and tonight's A&B lesson about the yellow paint.

"Don't laugh at me, okay?" I say, "This actually means a lot to me ... to share this with you."

"Why would I laugh at you?" He says, inching his chair closer to peek at my notes.

I shake my head, "I know we've never been religious ... but you know I didn't grow up that way. My parents brought me up in the faith."

"I remember." He says.

"Well," I continue, "Lately, I've felt really overwhelmed. The wedding, my classes, and other things are just really weighing down on me. So I talked to Kaya to figure out what some of her tricks are for handling life the way she does. She just has this beautiful grace about her, Adam. She glows in a way that all of us can see, but she has no reason to be so cheery. She lost her parents when she was young, and recently she's been diagnosed with some sort of cancer."

Adam remains attentive, even though I'm rambling. He knows this is how I have to sort out my thoughts.

"Anyway," I say, "I asked her what her secret is, right? And in a nutshell, she told me that bettering herself spiritually, one thing at a time, helps her stay focused and joyful. She said that she's seen the areas in her life that God has rewarded her for trying her best, and that when she prays, He helps her achieve her goals. But that it's not a one-way street. She has to strive for her best to bask in the blessings."

I look down at my notebook. Before I can talk myself out of it, I pass it to him.

He gently takes it and places it on the table in front of him. I watch his eyes go back and forth across the page, reading carefully through the scriptures I wrote. His eyes settle on the part of the page where I've circled "sexual immorality".

I'm not sure why, but sitting in silence as he reads over what I've written — and wondering what on earth he is thinking — is nerve-racking. He probably thinks I've gone crazy.

He clears his throat and flips the page over to my A&B notes.

I panic a little bit at the thought of him reading further before I get the chance to explain it myself.

"Those are my A&B notes," The words tumble out, "And basically the point of the message was that sometimes the devil can take something that's meant to be wonderful and twist it into something corrupt, that ultimately harms us — sometimes without us even realizing what's going on."

He glances up at me over his smart-looking glasses, and smiles in a way that sends a shiver through me, "I got that, honey."

I go back to being quiet while he reads through the notes, practically wringing my hands waiting on him to say something.

Finally he closes the book and places it gently in my lap, bringing his handsome gaze back to me.

"Seven months is a long time, baby girl."

My gaze falls to my lap, "I know ..."

He glances back at the book and then back at me, "And you're sure that's what you want?"

It's what God wants.

I nod, though I can't look at him when I do.

There's a long pause, and I can tell his eyes are studying me.

"Alright. If that's what you want then that's what we'll do."

Something in my stomach twists, and I briefly wonder what horrible thing have I done? Seven months *is* a long time.

I try to offer him a smile, "Thank you ... so much. I'm sorry if I ruined your plans."

He laughs, "We're still having dinner, Rae."

His laugh warms me, and I feel like maybe it'll be okay after all.

"Where's your skillet?" He says, scooting his chair back and offering me a hand.

I take it and pull myself up.

We continue our date together, stealing kisses and laughing over sizzling, lemon-spritzed salmon.

After he leaves for the night, my bed feels cold and seemingly bigger, but it's a loneliness I'm okay with. Because overriding that loneliness is a different, altogether stronger feeling: The feeling that I've done something good … and that maybe, just maybe, The Creator of the whole world is just a little bit proud of me.

17

Grace - Thursday

I loved everything about today. Marla came by for a follow-up appointment and informed me that the tincture I made for her migraines has been working. She was ecstatic to have finally discovered something that helps her and ordered five more vials. All of my other clients were also happy with their care and gave *Hyssop 'N' Sage* some positive reviews online. The last couple I saw asked me to do my favorite thing, which is create an essential oil synergy for their home that 'smells like purity'. When someone asks you to create a scent that doesn't already have a set smell associated with it, you have a lot of creative leeway. So I had a fun day of concocting new scents that could somehow convey the aroma of 'purity', and put the finished product in a spray bottle. The couple was thrilled with how it turned out.

It's days like today that I'm completely in love with my job. So to preserve the magic of this day, I deliberately try to think very little of what day it'll be tomorrow. Not just a regular old Friday — but a Friday that I will meet with my ex's lover for a chat. This week has me worn-out on worrying, so I push any thoughts of worry aside for the time being and remind myself that I deserve happy days too.

By the end of the day, all this talk about purification has me on a cleaning kick. My kitchen has transformed into an imaginary stage as I engage in my least favorite upkeep activity: washing the dishes. Grandma Jackie was too old-school to invest in a dishwasher, so ever since I moved in, I've had to do all of the dishes by hand. But seeing as though it is a necessary chore, it's always been my personal goal to make it enjoyable some way or another. I'll usually listen to a podcast or one of my favorite playlists, but this time, my favorite mix tape blasts from the old-timey radio I salvaged from Grandma Jackie's things. I belt out every lyric of *"Wouldn't It Be Nice"*, despite my inability to carry a tune. Suds and soap slosh around in the sink as I scrub the dishes, sending a few wayward bubbles flying into the air.

Amity touches her nose to one of the bubbles and spazzes out when it pops, sending me into fits of giggles. The cat's expression of pure disdain is priceless.

When I finish the dishes, I grab the mop nearby and begin slathering the floor with the natural cleaner I made this morning. The slippery socks I'm wearing are fully intentional, as I don't see any other way for a person to mop than to spin around and slide along the floor with your dashing, wooden-stick of a dance partner.

As the song fades to an end, I dip the mop low to the ground with a flourish and blow my adoring fans a kiss. If not for the song ending, I never would have heard my phone ring.

I pause my mix tape and go over to my cell, sliding the 'accept' icon without checking to see who it is.

"Hope there's a good reason you're interrupting my jam sesh," I smile, wondering whether I'll hear Rae's voice in reply or Aunt Kim's.

"Wow ..." is the reply I get, "You picked up,"

My heart falls all the way into my stomach at the sound of his voice. Deep, soft, and unwelcomingly familiar.

"Jayden," I say, sinking to the floor, "What're you ... why-?"

"Can you come get the door?" He says.

It takes me a minute to process.

"The door?" I say, "*My* door?"

"Yeah."

"You're *here?*"

"Yeah."

***

"I tried knocking," He says as I open the door.

"Yeah ..." I say, running my fingers through my hair, "I had some music going."

"I heard," he smiles, "The Beach Boys, huh?"

My cheeks redden and I suddenly feel self-conscious in my oversized t-shirt and capris, which evidently are covered in patches of soapy water. *This is not how this was supposed to go.*

I was supposed to look perfect the first time seeing Jayden after the breakup. The ideal meet-up scene consisted of me walking down Broad Street in some pretty high heels, a short red dress, and a pair of Gucci sunglasses with my hair falling glamorously down my chest. The ideal scene did *not* occur in my house, wearing no makeup — or a bra for that matter — with my hair restrained by a bandana.

"Can I come in?" He says.

"No." I shift, holding my place in the doorway.

"Grace," He takes a step forward.

"What?" I take one back.

"Please."

While my heart remains in my stomach, old feelings for Jayden rise up into my throat and choke out any words of rejection. I step helplessly aside, a slave to my own emotions.

The tension in his jaw slackens as he steps across the threshold and I shut the door. I'm frustrated with myself for granting him any feelings of relief.

"Make it quick, Jayden." I say, "What do you want?"

He holds my gaze, unsmiling, "Wow. You really must hate me."

I raise my brows, as if to say, *you think?*

He sighs, "I *want* you to hear me out, Grace."

Keeping my arms crossed and my eyes trained, I remain silent.

His eyes wander over to my collection of herbal plants spilling over the windowsill and he half smiles, "You have no idea how much I've missed you."

My brows knit together at his statement and I feel the knot in my throat bob when I swallow. He has no right to barge in like this. No right to make me feel anything.

Keeping his gaze on me, he takes a seat on my couch, motioning for me to sit down next to him.

I don't move.

An expression of hurt flashes briefly behind the screen of his light-colored irises at my dismissal.

"What's it going to take for you to believe me when I say that?"

I unfold my arms, throwing them up in frustration, "I don't know at this point, Jayden. You've lied to me so much, I don't know how you expect me to believe a word you say anymore."

He buries his hands in his hair, nodding down at his lap, "I guess I deserve that."

My face heats, and my anger suddenly overrides every other emotion, "You *guess?*" I take a step towards him, "You deserve that and *more.* You don't even deserve to be in this house, on *my* couch. How dare you come back here after what you did. After all of my questions you wouldn't answer — and say you *miss* me no less."

"Grace —" He starts.

"No."

He stands suddenly, closing the space between us. His eyes bore into mine with an intensity that burns. "I came here to answer all your questions, if that's what it takes. I came here to remind you what a good thing we had and can still have."

I try to step away from him, but his hands catch my hips and pull me back.

"Listen, Gracelynn."

His use of my first name stills me. He's only used it over serious conversations.

"My relationship with Hadley was obviously against all of my better judgment and it never should have happened. But it did, and now all I can possibly do is try to make it better with you."

He's so close, I can feel the warmth of his breath on my chest. The musky scent of his cologne mingled with the smoke of his last cigarette.

Could he really mean what he's saying? Moreover, can I bring myself to match the meaningfulness of his words with the face I'm looking at? The one who stared emotionless at me while tears streamed down my cheeks, blackening them with running mascara? The thought makes my body go slack and I wriggle away from his grasp.

I turn my back to him, willing myself to focus on what to say next. Instead, hot tears snake down my cheeks as I remember the bits of joy I used to feel with Jayden, and how at one point, our memories counted for nothing in his eyes.

I can't say anything right now. I don't want my voice to crack. If I speak, even if my eyes are red rimmed, my voice needs to be strong and resolved, so he gets the memo that I really am done this time.

But then, the persistent and insatiable part of my heart tugs at me to ask him the questions he wouldn't answer before, and to find comfort in his willingness to answer them now. It would be so easy to fall right back into his open arms and let him hold me the way he always used to. To listen to his whispers of love and regret as he strokes my hair with his strong fingers. Our memories wouldn't be for naught after all.

But the fact of the matter is, I tried this once already.

I cringe at how vulnerable I allowed myself to be when I first found out. I literally went right up to him — my shattered heart on full display — and asked *why.*

Why would you do this to us? You are my best friend. What gave you permission to get involved? After the first time you slept with her, did you feel guilty? How could it go on for so long if you felt guilty? Was it even hard for you to keep lying to me?

He answered none of these questions. He wouldn't even look at me. To me, *that* was his chance. *Not* this.

"I know I hurt you," he says softly, "and I know I betrayed your trust. I'm apologizing for that."

I squeeze my eyes shut, resisting the urge to wrap my arms around myself.

I clear my throat and will my voice to sound unfazed, "Are you still seeing her?"

Silence.

A couple beats pass.

I turn, "Are you?"

"No," He says quickly, "I mean, I was,"

"You *were?*"

"Yes, but *no.*"

"Which one?" I say, backing him towards the door.

He sighs, exasperated, "Yes, I was seeing her for a few days after you and I broke up, but no, I'm not anymore. I've cut off all communication with her."

I stop.

A flicker of something flares in my chest that I can't peg. *Sadness? Anger? Hope?* Possibly a blend of all three.

"Why did you stop?" I demand, keeping our eyes locked.

He shifts on his feet, "Because I'd rather have you. I *miss* you."

It then becomes clear what the flicker had been. *Anger.*

It rises up in my chest, grabbing hold of my words. It throws them up my throat and out my vocal chords before I can filter them.

"Oh, I see. You'd *rather* have me. What? After you've had a taste of something else? After you've finished your *sampling,* you decide you'd *rather* just stick with me?"

"Grace," He pleads, as I shove him towards the door.

"Get out."

"Please."

"*Get out!*" I shout, opening the door.

His handsome face looks startled at the sudden raise in my voice. It's unusually satisfying, but the tiniest piece of my heart still dares him not to listen. Dares him once again to stay and say exactly the right words to fix everything.

But he doesn't.

Of course he doesn't.

He averts his eyes from mine and without another word, proceeds out the door. I don't wait to see if he gets into his car and leaves. I slam the door shut behind him, lean my back against it and sink to the floor, heaving heavy sobs.

Why, Jayden?

Why, Why, Why?

Just leave me alone.

Just let me get over you.

18

Rae - Thursday

Grace had it right all along, picking a career that requires a couple certifications instead of a four-year degree. Not that she didn't have to work hard for them, but I think she genuinely enjoyed the process, which is more than I can say for myself right now. It's on days like today that I wish someone had told me to go that route with my career.

I sit in the front row of the class, quickly jotting down notes before Mr. Algray runs out of space and starts erasing the whiteboard.

I'm barely able to process what he's saying because I'm trying so hard to get it on paper, so when I look up at the board and realize I'm totally lost, I set down my pencil and raise my hand.

The teacher's monotonous drone pauses for a moment, bringing a satisfying silence to the class.

"Ms. Brooks?"

I lower my hand and squint at the board, "Why does it equal three?"

The teacher turns back to the board and examines his work, "What part of the equation are you asking about?"

Great, he wants me to name specifics?

I stare at the board which has a jumble of both words and numbers scrawled on it, complete with two sets of parentheses.

All of it – I want to say.

I clear my throat instead, "I don't get how we solved the last part."

He points to the equation on the board, which reads "Sin2(Θ)+Cos2(Θ)= 1".

"We simplified the problem by substituting sin squared of theta plus cosine squared of theta for one, and then since the equation asks for that substitution *plus* two, we added two."

I swallow, trying to take in the mouthful of mathematical terms.

"But …" I say, "Why did we substitute it for one?"

"Because that's the trigonometric identity." A student adds, as if to say *duh.*

"Oh," I say, backing down, "I get it."

But I don't.

It should never be allowed for a student to answer another student's question, because then the asker feels dumb for even bringing it up. As if the answer is obvious, and the entire classroom is getting it. Everyone but you.

My mind circles back to *'If I'd only just picked a career that requires a certification'.*

The courses you have to take in order to obtain a certification tend to focus on the subject you're actually interested in pursuing. For example, Grace dreamed of being an in-home, natural-medicine guru of sorts. So, she spent her time reading books about – if you can believe it – *natural medicine.* After about nine months, she became a certified herbalist and aromatherapist. Then she went on to obtain her associate's degree in business with the time she saved. Now she has both a job she loves and a brain full of knowledge she actually uses on a daily basis.

I, however, am filling my brain with fragments of knowledge about trigonometric identities. Which, of course, is entirely relevant to physical training. Obviously.

Soon enough, the class is over and I'm left staring down at my sloppy attempts to copy down the teacher's writing.

"Don't forget," he says as students begin gathering their things. "Your midterm test is coming up in one week. That's *this* upcoming Thursday, and it's forty percent of your grade, so study hard."

A whirlwind of dread comes sweeping through my stomach. I am so screwed.

Most of the students have dispersed from the room. As I am collecting my papers, a shadow appears on my notes. I look up to see who it belongs to, and a smiling, redheaded girl waves at me.

"Hi," She says.

"Um, hi." I say back, shouldering my bag.

"Do you feel like you're understanding everything so far?" She says, keeping step with my pace.

I give her a look. Not to be rude, but just because it's obvious to everyone in the class that I'm *not* understanding everything so far.

"Sorry if that's too invasive," she says, "I just thought you might be interested in looking over my notes."

I stop, looking over at the piece of paper she's offered me.

The notes are neatly written in light blue ink and are complete with not only the equations, but lines of explanations and arrows pointing to which equations they apply to. Much more orderly than mine.

"Actually," I say, "Yeah, that would be awesome. You don't mind?"

She shakes her head, red hair bouncing.

"Well, thank you." I say, folding the paper neatly in my binder, "Do you have more of these?"

She smiles, "One for every class session."

I scan her with interest. She has a sprinkle of freckles spattered across her nose.

"Why would you … I mean …"

She adjusts the bag on her shoulder, "The truth? I'm studying to be a math teacher, and I need to fill a certain quota of one-on-one student teaching hours."

I stare at her, my lips parted in amusement, "You're using me?"

She smiles a toothy grin, "Only if you agree."

I appreciate her candor right off the bat. Not only did I need all the one-on-one help I could get between now and next Thursday, but I'd be giving her something she needs too.

"Yeah, that would be good." I say, "Let me give you my number."

She smiles and gives me hers as well, telling me her name is Claire before we go our separate ways. When I get to my car, I look back at her notes again. They're exactly what I need to understand the lesson for today.

I turn my eyes upward as I ignite the engine. *Could this be my reward for trying to do better? For suggesting abstinence last night?*

***

I'm so excited to take a left turn at the stoplight instead of a right turn, which would normally take me in the direction of home. The left turn leads me to the gym, where I've been dying to try a new barbell workout. It's been far too long since I've been here, but my work and school schedule just wouldn't allow for it.

When I step into the building, I feel like I'm in a secondary home. A place where I can focus on becoming the best version of myself. Where I can push my physical limits toward something more resilient. Where I can tune out every last thing besides the sound of my own breathing.

I go over to the barbell station, switch my phone off, and begin my work.

To say that time passes quickly in the gym because I'm doing something I enjoy would be a lie. In fact, during the moments where I'm really pushing myself, five minutes feels much closer to an hour. But when I finish my last rep of the new barbell workout and my body feels warm with aching muscles, I love it. Something about that feeling is liberating to me.

I place the weight back on its rack and pause the music beating through my earbuds. I pull them from my ears as I turn from the station, and preoccupied with wrapping the earbud wires around my iPod, I bump right into another person.

"My bad," He says.

"No, I —" I start, but my words are cut short as the tumble of blonde hair and friendly blue eyes in front of me begin to register.

Recognition dawns on his face at the same moment.

"Rae?" He smiles.

"Oh my gosh, *Sam?*"

"Yeah!" He laughs, "What are you doing here?"

I smirk, looking around, "This is my sanctuary. What are *you* doing here?"

He scratches his neck, glancing briefly at my body, which is glistening and toned from years of coming here.

"I guess that *is* the better question. I don't know, I just figured it was time to get into some new habits — you know, get buff for my lady."

"Ooh, your *lady,* huh?" I punch his arm, "Who are you seeing now?"

"Rosie Martin," He waggles his eyebrows at me.

My lips part in a wide-open smile, "No way! You and Rosie? You have no idea how happy that makes me."

Me, Rosie, Grace, and Samuel Ross used to all hang out together in high school. I lost touch with Rosie around the same time I stopped talking to Sam, so I guess shortly after graduation. The four of us certainly had some great times together back in the day. Oddly enough, even though Jayden was technically in our circle. We never saw him as much because he went to the high school across town, which was *my* old high school before the transfer. We pretty much only saw him during after-school double dates or school formals, to which Rosie usually took some upperclassmen, and I always took Sam (even after we broke up).

Our breakup was lighthearted and mutual. It wasn't that we had some horrible fight or disagreement, it's just that we honestly got bored of being a thing. Sam was my friend, and I was his, but the romantic feelings didn't last that long. Neither of us ever said this, but now that I'm older, I think he and I were each other's experimental boyfriend/girlfriend — to practice kissing on before we were with someone who would judge our beginner-level skills and whatnot. Boyfriend and girlfriend or not, Sam and I always had fun together.

"Yeah," He smiles, "I've been seeing Rosie for just under two years now,"

My eyes crinkle at the corners, "Wow, I'm really happy for you guys."

"What about you though?" He says, eyeing my ring finger, "Is that a rock I see?"

I look down at my engagement ring. The diamond sparkles in the light and I smile.

"Are you blushing right now, Brooks?" Sam laughs, "You don't blush."

"Am not," I say defensively.

He continues to tease me as though we're sixteen years old again until I shove him.

"Wanna get out of here?" I suggest, "Sounds like we have worlds to catch up on."

He tosses his brand-new membership card, "What is fitness? I don't need to be sexy."

I laugh, inching toward the door, "You gonna pick that up?"

He frowns, staring at its place on the floor.

"Yeah ..."

***

"Where do you wanna go?" I say.

Rays of warm autumn sunshine spill from the sky as we exit the air-conditioned gym.

"Is that even a question?" He says, nodding his head at the quick mart across the street.

I chuckle. Remmy's Quick Mart, which is also just a short distance away from our high school, is an old favorite of ours. There's nothing special about it — It's just a run-down, gas station-like store that desperately needs a paint job — but it *does* consistently carry those little retro wax bottle candies that seem to be absent in every other store.

"So tell me about your guy." Sam says, giving the store owner a quick wave as we enter the building.

I tuck a lock behind my ear. "His name is Adam Compton. We met at the park."

"Gevali park?" He asks, selecting a package of wax bottles.

"Yeah," I smile, "It's kind of a funny story actually."

He tucks the package under his arm and selects a bag of Pop Rocks and a couple bottles of Coke from the fridge.

"These snacks," He says, tossing a bottle to me, "Were literally *made* for stories."

I laugh.

We proceed to the counter and Sam buys our goodies for us. In our circle of friends, this snack combo was iconic. As teenagers inspired by the Green Day song, we were curious to know what *"Poprocks and Coke"* really tasted like together, even though the song never actually mentions anything about the two items.

Turned out, Sam and I loved the explosively fizzy combo. Rosie and Grace, however, were not fans. So whenever Sam and I hung out, we got them for the two of us, and we never failed to get a package of wax bottles along with it, just because.

"Thanks man," Sam waves to the cashier as he opens the door for me.

We decide to partake of these legendary snacks at the docks — a five minute drive from here.

"So you met him at the park huh? And a story ensued?"

I smile, "Yeah. It was two summers ago. He was helping host his little cousin's birthday party at one of the pavilions. On that particular day, It just so happens that I decided to take advantage of the park's walking trails instead of hitting up the gym for my laps. Nice weather and all that. But, the thing is ... pause for effect ..." I raise my brows dramatically, "I forgot my water bottle."

He gasps, "No."

"Yes ... So I remember slowing my jog upon seeing the party. Mind you, I had gone pretty hard already, and the sun was beating down no less, so I was feeling pretty desperate for some water."

Sam raises an eyebrow suggestively, "And hottie offers you some water?"

I shake my head, "Hottie offers me some *cake*."

"Classic." Sam says solemnly.

I pull into a parking space in front of the lake, sighing wistfully, "So I declined the cake, but asked if I could bum on their party for a little water. *Then* I accepted the cake."

"And the rest is history." Sam shakes his head, "Ole' Rae — putting out for the first man who offers her cake."

I punch his arm, mouth gaping, "*No.* Jerk."

Sam laughs, "I'm sorry."

We get out of the car and make our way down the grassy hill to the old wooden docks.

"*Actually,*" I say, "Adam's aunt had forgotten to buy some important item for a game she had planned out and was making a store-run to pick up said 'item'. Adam was left to fend for himself as the responsible chaperone over about twelve screaming third-graders, and I picked up on the fact that he looked a little outnumbered. So I offered to stay with him and rally the kids until his aunt got back from the longest trip to the store *ever.*

Sam snorted, "She actually just ditched you guys."

"I know right? But it all turned out right in the end, so I really have his aunt to *thank* for my upcoming marriage plans."

"So what happened next?" Sam says, "He was just like, 'Hey, you're pretty cute. Let's get married.'?"

"Naturally," I laugh. "Long story short, Adam and I decided we made a pretty good team that day by rallying all the third-graders. So he asked me if I wanted to do it again sometime, and I said yes."

"Babysit a bunch of eight-year-olds for free?" Sam prods, "Sounds like a solid date idea to me."

I roll my eyes, but the smile doesn't leave my face, "It was actually pretty fun. And honestly, he nailed our first *actual* date, so I don't want to hear it."

He throws his hands up, "I'm sure he did. I'm just saying it doesn't sound like *my* idea of a good time."

I squint at him, "That's because your idea of a good time is sitting around playing Mortal Kombat all day."

"Hey now ... This is feeling like a personal attack."

"Or Pac-Man World 2." I add.

His face goes serious now, "Don't you ever insult Pac-Man World 2 to my face. That is straight blasphemy."

I laugh, shaking my head "You haven't changed a bit."

"I have too. Only where it matters." He smiles taking his seat at the end of the dock.

I take my place beside him, dangling my feet over the edge, "Like joining a gym?"

He points at me with the cap side of his bottle and winks, "Exactly."

We crack open our bottles and he pours a few pop rocks in my palm.

"Tell me about you and Rosie though," I say, tipping them back in my mouth, "What happened there."

He shrugs, "You know, it's kind of weird because I feel like after graduation, our group just sorta split. I assume you and Grace kept up with each other while Rosie and I gradually grew closer. A douchebag at her college is what really sealed the deal for me."

I wait as he takes a swig.

"It was her first semester at UVM, and she thought she was in *love.* She and I were mostly keeping up through e-mails and texts at the time, but every once in awhile she would give me a call and tell me about college life. I wasn't liking the sound of this guy from the start to be honest with you."

"Intuition kicking in?" I say.

"*Way* in. She called me one night in tears. I didn't have to ask a lot of questions to know I needed to go up there."

I frown, "Really? You kick his ass?"

"*Yeah* I kicked his ass. Got it kicked right out of UVM too."

I smile, amazed at my friend, "Damn, Ross."

He shrugs like it's no big deal.

"It didn't take long after that for me to fall in love with her. I liked her for a little while leading up to this, but the *love* part didn't kick in till later. She, on the other hand, took even longer to realize that I was her man."

"Oh yeah?" I say, biting off the wax tip off of a bottle and spitting it.

"Yeah," He stretches his arms back, "But she finally came to her senses."

I smile, taking a swig of my drink. The bubbles intermingle with the snapping rocks in a popping frenzy.

As I stare out at the calm, ever green lake as it shimmers in the sunshine, I briefly recall a bright idea Sam and I once had to kiss with Pop Rocks in our mouths. It was the strangest sensation that ended in a fit of laughter and Rosie calling us gross.

I steal a quick glance at my friend. I told him he hadn't changed a bit, but he really had in subtle ways. His jawline is more defined now, and he has a hint of stubble. His demeanor has lost its charming boyish vibes and taken on one of strength and masculinity. My friend, who once hated the idea of confrontation or causing any trouble, has now gotten someone kicked out of a college and since claimed his woman. I suppose it's his confidence that has heightened over the years. Sam is the same ... yet he's different.

"How is Grace doing? Have you heard?" He says, tearing me from my thoughts, "Are she and Jayden still going strong?"

I wince, "No ... definitely not."

"I kinda figured." He says, "My intuition is never wrong about these guys."

"They held it together for like, four years, though." I say, "The breakup was recent."

"Really? Now that actually does surprise me. Didn't think Jayden had that kind of loyalty in him."

I frown, "He doesn't."

"Oh," Sam winces, "I got you."

We sip our drinks in silence for a few moments, soaking in all of this new information.

"Oh, what was I thinking?" Sam says suddenly, "I should text Rosie. I bet she'd love to see you again."

I smile, "Yes! Please. If she's into it, I'd love to have her as a bridesmaid."

"I'll call her real quick," Sam says, reaching for his phone in his back pocket.

As he gets up to call her, I pull out my phone to check any messages. It's been off since I entered the gym, so it vibrates with notifications as it boots back up. What I find is three missed calls from Zoe and a text.

From: Adam

Sent: 10/10/19

Time: 12:03

"Where you at, honey? We need to leave soon."

My eyes widen as I remember the photoshoot we scheduled for today with Zoe. And the text was sent a full HOUR ago.

I tap out a quick text that I'll be right there and pocket my phone. Sam is striding back towards me with a smile.

"Rosie's on her way. She's excited."

"Oh, I'm sorry, Sam," I say, "I totally forgot, but Adam and I have a photoshoot today and I really should get going."

Sam smirks, "A photoshoot? You hate taking pictures."

"I know," I sigh, "But we need a good one to put on our invites."

"Ah," He says, "Wedding stuff."

I smile sadly, "Please apologize to Rosie for me. I want to catch up with both of you guys soon."

He laughs, "Go on, Brooks, we'll find something to do."

"Alright," I say, giving him a quick side hug, "I'll see ya."

"Run, girl, run." He says after me.

***

My house isn't even far from here, but of course I hit every red light possible on the way home. When I pull into my driveway, I am relieved to see Adam's car in the space next to mine. I hurry inside.

He's sitting at my table with piles of papers all around him. He looks at me unsmiling over the top of his glasses.

"Did you forget?"

His voice is calm as ever, but I can tell he's displeased.

"I'm so sorry. I totally did, and I had my phone turned off."

He continues reading over his papers.

"Are you pretty much ready to go?" I say, fiddling with my car keys.

"We're over an hour and a half late, Rae," He says, "I called Zoe to reschedule."

"You — Oh ... okay. How'd you get her number?"

He nods over to a note stuck to my fridge that has today's date and Zoe's number written on it, followed by a doodle of a camera.

"Oh ..." I echo, "But ... you're still here. And it's a Thursday."

"Yes," He sighs, "I took off work for this, remember? You told me Zoe's only available on weekdays."

"That's right ..." I say, approaching the seat next to him, "I'm really sorry."

He's silent as he straightens a stack of papers. I can see now that they are ungraded quizzes for one of his classes.

"Where were you?" He says finally.

"Well," I say, folding my hands, "I had trig this morning of course, and then I went to the gym. I ran into an old friend there."

He writes something in red ink on one of the pages in front of him, "Anyone I would know?"

I clear my throat, "Do you remember me telling you about Samuel Ross?"

His ink pen stills. "Your ex?"

Suddenly, I feel uncertain.

"I mean, I guess. He's hardly an ex, Adam. We were sixteen."

He clicks his pen and sets it down on the table, turning toward me.

"Hold on. Let me see if I have this straight. You were late for something *you* really wanted to do in the first place, despite what I said about the other pictures we have being just fine. Something you asked me to *take off* work for. And that tardiness caused me to have to cancel the shoot and reschedule it for you so that I'll have to take yet another day off work. And your reasoning behind doing that to me is because you were busy catching up with your ex?"

I blink. It sounds terrible when he says it like that.

"During which," He continues, "Not to mention, you had your phone turned off, making it impossible for me or anyone else to get a hold of you."

"It's not like that, Adam, I turned my phone off at the gym *way* before I ran into Sam. You know I do that."

His eyes narrow, "So I suppose it'd be perfectly reasonable for me to not show up for something I asked *you* to take off work for because I'm busy catching up with Lexi, is that what you're saying?"

"*What?*" I gape, "Okay, that is *not* the same."

Alexis Reed was Adam's most serious girlfriend, second of course, to me.

"Sam and I were just like ... you know ... after-school study-buddies." I say, "Someone to go to formals with each year without all the drama."

"After-school 'study buddies'." Adam remarks, collecting his papers, "Sure, babe."

I open my mouth and then close it, realizing I've probably shared way too much information about my relationship with Sam in the past.

I watch him gather his things and organize them into his satchel.

"I'm not sure why you're trying to compare what Sam and I had to what you and Alexis had." I say, "As far as I know, weren't you two preparing for a future together? How is that the same as a high school fling?"

He says nothing and heads for the door.

"Not that you care," I add, following him, "But we pretty much just talked about you the entire time. And also, Sam has a girlfriend now. A really serious girlfriend."

He turns at the doorway, exhaling. He says nothing, but gives me a brief peck on the cheek before opening the door and leaving.

I'm left shell-shocked, standing in the foyer.

I'm not sure what just happened, but I definitely did not like it.

19

Grace - Friday

I tossed and turned all night. My mind kept replaying what happened with Jayden and coming up with better ways I could've handled everything. I should've just acted neutral about seeing him again; Like I had already moved on and he no longer has any power over me. Why did I let him see me cry?

The worst part is how badly my body wanted to just give in. What if that was God's way of telling me to accept Jayden's repentance and forgive him? Would that mean welcoming him back into my life?

I stare at his number on my phone screen, so tempted to press the call button. To tell him everything. But then I remember something that he said last night that didn't add up: That he wasn't seeing Hadley anymore. That he'd cut communication with her.

Last I checked, his Facebook didn't back up that claim, but out of pure curiosity, I type his name into the search bar.

To my surprise, nothing comes up. I apparently no longer have a Facebook friend named Jayden Grayson.

This, of course, could mean one of two things: Either that Jayden *is* telling the truth, or that I am officially blocked.

Probably the latter. I throw my phone across the bed, choosing to shove Jayden from my mind.

It's Friday. The big day. Meaning I need all the mental strength I can conjure.

I spend a little extra time getting ready for the day. I outline my nails with perfect French tips and apply a layer of beige lipstick. I slip on a close-fitting black skirt and a white button-up shirt. From my jewelry box I select a classy, jeweled watch and some conservative hoop earrings along with my favorite black heels. I turn to see my profile in the mirror as I twist my hair into a neat bun. I'm going for a no-nonsense, businesswoman look, and I feel like I've nailed it. My gaze flicks over to the circled date on my wall calendar: Hadley - 11 o'clock - Vanelos.

My eyes drop down to the handwritten note pinned to my bulletin board. The apology and phone number from Liam. I almost thought the note would've inspired me for the day ahead — made me feel desirable and untouchable — but instead, I find myself burning with fury. Why had I kept any evidence of someone else's infidelity, and used it to make myself feel good? I must really be at an all-time low. I rip the paper down from my board and pick up my cell phone, pressing the numbers on my phone digit by digit.

The dial tone beeps five long tones before the answering machine picks up, "You've reached Liam Cross. Please leave your name, phone number and a brief message and I will get back with you as soon as possible." I expect the beep to follow directly after the message, but instead I hear what sounds like the same message repeated, but in some other language — Italian maybe? Then the beep.

I shake my head to clear it and make my voice firm.

"Liam, this is Grace. We met a few days ago in the Café, and you gave me your number. I just wanted to say how highly inappropriate that was, seeing as though you have a girlfriend – who I would be more than happy to contact for you about this, by the way. Please do not use this number to call me back," I say, "and for goodness sake, quit handing out your number to random girls."

I tap the 'end call' button and throw my phone in my purse. I crumple up the note and toss it in the trash can once and for all as I take one final look in the mirror. I press my beautifully beige lips together in a pucker before grabbing my keys and heading out the door.

***

I pull up to Vanelos and pick a stool at the bar. I was never much of a drinker myself.

I've only been to Vanelos on nights when Rae dragged me, and I was usually the designated driver. But I figured today ... with the topics I'd be drudging up, and moreover *who* I'd be drudging them up with, might call for a little alcohol.

Shortly after my arrival, the familiar blonde comes in and shoots a smile at the bartender, who waves at her. I plaster on a smile when she joins me at the bar.

"Hey!" She says, reaching over for a hug.

"I guess you come here quite a bit?" I say, hugging her back.

She laughs, "That's a fun story. I was nineteen when I moved here, and I thought I had a pretty convincing fake ID, but Joshua here," she nods to the bartender, "Called my bluff immediately."

My eyes widen, "Oh no."

She waves her hand, "He let it slide. Still gave me my drink and everything."

"Shhh," The bartender cuts in, "Don't make me regret it, Harris."

She laughs, "But not before giving me an all-responsible talking to of course. About how a young girl shouldn't be lying about her age."

I watch as the two share comradery and after a few minutes we order margaritas.

I try to act natural as we make small talk and sip our drinks for the next ten minutes, but I'm not sure how much more avoiding the topic I can do. I wait for the small talk to come to an awkward silence before gaining the courage to broach the reason we're here.

Folding my hands in my lap, I realize being direct is the only way I can do this.

"I know it probably seemed weird that I contacted you out of the blue," I start, choosing my words carefully, "But to be honest with you, I wanted to ask you something specifically."

A look flashes across her face. It isn't malice or feigned innocence, but genuine curiosity.

I take a deep breath. "Do you know someone by the name of Jayden Grayson?"

She gives me an inquisitive smile, "Yes, he's my boyfriend."

My chest squeezes tightly. That's when I know for sure; she has no idea who I am to Jayden.

"Like, you're currently seeing each other?" I say.

All traces of a smile disappear, "Yes ... Why?"

Her confirmation twists my stomach in knots. That low life lied to me again.

Hadley sips her drink with a sudden look of uncertainty, waiting for me to continue.

"I don't know how to say this, Hadley. You're clearly not anymore to blame than me, but Jayden was my boyfriend too."

She studies me carefully, "Okay?"

"Not like, a long time ago ... we broke up a little over three weeks ago."

I can see the gears in her mind turning as the color bleeds from her face. There is silence between the two of us as her light eyes stare at me, guarded, "What are you saying?"

I shake my head, sorry that I have to be the bearer of this news, "I'm saying that we were played. Both of us."

She sits back in her chair, watching me, and I almost wonder if she feels skeptical of what I'm saying.

"I naturally had a lot of questions for him when I first found out about you, none of which were answered." I continue, "But when I saw you that first time at A&B, I recognized you immediately. I thought you knew who I was, too. But I guess ... I was wrong about that?"

"You thought I knew you? As in, took your man from you on purpose?" She says, somewhat defensively. Then her face softens. "Damn, it feels weird even referring to him as someone else's man."

My shoulders ease down as I realize in her mind, Jayden belongs just as much to her as he does to me. This must be a lot to take in — that she's not the only girl he's been whispering sweet nothings to.

A new bartender—Not Joshua—comes up and whisks away her empty glass.

"Another ma'am?" He asks her.

She regards him with a half-hearted nod, and my heart just aches for her. All at once, I begin to feel that she's a lot like me. The bartender slides over her drink, but Hadley only considers the glass, brushing it with her finger tips.

"The truth is," I begin again, "I was really hoping I could ask you some questions about the whole thing," I say, taking my guard down in hopes that she will do the same. "Not just because Jayden wouldn't answer them, but because the idea of seeing him again just… hurts a lot. I'd like to keep him out of it."

"You're not trying to get him back?" She asks.

I shake my head, "Definitely not."

Not after he lied to me last night about not being with you anymore. Right after basically promising me no more lies.

"I don't blame you…" She says, finally sipping her drink.

It dawns on me that she might have questions for *me.*

"I'm happy to answer anything you want to know as well. I was just hoping you could give me some closure."

She nods, "Okay. I can try."

I recall the list of questions I'd written down to ask her, trying to decide which ones were crucial and which ones were unnecessary heartache.

"How did you guys meet?" I conclude.

I see a hint of a smile play on her lips before it disappears, "A couple months back, my sister invited me to come see her and her new husband in Nevada. I had just adopted my little Pomeranian, Hudson, at the time, and it was too expensive for me to take him on the plane with me, so I hired my cousin to take care of him while I was gone."

I nod, interested.

"I really should've known better than to ask my cousin to watch him. I should've just asked Kaya to take him for awhile so he could hang out with Coco. But long story short, somehow Hudson got out of the house on my cousin's watch and tore off down the street. He was still missing by the time I got home. Of course, my cousin was sick about what happened, but we couldn't find him anywhere. So naturally I printed about fifty 'lost puppy' posters, attached my number and a cash award, and hung them up all over town. A few more days went by without any calls and I was starting to lose hope, when finally my cell rang, and guess who it was."

I try to bite my tongue and listen, even though every new piece of information rips a thread from my precariously sewn heart.

"I had Jayden send me pictures of Hudson first, just to make sure that he *did* have him, and the pictures I got of my sweet boy were heartbreaking. He was covered in dirt and his tongue was lolling to the side like he'd been panting. So I gave Jayden my address and he showed up with my puppy that night. To my surprise, however, Hudson had been groomed to perfection and was wearing a little bowtie collar, complete with a new license that had his name and my address engraved on it. I told Jayden he didn't have to go through all that trouble, but Jayden insisted that Hudson was far too loved by his owner to risk being lost again. I offered him the cash reward, but of course, he was a gentleman and declined, so I insisted on him taking at least reimbursement for the trip to the groomers. He told me that wouldn't be necessary, because he had washed and brushed Hudson himself, and it was no trouble to do so."

I fidget with the fabric on my skirt, all too familiar with Jayden's random bouts of thoughtfulness.

"I was … charmed … that he had such love for animals. That he took time out of his day to do something that benefited him in no way. I asked multiple times if he was sure there was nothing I could do for him. That's when he said the only thing he could think of was to allow him to take a 'pretty thing like me' out to dinner …"

I purse my lips and look away, trying not to think about that too hard.

"I'll stop." She offers.

I just nod. I'd been drinking in the story, but it was blackening my heart. I crave to know more, but I don't *need* to know more. I have to distribute my emotional taxing wisely with these questions.

"Mind if I ask you a question now?" She asks.

I shrug, "Shoot."

Her throat bobs, "How long were you two together?"

I wince inside, "Just about four years."

"*Four?*" Her eyes widen.

I nod, taking the last sip of my drink.

She pushes the remainder of her second margarita toward me, "You need this way more than I do."

I smile at her weakly and accept the drink.

A few beats pass between us as we soak up all the new information.

"Did he ever mention me?" I manage.

She shakes her head, "Never."

"Wow."

I would probably be upset about this on a normal day, but I feel like I've cried all my tears and all that is left is the hollow, empty drum in my chest.

She shifts in her seat, "Earlier you said you recognized me at A&B … did Jayden mention *me*? How'd you know what I look like?"

I tuck a lock of hair behind my ear, "He didn't. I saw your pictures in his gallery."

Her cheeks redden, "All of them?"

I wince, "Yeah … sorry."

She squeezes her eyes shut and wrinkles her nose, "What an *idiot.*"

At that, I laugh, "I know right. Isn't that like, the most basic and obvious rule of affairs? If you're gonna cheat, at least don't save girl number one's nude pictures in plain sight for girl number two to find."

She smiles and hides her face with her hands, "Oh my word, that's so embarrassing."

The bartender comes back over to us, "More drinks, ladies?"

"Mm, I better not." she says.

I smirk, "Can we get two shots of Jack Daniel's Single Barrel Whiskey?"

The bartender nods and Hadley raises an eyebrow, "You have some good taste."

I scoff, "In everything but men apparently."

She sighs, "Same."

A few beats pass.

"I'm really sorry this happened." Hadley says, her body wilting slightly.

"I am too," I sigh, "I know this isn't any fun for you either."

She shrugs, "I'm just trying to take in the idea that I'm the *other* girl, you know? Everything felt so real, but in reality, you were the main attraction … I was just the side chick."

My brows furrow in sympathy. I hadn't even thought about that; how painful that must feel. Part of me wants to comfort her, but I don't know how. I can't tell her she's wrong, and I'm in no place to reassure her of Jayden's love for her.

"I mean, what do we do now?" She says, "I feel like it's more of your right to decide than mine."

I shake my head, "I don't think that's true. I think you can feel the same intensity of love for someone you've only been with for a few months as someone you have been with for a few years."

She exhales through her nose, "Yeah ..."

The bartender returns with our shots.

I take one and pass the other to her.

"Who says we have to say anything?" I say, "He doesn't know we've talked. What if we just let it be ... let it take its own course?"

"Let it be." She scoffs, swirling the whiskey around in her glass, "Not a chance. Not with me as his girlfriend anyway. I won't say anything about our talk though ... I'll leave that up to you."

I smile in sympathy. I don't blame her for wanting to leave him. I did, after all.

"Whatever," She says, becoming resolute. "I'm not gonna wallow about this, and neither should you. We're two young, sexy, *single* ladies with our whole lives ahead of us. It's a shame that he doesn't get to be a part of that, for his sake."

I nod my head, loving her vibe, "Hell yeah."

She holds up her glass and I clink mine with hers.

"Cheers."

We tip our heads back in unison and let the whiskey burn down our throats.

20

Rae - Friday

I'm in a hurry as I lather my hair with soap.

Adam had been in such a mood last night that he forgot to tell me that he rescheduled the photoshoot for *this morning.*

"Can you be ready in forty-five minutes?" His voice spoke over the phone earlier.

I'd just come back from my morning jog. I glanced in the mirror, a few wayward strands of hair sticking out from my ponytail and clinging to my neck, shiny with perspiration.

"Do I have a choice?" I said.

"Not really." He sighed.

"I had work today, Adam."

"I had work yesterday ..."

I peek at my watch and sigh back at him. "Okay, I'll be ready."

I called SportsTop and apologized for not being able to come in, and then hopped in the shower.

When the warm spray clears my body of soap, I turn the shower knob and wrap a towel around me. My hair drips as I try to comb through the tangles. The shower alone had taken fifteen minutes of my time. It's only half-way blow dried when Adam appears in the bathroom doorway.

I smile at him sweetly, "Could you pick me out something to wear while I finish?"

"You don't have something picked out already?"

"I trust you." I say, hoping to soften him a little.

The corner of his mouth twitches as he disappears into my room. It's clear that we're going to need to discuss what happened yesterday.

My hair dries with a natural wave that's surprisingly perfect. I apply a little mascara and then step into my bedroom to see a short white dress laid on my bed with matching earrings and heeled cowgirl boots.

I smile absently at his choice. Despite the fact that I don't usually like dresses, may as well go a little extra for a photoshoot.

Adam hadn't, however, picked out any bracelets for me, so I go over to my dresser and slide on a few matching wristbands. I may be wearing a dress, but the fabric athletic bands make me feel more like myself.

I step into the living room where Adam is waiting. "Time?"

His eyes lock on my figure and he smiles, "Look at you."

I smile, rolling my eyes, "*Time?*"

He glances at his watch, "five minutes to spare."

I cross my arms, "See that? *That's* why you're marrying me."

He laughs, "It is."

In the car on the way over, we are quiet. Our comradery had been short-lived, and now there's this unnatural tension hovering in the air between us.

"Can you at least act like you like me for the photoshoot?" I say finally, "If you're pissed off at me, it's gonna show through the pictures. Which are going on our *wedding* invites."

He sighs, keeping his eyes trained on the road, "Forget liking, Rae, I *love* you. Which is why I need you to be honest with me."

I throw up my hands, "How was I dishonest? I told you exactly where I was, and I had no problem telling you who I was with."

He laces his fingers through mine, "Okay, fair enough. But can you at least try to see how that looked from my perspective?"

I stare out the window, frustrated. But I really do for the first time consider his point from yesterday. If the tables were turned and he'd been out with Lexi with his phone off, I'm sure I'd also be a little upset, even though he's assured me there's nothing between them anymore.

But isn't it different? Me hanging out with Sam is more like him hanging out with a good guy-friend. Just then, my phone vibrates. I peek down at the screen and see that it's from — speak of the devil — Sam. I peek over at Adam, whose eyes are trained on the road ahead. I look back at my phone and open the text.

From: Samuel Ross

Sent: 10/11/19

Time: 9:25

"Rosie and I are going to the Café today - you should come! You can ask Rosie to be a bridesmaid in person :)"

I quickly close the text, unsure of how to deal with it now.

Adam has made his opinion clear, and I'll have to respect it. But I still can't shake how unfair his comparison feels: Sam and I are *not* like he and Lexi.

"Sorry for the surprise this morning ... I didn't mean for it to be so last minute," Adam smiles, "It didn't even phase you, though ... Just look at you. Gorgeous."

I smile, glancing down at our hands as he interlaces them.

"I love you, Adam Compton."

He turns into Zoe's driveway, "And I love you, Lacey Rae."

21

Grace - Friday

I wish I'd learned sooner how cool a girl Hadley is. It turns out she too is a bookworm, and we spent the rest of our time together sharing passionate fandom theories and recommending certain authors to each other — something I've never been able to do with Rae. These topics would bore her to tears, but I find myself grateful she encouraged me to meet up with Hadley in the first place.

In a way, I am envious of my new friend. She is feisty and confident and has a careless ease about her. The way she was able to bounce back from the news I delivered and still enjoy the rest of her day is something I can only aspire to do.

After Hadley and I part ways, I go ahead and updated her name in my phone. She said we should keep in touch, which I thought was pretty awesome of her. Find out your boyfriend was with someone else the whole time, and Hadley's logic is to become her new best friend. Rae would certainly shoot me a smug look about this after the big deal I made of everything.

There are two other notifications on my phone: A missed call from my mother, and one from — wouldn't you know it — Jayden.

I smirk.

Feeling inspired by Hadley's flippant attitude, I tap the call-back button with no hesitation.

"Grace," comes his low voice after the second ring.

"You called?" I say, my heels clicking as I make my way to my car.

"Yes … Thank you for calling back. I didn't think you would."

I roll my eyes.

"I just wanted to apologize for showing up the way I did last night … I should have called or something."

"You did call," I point out.

"Yeah, but you know what I mean." He says, "I should never have expected an answer from you right away. Especially after … everything. If you need time, I'll give you time."

Jayden. Jayden. Jayden. Ever charming.

"In my experience," I say, enjoying myself, "You're not a patient man."

"But I will be for you, baby. I have all the time in the world."

I laugh humorlessly, "Okay, first of all, I'm not your baby, so you can quit with that. Second of all, I'm gonna need you to go ahead and confirm something with me before this conversation continues."

There's some shifting on his side of the line, "Anything."

He says it almost seductively. As if I can be swayed.

"You broke up with Hadley … right? I need you to promise me I won't ever have to worry about her again."

I can practically hear his wry smile, thinking that he's got me. "That's right, love. Ancient History."

I narrow my eyes, deciding to ignore the 'love'.

"Well, she will be happy to hear that, seeing as though I just spent the last couple hours with her."

At the silence on his line, my lips stretch into a smile.

"You … what?"

"Mm-hmm," I sigh joyously, "I can see why you like her. Turns out we have a lot in common."

"You — "

"Like books and drinks and *terrible* taste in men. The whole shebang, really."

"Grace, I swear, if you're bullshitting me — "

"No, darling, I'm afraid I'm not. She should be arriving at your house right about now actually. I should really let you go handle your business like a grown man."

Right then, I hear the doorbell ring on his line. Something resembling a laugh almost escapes me, because I couldn't have chosen a better timing for Hadley's arrival.

"Shit." He says, and the line cuts.

I smile and open my car door, confident that Hadley can take it from here.

* * *

My phone call with Jayden gave me such a high that I actually *felt* like calling my mother back. With a smile on my face, I tapped out her number as I pulled out of Vanelos.

"Corinne," she answers.

"Hey, mom."

"Oh hey, thanks for calling back."

"Guess what I just did." I bite my lip.

"What?"

"Totally told Jayden off. Gave him a big ole' middle finger."

"You did what?" She sounds concerned.

"I told him to get lost, mom." I say, "You know, the jerk you never liked in the first place? Why aren't you thrilled?"

There's silence on the line for a moment.

"Grace ... did you ever take a pregnancy test?"

I sigh. Why won't she hear what I'm saying?

"Yes, mom, like, two days ago. We're all good."

"Have you taken one since then?" She says.

"Um ... no? The first one was negative."

"Jesus," I hear her whisper, which actually kinda bothers me.

"*What,* mom? What'd I do wrong now?"

"You need to take another test, baby. *Especially* before you go telling off the potential father." She says.

"What? Why?"

"The results of those tests depend on so many factors ..." She says, "How closely you followed the directions, how long you waited before checking your results. In fact, nine out of fifteen women will get a false pregnancy test until their eighth week of pregnancy, and you're only in what? *Maybe* your fourth? I wouldn't trust any reading you got."

My heart falls. I thought I had rid myself of this nightmare, and here it comes creeping back?

My mother tsks, "Today is the 7th day late from your period, right? That's perfect, actually. Even though it may still be too early to tell, tests are supposed to be way more reliable a week after your supposed start date."

I want to blurt, *That's what I originally thought!* But for many reasons, I keep it in. I don't want to believe that my test results were false, or that I'd put too much hope in Rae's judgment. I just want this whole thing to be over.

"Why don't you come down to the clinic?" She says, "We have plenty of tests here. I could snag one for you."

The thought fills me with dread.

"I don't know, mom. Maybe I should just get one down here. My car's acting funny, anyway."

My Volkswagen shudders in response and I lightly tap the brake so she will stop. Persia has had transmission issues in the past. I'm hoping I won't have to go through all of that again.

"Quit making excuses," She chuckles, "Really. Come to the clinic. I seriously doubt you want Rita spreading word about you buying a pregnancy test — do you?"

I sigh, because my mother is right. Rita is the owner of Gevali's local pharmacy, and she happens to be the town's biggest gossip.

"Alright, I'll head over."

"Cool. I might even take a lunch today if you do."

Which is a big deal. My mother never takes breaks from her work.

We hang up and I turn on to the interstate.

My car shudders again as I accelerate the gas pedal, and I try tapping the break again. Usually, that snaps her out of it, but this time she protests a few seconds longer.

"Oh please, God, keep her running," I whisper.

And He does.

For about ten minutes.

I pull into a gas station off the Waterbury exit, too cautious to continue.

I open my wallet and remove my car insurance card, which boasts one free tow to any location within an hour of my current location. I dial the phone number and explain the situation to the man on the other end. Luckily for me, my insurance also provides a free taxi service when you utilize your one free tow, so the man assures me he can get my Volkswagen back to the Mechanic in Gevali, and arrange a ride for me to my house.

"No," I say, "Actually, I need to go to Montpelier if possible. To the Oakland Clinic."

"Alright, we'll send someone your way!"

I thank the man and pocket my phone.

I figure my mom can give me a ride home when we're done.

* * *

The kind-faced man who tows my car offers to stay with me until my taxi arrives, but I politely decline. He relents only because we're both certain it can't be that much longer. Gevali's not even that far from here.

I utilize my time by updating the *Hyssop 'N' Sage* website while I wait. I got three new subscribers to my site over the past few days. So I send a few pictures of the new products I'll have in stock shortly and hit send on my e-mail list. When my phone battery dies, I buy myself a green tea and wander around the small convenience store attached to the station.

At least three times, I walk past the small aisle that no one wants to be caught in for long – the one that dutifully contains cheap bottles of aspirin, Trojans, and of course, pregnancy tests.

At first, I find myself wondering why I hadn't just come here instead of trying to go all the way out to Montpelier to take my test. My mother's main argument had been for Rita's loose lips after all. But I push the idea from my mind and continue browsing the store. For one thing, they may only cost ten dollars, but those may be ten much needed dollars after I get the bill for my car repairs. On top of that, my phone is dead, and the last thing my mother heard from me is that I'm on my way to see her. If I took a test now and used the taxi service to go home, she'd have no way of knowing why I never showed up. At least not until way later after I got home, and she'd be worried about me by that point.

I search the walls of the store for a clock, but don't see one. It feels like I've been waiting forever for this taxi.

I peek back over at the forsaken little aisle. What if I still went to Oakland, but just took one of these cheap tests until then to ease my conscience? Heavens know I've had plenty of time to kill. I glance over at the cashier, double-checking to make sure I don't know him — which I don't. I cradle one of the little pink boxes in my palm.

Fast Acting Response!

That's when — finally — a glimpse of yellow flashes in my peripheral. Outside the glass wall of the store, the taxicab pulls up to the curb and waits. I set the box back in its place and toss my empty bottle of tea in the trash before plastering on a smile and greeting my *late* driver.

A young man with tossed blonde hair and a lopsided smile greets me, mentioning nothing of an apology for the delay. He opens up the back passenger door for me though, so I do allot him a few points.

But when I slide into my seat, my body literally jolts when I register whose face is staring at me from across the bench.

Chestnut eyes, dark spiky hair, and for a split second, an expression that mirrors the surprise in mine. He suppresses it quickly, assuming a neutral expression. I follow his lead, reaching for my door to shut and clearing my throat.

"Grace," Liam says coolly.

I regard him with the smallest of smiles, without taking my eyes from the view outside my window.

"Alrighty!" The driver says, joining us in the car, "To Montpelier. Oakland Clinic, right?"

"That's right," I say stiffly, wondering just what kind of odds these are supposed to be — that I would somehow end up in the same taxicab as Liam Cross.

22

Rae - Friday

Though I usually hate photoshoots, Zoe found a way to make ours fun. Before we left, she let us see a sampling of the shots she got, and judging by our photos, you'd never be able to tell there was something going on between me and Adam. Absolutely zero tension showed through our picture-perfect faces.

Afterwards, Adam had to rush back to work to chaperone an activity, and I was left with a cleared schedule and a predicament: should I go to the Café with Sam and Rosie?

Does Adam's problem with Sam mean I can no longer ask Rosie to be a bridesmaid?

That doesn't seem fair. His issue with Sam has nothing to do with her. In fact, going out of my way to reschedule a meet-up with *just* Rosie felt borderline obsessive of Adam. You don't see Rosie acting this way about *Sam* spending time with me. And surely Adam wouldn't care if I popped in for a brief moment, *just* to ask Rosie and then leave.

Yes. That's what I'll do. In - out - done.

I felt terrible for the way I ditched them both yesterday, and Adam's main issue was with Sam and I being alone anyway. It's not like I'm about to go see *just Sam.*

When I arrive at the Café, I make sure to turn my phone volume all the way up, remembering how that'd been a problem last time. I pocket my phone and enter the building.

Right away, I hear my friends call my name. Two smiling faces wave me over.

As I'm walking to their table, it suddenly occurs to me that Rosie has every reason to not feel comfortable around me anymore, seeing as though she is now in a serious relationship with my ex. But as she stands and spreads her arms out to me for a hug, I realize that's nonsense.

"Rae!" She says, practically jumping as she hugs me, "It's been *way* too long!"

I'm laughing now, "Rosie, look at you. You finally got that booty you always wanted."

She smiles with pride, "Isn't it great? Squats for days."

Much like Sam's subtle changes, Rosie has a few of her own. While she still has the same green eyes and short strawberry-blonde hair, my friend who always had a slight figure finally started filling out, and it looks amazing on her.

"Couldn't have her looking so incredible without me," Sam says, giving me a side hug, "Hence, the gym membership." He says.

I smile taking my seat, "It's so good to see you guys again. Sorry I had to run out on you yesterday."

Rosie leans in, "Sam says it's because you had an *engagement* photoshoot! What on earth? I'm missing out on your life!"

I laugh, "Not anymore you're not. I would love for you to be a bridesmaid."

She beams, "Um, yes! Yes a hundred times. When is your day? Is the wedding local?"

Her enthusiasm is contagious.

"Just over seven months now, and yes, all local. We're having it in Mr. Cane's old barn. He offered it to us for free."

"Wow," She says, "That's going to be stunning with all those maples and the lake!"

"I should've known this would turn into you girls 'talking wedding' the whole time." Sam says, taking a leisurely sip of coffee.

"Sorry, sweetie," Rosie says, squeezing his hand, "You two talk. I'll be right back."

"Where are you going?" I say.

"To get my beautiful bride friend a cup of coffee. And when I get back, I wanna hear about your guy."

I laugh, rummaging through my purse and producing a few dollars, "You don't have to do that, Rosie. Here."

"I insist." She waves me away and flounces off to the other side of the Café.

I shake my head, smiling, "I forgot how wonderful she is."

"I didn't," Sam says, eyes trailing her as she walks.

"Sooo," I lean in, raising my brows suggestively, "Are you gonna make your move on her any time soon?"

He smiles, "If marriage is what you mean, I'd like to, but not any time soon. Rosie wants to finish her degree first, and I wouldn't mind having mine out of the way either."

"That's fair," I agree, "I guess I kind of lucked out with an older guy. I didn't have to wait for him to finish anything before we made the next move."

"How much older are we talking?" Sam says.

"Twenty-five. Nothing too crazy."

"Old enough to have a steady job in the real world before settling down?" Sam nods, "I like that for you."

"Me too," I say with pride, "Trust me."

He smiles, "Well, I know Rosie is thrilled to have a part in your wedding,"

The door to the Café jingles as it opens.

"And if there's anything I can do for you too," Sam continues, "don't hesitate to let me know."

"Thanks, Sam, I definitely will."

The door to the Café never jingled close and the chilly autumn air wafts over to our table. I peek over to see who's holding the door open for so long and see Adam's face staring right at our table. He looks pale as he stands in the doorway and his lips are pressed in a thin line. The moment I've registered who it is, I also register that it appears as though Sam and I are alone at this table.

I stand, intending to go to him. But in a serene sort of way, he turns and exits the building.

Shit.

I'm frozen in my tracks, thinking a hundred miles an hour.

Rosie comes bouncing back to our spot and hands me a hot to-go cup, "Here you go, Rae. Who was that?"

"Um," I say, barely able to focus. I can feel the warmth of the coffee in my hand, but it's the only thing keeping me present.

Adam thinks I'm cheating on him.

"Rae?" Sam says.

"That was Adam," I say looking between them, "Thank you so much for the coffee, Rosie, but I should probably go talk to him."

"Oh sure," She smiles, "You're coming back, right? He's welcome to join us!"

"Um," I say, shaking my head to clear it, "I'll text you, okay? It was so good seeing you guys."

"Oh, okay," She says, shoulders falling, "Talk soon then."

"Definitely," I say, giving them both hugs before I leave the building.

I apparently didn't make it out quick enough, because all I see are the taillights of Adam's car rounding the corner, going in the opposite direction of home.

23

Grace - Friday

I am thankful for the emergency book I keep stowed away in my purse. Since my phone died, I'm glad to have *something* to focus on while we drive. *Anything* but Liam.

Just a few more minutes, I tell myself, *and it'll be over.*

That's when the cab begins to slow down on the interstate. *Way* down.

I glance up from my book to investigate the problem, and to my dismay, I see a long line of red brake lights as far as the road stretches ahead.

My lips part slightly as the car comes to a complete stop.

"Ooh," The driver says from the front, "Bummer, dudes. Looks like a showstopper."

I suppress the need to let out a deep sigh. You *cannot* be serious right now.

"Did you have an appointment?" He says to me, "You may want to call and let them know you'll be late."

I release the sigh now. "No, I didn't. I was just visiting — oh, it doesn't matter. My phone is dead, anyway."

"You can borrow mine." Driver says from the front. A sticker hanging down from his rear-view mirror says "My name's Terrance! Tips appreciated!"

"No," I say, "Thank you, Terrance. I may take you up on it after awhile, though. If this doesn't let up soon."

He smiles and flips the radio on, keeping the volume low.

I resume my book reading, determined to appear interested despite not actually processing a word. Out of the corner of my eye, I can see him watching me, but I *feel* his gaze more than anything. I flip the page in my novel, making my eyes move from the left side of the page to the right, line after line.

Suddenly, a soft laugh comes from my left, and I can't help but look over. His eyes are still fixated on me, and he wears an expression of amusement — the same one he wore in the Café when I placed myself across the table from him.

I narrow my eyes at him and flick my gaze down and up his form, "What?"

He smirks, "Are we just gonna pretend you didn't leave me a nasty message this morning?"

I snap my book shut and give him a face, like *seriously?*

He holds his hands up in surrender, ever smiling at me, "Hey, you have *way* more explaining to do than I do."

"*Excuse* me?" I snap, "Are we just gonna pretend you don't have a *girlfriend?* Or that it's okay for you to go passing around your number to any girl who bats an eye your way?"

So I may be a little heated. So what. Our bad experiences can help us discover what we're passionate about.

"Well, if by 'girlfriend' you mean Sakura, she's my sister."

"And since when did it ever become okay for — wait ... what?"

He throws up his hands again, raising his eyebrows in innocence, "Oh no, go right ahead. You're on a roll."

I narrow my eyes at him, "You mean to tell me that the girl who met you at the Café the other day is your *sister*?"

He crosses his arms, "Is that allowed?"

I shake my head, "You can't *seriously* expect me to believe that, Liam," The girl's features appeared richly Asian American. "You two look nothing alike."

"If you're referring to the fact that she's Japanese and I'm clearly not," He says, not skipping a beat, "She was adopted. Just a few years before I was, actually."

"Oh," I say, nodding my head in a mocking way, "The two of you were adopted. How convenient. And what about the fact that she kissed your cheek when she saw you?"

"It's a ... family thing," Liam says, "But even if it wasn't, that's just Sakura. She's really touchy-feely."

My smile doesn't reach my eyes, "Oh, I'm sure. That's just *how she is*."

He uncrosses his arms, "This conversation is starting to feel really unfair."

"Unfair?"

"Yes."

I squint, "How do you figure?"

He spreads three fingers, ticking each one as he makes a point, "For one thing, you have some preconceived ideas about me that are totally arbitrary. For another thing, you're basically coming at me with accusations based on your own assumptions about me, thereby not allowing me to defend myself or ask you any questions in return. And for a final thing, I never even got to formally introduce myself."

I pause, blinking at his formal word usage. I can't argue there isn't validity to what he's saying.

"Fine." I relent, "Introduce yourself."

He laughs, "I mean, shoot, girl, I don't know if I want to."

Really? He is being so frustrating.

"Fine." I say again, reopening my book and positioning myself away from him.

I see him shake his head and he resumes scrolling down his phone.

A few minutes pass as "*Margaritaville*" plays softly from the radio and Terrance tries to act like he hadn't heard anything. Traffic has moved maybe an inch.

I peek over at Liam, starting to question the randomness of this encounter. Don't taxis that are employed by car insurance companies usually not have passengers already in the car when you call them to pick you up at a specific location?

"Where are you even going?" I say quietly.

"Oh," He says, smirking down at his phone, "So you get to keep asking questions, do you?"

I cross my arms, looking out my window at the still trees.

"Montpelier." He says, smiling over at me.

I roll my eyes, "I know *that*, I mean *where* in Montpelier? Why do you need to go there?"

"Ah, you see, Grace, *this* is usually how conversations work: two people take *turns* asking questions — so I believe it would be my turn."

I press my lips together, narrowing my eyes at him.

He studies me, "Why do *you* need to go to Montpelier?"

"Well," I say, "That is, of course, none of your business. But if you must know, I'm going to visit my mother."

"Ah ..." His face becomes serious, "She's at Oakland?"

"No, no," I say, "Not as a patient. She's a nurse."

"Ooh," He says, "Bet that doesn't set well with you, does it?"

I furrow my brow, "What do you mean?"

He nods down at my bag, "Well, for one thing, your bag says Hyssop 'N' Sage. Those are both essential oils, aren't they?"

I stare down at my promo bag, "Uh, well, they're both flowers. But yes ... also oils."

"Okay," He says, "And am I correct in saying that traditional medicine and essential oils are like, on two opposite ends of the spectrum in the world of pharmacology?"

I nod, slightly uncomfortable with his intuition.

He looks smug. Impressed with himself.

"Okay," I say, "You got *two* questions. Now answer my one."

"Ah, let's see, why do I need to go to Montpelier? For work purposes."

I nod, "Okay, better question: How did you end up in this Taxi with me?"

He winces, "I *do* have a car, if that's what you're implying. My sister, however, does not, and she begged me to borrow it for a day trip with a girlfriend. I was supposed to have the day off, so I let her go. But this particular client that I'm working with is ... difficult sometimes ... and changed his mind about not needing my services today. So, alas," He holds up his hands in a sweeping motion, "Here I am."

I adjust my glasses, "I see ... and you didn't have like, a *friend* or something that could take you? You had to call a *taxi*?"

He holds a hand to his chest in offense, "Alright, first of all, ouch."

I roll my eyes, trying not to smile.

"And second of all, yes, I *do* have a friend."

He nods his head toward Terrance, who salutes me in his rearview.

"You guys are friends?" I say.

"That guy?" Terrance says, eyeing Liam with mock disgust, "No way."

I narrow my eyes at him, "Is he the reason you were so late?"

Terrance looks triggered.

"You were picking *him* up on the way to pick *me* up." I say, "Which is basically like using my money for a free ride."

Liam squints at me with a smile, "Isn't your insurance covering this?"

I wave my hand, "Irrelevant."

"And if it weren't covered by your insurance, don't go thinking for a second I wouldn't cover the entire thing for my riding companion, no matter who they turned out to be. Because that's what a *gentleman* does."

"Well," I counter, "It still made *Terrance* late in picking me up, which, in a way, is robbing me of my time."

"Oh please, my house was *on the way* to where Terrance was picking you up. It just so happened that he was scheduled to take you to the city that *I* needed to get to, so it was a perfectly convenient situation." Liam says, "But the fact that, of all people, *you're* the person who needed the taxi in the first place ... is an anomaly."

I open my mouth to say something, finding some level of enjoyment in our banter, but in that moment, the traffic begins slowly moving along, inch by inch.

"Ah, it lives," Terrance says as we begin to speed up.

It's just a short ride to the clinic after we get going again, so we spend it in silence.

Terrance makes a right turn into the large parking lot for Oakland visitors.

I feel the need to say something before exiting the vehicle for good. Something other than, 'Well, bye.'

"I still don't believe that girl is your sister." I say, keeping my face neutral as Terrance pulls into a parking space.

"Oh my word, Grace, she *is*."

"I don't believe you." I shrug.

Liam stares at me for a moment, then lets out an exasperated sigh. "You know what? My folks are having a big dinner tomorrow night. Come."

My eyebrows raise so high I'm sure my forehead wrinkles. "*What?* You're inviting me to *dinner?*"

"With my family." He rolls his eyes, "Not a big deal. Sakura will be there, and she can tell you for herself that we're related."

I glance over at Terrence, who is making honest efforts at minding his own business, then back at Liam.

"You can't be serious ..."

He crosses his arms, "I am. I will not have someone so openly questioning my morale. If you've got to hear it from the girl herself, fine. Here's your opportunity."

I pull on the door handle and step out.

"No. I can't do that. It's weird."

He stares back at me, saying nothing, so I shut the door.

The back window rolls down slowly, revealing his smiling face, "That's fine with me, Grace. It doesn't matter to me either way. But just know, with that invitation, I have done literally everything I can do to clear up my good name with you. So at this point, if you continue to think so poorly of me, that's entirely on you and *your* character — judging a perfectly good man so harshly, without any due cause."

He flips the sunglasses propped on top of his head over his eyes, and Terrance hits the gas.

I'm left speechless in the parking lot with my lips slightly parted ...

What just happened?

* * *

The automatic doors slide open as I approach. The temperature inside the clinic drops down about ten degrees from the outside air and induces a shiver.

The lady at the front waves at me and asks for my name and insurance card.

"Actually, I'm here to see my mom. Corinne Rains?"

The lady squints at me and then smiles, "My goodness! Of course you are. You two have a striking resemblance."

I smile politely as she pages my mother to the waiting room.

Everyone who says my mother and I resemble each other means it as a compliment. She has aged gracefully and still catches the eyes of many men, but she's far too independent … far too busy, to ever let one in. To my knowledge, she's only ever let one man into her life intimately, and he left her high and dry. It's to this man that I owe my hazel-colored eyes and my cream-colored skin — the only obvious differences between my mother and I, who is much paler than I am and has stark blue eyes.

The double doors by the front desk open and my mother appears wearing dark blue scrubs. She smiles curtly when she sees me.

"Grace,"

"Hey mom. Sorry I'm so late. I probably missed your lunch, didn't I?"

She looks down at her smartwatch and winces, "Oh … well, to be honest, I never took one. I was waiting to hear from you first, and I guess since I never did, time just got away from me."

Oh.

"I'll tell you what though. Let me see if I can go home early today and we'll spend some time together there. That sound good?"

"Okay," I say.

"Amber," she says to the lady at the front, "Can you check my schedule for the day? When is my shift over?"

Amber shifts through a couple papers, "An hour ago."

"Oh," mom chuckles, "Well that settles that. Let me just go clock out and we'll be on our way."

"Okay." I say.

* * *

When we arrive home, my mother gives me a pregnancy test first thing. She also gives me a more thorough rundown than Rae had of what to do with it.

"Don't forget to time it," She calls to me, "That's really important."

I roll my eyes, but still take notice of the time on my watch before I begin.

"Round two," I breathe to myself as I dip the new pregnancy test in the prepared plastic cup. I refuse to do what I did last time ... that is, literally watch the test for as long as it takes for a result to pop up, killing myself with anticipation in the meantime. So I leave the scene, distracting myself with making a cup of tea.

My mom is mainly a coffee drinker, so the small amount of tea I find in the cupboard is the same box I had stocked in here before I moved out almost two years ago. I pace the kitchen, trying to enjoy my drink until it's time to check on the test.

I venture back into the bathroom and remove the stick from the cup.

I blink at the status screen.

It takes a second to register what I'm seeing. And when I do, I spit my tea.

There's one really prominent red line … and then next to it, a faded, barely visible second line. The universal result of a positive pregnancy test.

24

Rae - Friday

I didn't go home — I went straight to his house and let myself in. I called him four times before resigning myself to the idea that wherever he is, his phone really is turned off. He had to come home at some point, right? So I would just wait here for him, at least until I get the chance to explain.

I feel so fidgety for someone who hasn't done anything wrong. I guess it's because I didn't picture it happening that way.

I thought if my meeting with Sam and Rosie came up in conversation, I could explain that I was there to ask Rosie to be a bridesmaid. *I'd have to tell him at some point, right?*. Or if he called or texted me, I could quickly answer back and let him know where I was *then.* I didn't expect him to *show up,* see Sam and I alone at a table without any explanation, and turn around to leave before I could introduce him.

I hate feeling this guilty over something I shouldn't, so I glance around the house and busy myself with little jobs here and there — helping him run a few loads of laundry he's falling behind on, washing dishes, and sweeping the floor. When I run out of busy work to do, I settle on his couch and turn on the TV.

It's a fair distraction for the most part. Until of course, the clock strikes 10 p.m.

I begin to wonder where exactly he went, and what reason he could have for coming home so late. My mind begins to wander, creating terrible images in my head: Adam assuming the worst about what he saw, and deciding to make a counter move — a visit to Lexi's house to level the playing field. Lexi's house *is* in the direction he was headed towards ... isn't it?

That's when I hear the front doorknob twist. I click off the TV and stand. Adam steps in, regarding me with little expression. His acknowledgement is bittersweet — I know he's upset with me, but at least he's *home.*

"You need to go home, Rae." He says.

"Let me explain," I say quickly when he starts to walk off, "Will you let me explain?"

He shakes his head, continuing for his bedroom.

"If you won't listen, fine," The words spill, "I know I'm innocent in this. But at least answer me when I ask where you were just now."

He spins on his heel and eyes me incredulously. He's finally lost his cool.

"Answer *you?* What about your actions these past few days makes you deserving of answers?"

"I've done nothing wrong! *You,* however, I'm kind of starting to worry about. Why won't you tell me where you were?"

"It's not a good feeling, is it? Wondering what the hell your fiancé is up to."

My cheeks heat at his accusation and I open my mouth to say something, but I bite it back.

He thinks he's got this all figured out and it's infuriating. He couldn't be more *wrong*.

I inhale deeply and force my voice to soften.

"Listen, honey." I sit lightly on the couch and rub the seat next to me, "Will you come over here and listen?"

He crosses his arms, a stone pillar in his doorway, but at least he's willing to hear me.

I sigh, "First of all, it wasn't just me and Sam there, even though that's what it looked like. Rosie was at the Café too. I had just asked her to be a bridesmaid in our wedding. In fact, that was my whole reason for being there. She was at the counter getting me a celebratory coffee when you came in. Sam and I were only alone together for a minute or two."

"But she wasn't there with you the other day." Adam counters.

"That's right. Admittedly, she wasn't there. But she *was* on her way, and remember that took place before I knew you'd have such a problem with it."

"Okay, and what about today? You knew I had a problem with it at this point, and you *still* went and did it."

"*No,*" I say, "I knew you had a problem with Sam and I being alone … I didn't know you'd still have a problem if Rosie was there with us."

"Why is this girl your chaperone when you two are together? It just proves that you *knew* I'd be pissed about you seeing him."

I laugh a humorless laugh at that, "Quite the opposite, Adam. If anyone's the chaperone, it's me. Rosie is Adam's girlfriend now … his really serious girlfriend."

"Are they engaged?"

I frown, "No."

"Planning to be engaged soon?"

I pause, remembering my conversation with Sam.

"No ..."

"Then that means nothing. 'Really serious girlfriend' is not a title. 'Girlfriend' is, and 'fiancée' is, and of the two, 'girlfriend' requires the least amount of commitment."

"Adam, come on. I had my phone on and turned all the way up in case you needed me. I can't believe you showed up at that exact moment that Rosie left to get coffee."

He squints. "I can't either."

My heart skips a beat. Does he think I'd lie about this? Suddenly I feel defensive.

"What were you doing there, anyway? I thought you had an after-school activity."

He stares at me as a thought occurs in my mind.

"Were you *spying* on me?"

"*What*? No! The activity got canceled and I wanted to grab a coffee before home. Is that so hard to believe?"

"No, it's not. Is *my* side of the story? I have *never,* not *once* lied to you."

He pinches the bridge of his nose and lets out a long, exasperated sigh.

"No," He says finally, "It's not."

"Okay," I say, my voice wavering a little, "Then why are you fighting me so hard?"

His shoulders slack and he hesitates before coming to sit next to me.

"Rae, try to see this from my perspective. I need us to back this up to last Wednesday."

I turn to face him.

"First things first, you tell me you want to stop having sex. Strange request in and of itself if you ask me ... but then, I hear you've been hanging out with your ex —"

"It's not like you heard it from the grapevine ..." I interrupt, "*I* told you myself —"

He holds up a hand, "Let me talk. I won't go into Thursday's fiasco with the photoshoot since we've exhausted that discussion already. Basically, I leave the actual photoshoot today thinking we've reached an understanding about this — only to find that you're out at the Café, *alone* with the very guy we talked about *yesterday.*"

"We weren't alone!"

He shakes his head, "I believe you. But that's what it looked like to me."

I sit back and look down at my spread palms. I don't know what else I can say.

"Adam ... I ... You know I couldn't live with myself if I'd really done something to hurt us, but I can promise you that I didn't. If my word isn't enough for you, then ..." My voice hiccups on the last sentence and I hate myself for it.

He softens and takes my hand, running his thumb across it. Warmth brims in the corners of my eyes.

"None of those things you mentioned are correlated," I continue, "The sex boundaries and my run-ins with Sam."

"I believe you, honey." He repeats.

My countenance falls, a tear trickling down my cheek, "Where *were* you tonight?

"Tyler's." He says. His buddy from college.

My heart lets go of the breath it'd been holding, sighing in relief, but the anticipation of waiting for the answer takes its toll on my emotions. "Geez, Adam, I thought you were with Lexi."

A line appears between his brows, "Um, *definitely* not. I couldn't care less about Lexi anymore, Rae. You know that."

"But I *didn't* know that." I breathe, "All I knew is what *you thought* I did with Sam, so I was second guessing everything I know about *you.* I thought you might validate some sort of revenge …"

He smirks, pulling me into him, "Well that would be incredibly childish of me, wouldn't it?"

I suddenly feel years younger than him for even suggesting such a thing. His embrace dries the escaped tear and I stay there, wrapped in his arms.

We stay this way for about ten minutes, until I realize I'm incredibly tired now.

I want him … but we can't.

"I should head home," I say to him.

He stands and holds out a hand to me, "I'll walk you to your car."

We walk out together and he opens the door for me, "Are we all good?" I say.

He sighs, nodding slowly, "We're good."

25

Grace - Friday

My heart plummets to the floor, skipping my stomach completely.

No. No. *No.* That can't be right.

I continue staring at the two lines on the pregnancy test, wondering if the faintness of the second line matters. It's *barely* there, after all.

I hear a knock on the bathroom door, "How's it going in there?"

She slowly inches the door open but stops short as she sees me stationed on the floor, pregnancy test in hand.

I angle the screen facing her so that she can see the verdict.

"Oh ..."

She doesn't try to help me up. Instead, she sits right next to me on the bathroom floor.

"Does that line count?" I say, "It's so faint."

She stares down at the test, hesitating, "Well ... I think it's safe to assume that it does count. False negatives are common ... but false positives?"

She shakes her head.

I can't seem to find any words for what I'm feeling right now, so I just sit there blinking at my test.

My mother tentatively places a hand on my shoulder, letting me process the reality of my situation. What I really need, though, is someone's arms wrapped around me.

The test is positive. The father is a cheat. And I just basically told him to eff off.

When I look at her, her blue eyes hold no judgment — but definite concern. My next thought hardly feels like it should belong to me, but for a brief moment I wonder if the baby will have the same hazel-colored eyes as my father and me, or Jayden's light grey ones. Suddenly I feel like crying.

My mother gently smooths my hair, treating me like a fallen leaf that could crumple at any moment. Her gestures are almost tender… the most maternal I've ever felt from her.

"What can I … what do you need?" She says.

Pulling away and wiping my nose on my sleeve, I consider the question. The truth is, at this moment, what I need is not what I thought I would need. I just need someone to tell me they're proud of me. That I'm not a total failure. That I've done well with my in-home business and with trying to be a good friend to Rae as she gets married while I'm mourning a breakup. That I was a good girlfriend when I was one … that I'm brave for taking this on by myself.

But I know that I can't ask that of her right now … to tell me that she's proud of me when I'm in this sort of mess. So instead, I ask an easier question.

"Are you mad at me?"

She folds her hands together, "No, honey, of course I'm not mad …"

A brief weight lifts off my shoulders.

"I'm just ..."

I look up at her. Please don't say it.

"A little disappointed."

Damn it. Tears threaten.

"It's just that I raised you to be better than this, Grace ... to be better than me. But I know that's not fair of me ... I can't expect you to learn from my mistakes. Everyone has to learn from a few of their own."

I'm taken aback. I stare at her with my lips parted.

"Mistakes?"

She rolls her eyes, "Not you, baby. You weren't a mistake. Just deciding to be with the man I was with was a mistake."

"But if you weren't with him, you never would've had me. *I'm* the *result* of that mistake."

She shakes her head, "Good things can come from bad things, Grace. All I'm saying is that if this is too much for you ... you don't have to do it. You're so young ... a baby is so much responsibility ..." she shifts, "I'll support whatever decision you make."

My brows crease, "Wait, *what?* What are you *talking* about?"

She is silent.

I pull away from her. "You're not saying to abort the baby, are you?"

She holds her hands up, "I'm not telling you what to do. I'm just saying I would support that decision if you decided that's what's best for you."

My mouth falls open. She knows how I feel about this topic.

"Are you serious right now? First you say I was a mistake, then you suggest *killing* my baby? Was I really so horrible for you to raise that you would rather see your very first grandchild terminated than me go through with the pregnancy?"

"I didn't *say* you were a mistake, Grace, I —"

"But I was!" I retort, "I wasn't in your plans. Hell, sometimes I wonder if you even want me *now.* I rarely hear from you, mom. And when I do make time to see you, you aren't even concerned with normal motherly things!"

She turns her body toward me, all business now, "What are you *talking* about, Gracelynn?"

"I was late today mom. By a few *hours.* Did you worry? Did you even care? You never even asked what happened!"

Her jaw sets, "That's only because I want to respect your privacy."

"I could've been abducted, mom, and you would never know. Because you're too busy *'respecting my privacy'.* I don't have a boyfriend anymore, okay? That's the fact of the matter. So *someone* has to look out for me, and I would hope that someone could be my own mother!"

"Damn it, Grace! That's something my mom *never* gave me. She was always in my business, trying to make my decisions for me. I'm just trying to give you the freedom to live your life the way you want to. You're a grown woman — so if you had a reason for being late, that's *no* business of mine."

"You're talking about Grandma *Jackie?*" I say.

"Yes!" She says, her eyes beginning to glisten.

I stop short at the sight her tears.

She gets up, squeezes her eyes shut and sighs.

"It's been a long day. Why don't you stay for the night and I'll drive you to where you're parked at the clinic in the morning."

"I'm not parked at the clinic," I snap, "You thought I was kidding about my car acting funny? It quit on the way here. Got it towed back to Gevali. *That's* why I was late, thanks for asking."

The usual tightness around her eyes and mouth fall. It's clear that comment hurt.

"Well, I suppose we'll figure something out in the morning. You know where everything is ... blankets in the closet if you need them."

With that, she turns on her heels and walks straight to her bedroom, closing the door behind her.

Suddenly I feel terrible. Like my situation can't possibly get any worse.

I get up from my seat and traipse down the hall to my old room — the one my nineteen-year-old self had decked out with dream catchers and framed book quotes.

I finally let the tears stream down my face as I go over to my roller desk and pull open the middle drawer. My old iPod lays faithfully in the corner.

I grab the device, unwrapping the earbuds from around it.

There's a playlist I made on here years ago that has only three tracks on it, affectionately titled, *"Rainy Days"*. Turns out, it's exactly what I need right now ...

The songs carry me through their melancholy tunes, while my mind remains a dark, empty place. I am burdened by no thoughts, as tears streak down my cheeks.

When the last track ends, I go back to the beginning of the playlist and listen numbly to the same three songs, over and over again.

26

Rae - Saturday

I hated leaving Adam last night, but being alone in my bed afforded me some time to think about everything. Throughout my whole correspondence with Sam, I felt like I wasn't doing anything wrong, but if that were the case ... why was I feeling so guilty?

God, give me clarity ... where is this feeling of guilt stemming from? Was I out of line? Please ... tell me anything I might be missing.

Moments after I uttered the words, a thought popped in my head:

I had to justify going to see Sam and Rosie pretty hard before I did it. Then I came up with a game plan of how I would explain my actions to Adam before it was even an issue ... which meant I had a pretty good idea that it *would* be an issue if he found out.

I didn't exactly let him know where I was going beforehand ... and why didn't I do that, knowing that it was a sensitive spot for him? Adam probably wouldn't have had an issue with it if I'd just communicated with him. But the fact is, I *wasn't* expecting him to show up at the Café. In fact, I was *banking* on him not showing up.

I certainly wasn't cheating on him, nor did I have any desire to. But I was being secretive ... which is something I promised I'd never be towards him.

Is being secretive a mindset I can reasonably ask Adam to accept from me going into a marriage? It's certainly not one I'd want from him.

On top of that, when I saw Sam that first day in the gym and we decided to go to the docks, I'd allowed my mind to wander. Memories of our past relationship surfaced — even of us kissing. Even though they aren't significant anymore, I never should've allowed those thoughts. Sam is *another man* ... significant or not.

My heart beats loudly. Adam would *never* do that to me.

Before I went to bed, I sent up another prayer.

Lord ... I'm sorry for anything I've done to hurt my relationship with Adam. I'd been trying to edify it with our new goal to abstain until marriage, but I ended up finding a new wedge instead. I know I am not entitled to a relationship with him, and that he is a gift from you ... please help strengthen what we have together to make for a strong marriage. Thank you, Lord, for your clarity.

I slowly drifted into sleep. A peaceful conclusion to my otherwise crazy day.

* * *

Early this morning, a text jolted me into consciousness.

From: Grace

Sent: 10/12/19

Time: 7:04 am

"Hey, would you mind checking on Amity for me? I stayed the night at mom's, and I guess I forgot to lock up the art room. Of course, the one time I do this, the nanny cam goes off lol. It's probably nothing — I'm sure her spoiled self is just freaking out because she hasn't gotten breakfast yet. I owe you."

Awhile back ago, Amity slinked her way into Grace's art room — the place she makes most of her Hyssop N' Sage products and occasionally paints a piece. The cat had managed to paw several books off of the bookshelf and knock over a freshly potted plant. After that, the art room became the first officially off-limits area for Amity. The next day, Grace ended up buying a cheap nanny cam for the room. Not only is she able to record herself making products for her business and upload them directly from the cam to her website, but if Amity slips inside again, the cam sends an alert to her phone that there is motion in the room. There's supposed to be a feature where it sends an image along with the alert, but it's broken. So she knows something is up when it goes off, just not *what* exactly.

I tap out a message, telling her *"I've got it"*, but I find myself pondering what she is doing in Montpelier. Grace spends very little time with her mother, mostly because of how scarcely Corinne seems to have time for her daughter. As I hop in my car to head over there, I make a mental note to ask Grace if everything is okay.

I walk up to Grace's sage-green door and twist my key to her house in the lock. It's quiet inside and Amity is nowhere to be found.

"Here kitty kitty," I call.

No response.

I pad over to the art room, where the door is slightly ajar.

I push the squeaky-hinged door wide open to discover somewhat of a horror scene.

There are several small cans of paint that've been tipped from the desk to the floor. They look as though they'd been re-sealed with plastic wrap, which of course didn't hold very strong when they fell onto the hard wooden floor. The colors of paint pool together in the middle of the floor, and Amity sits smack in the middle of it, looking both pissed off and pristine at the same time. Her ears are bent back and her tail flicks angrily, while her black coat is covered yellow, blue, and red patches. She looks as though she's trying to maintain some level of dignity as she raises her front paw to lick the paint off the front.

My eyes widen and I lunge for her, "No, Amity!"

This startles her and she jets off past me and out the art room door.

"Damn it," I mutter, chasing after her.

She leaves colorful little paw prints everywhere she scampers.

I quickly tackle her on the ground and she yowls loudly. I grab her by the scruff of her neck as she bats her paws and hisses wildly.

I frantically look around, trying to think of what to do next. I make for the sink and plunk her in it. She's already furious with me for holding her down, but when I turn on the water, she becomes a monster. An all-new rage bellows out of her mouth as she bites my hands and scratches the shit out of my arms.

I try to keep my cool and get a better grip on her legs so she can't attack me anymore.

When the temperature shifts into a warmer, more comfortable temperature, she gradually stops fighting me. I'm able to loosen my death grip on her and gently wipe the paint from her fur with a warm, soapy cloth.

"You're a little shit, you know that?" I say as the water washes my blood away along with the paint.

She glares at me hatefully. I've never met a creature more undeserving of their name.

When all the paint is removed, I pat her dry and she wriggles from my grasp, running from me as quickly as possible into Grace's room. I roll my eyes and go back into the art room, snapping a picture of the disaster to send Grace before kneeling down to wipe up what I can. The spill is still pretty fresh, so if I work quickly, the damage may not be too bad. The paw prints in the hall came up easily, but after thirty minutes of scrubbing the main spill, I realize there will be some permanently blue spots.

I eye the paint cans warily. The label says "non-toxic", so I'm assuming Amity will be okay if she consumed any, but I still head over to the little devil's food bowls and fill them up just in case. I close the art room door and lock it up tight before heading out, trying to think of the lightest possible way to tell Grace what just happened.

To: Grace

Sent: 10/12/19

Time: 8:33 am

"So, I am renaming your cat Vincent Van Gogh. Partly because she's undeserving of a name that means 'Friendly and Peaceful', and partly because she took Van Gogh's analogy about eating yellow paint a little too seriously. Good thing you bought non-toxic. I fixed her up with food and water, but Google says she might have some tummy problems this week — so you have that to look forward to."

I send the picture of the paint mess, along with a one of my battle wounds and one of a very wet, very *angry*-looking Amity.

Right after I hit send, another text comes through. This one's from Zoe, containing a link to the photos from our shoot.

* * *

"They look amazing," I say to Adam over the phone, "You should come by after work and pick out your favorites with me."

"You can just send them to me real quick, babe." He says.

"No." I pout.

"No?"

"I miss you. Come over."

He laughs, "Okay, honey. After work, then."

I smile.

I always miss Adam, but especially right now. Maybe that's unreasonable since I just saw him yesterday, but we've just been fighting so much lately. The absence of adoring comments ... the lack of physical affection ... it's getting to me. It's been nine days since we were last intimate, and I'm starting to feel like this goal will only work if we're making up for that loss by going above and beyond to express our love in other ways. But if we're going without sex *and* simple romantics because we're fighting ... there's no way I'll be able to keep this up.

I busy myself with my studies while I wait for him to get here, but I can't focus for crap. How am I supposed to solve integral equations or whatever they are when all I can think about is Adam.

There's no knock at the door, just suddenly his presence in the living room doorway. I jump up from my task without a second thought and wrap my arms around him. He smells like cedar and cinnamon and warmth as I press my lips into his.

When I pull away, his eyes are smiling. "Well, hey beautiful."

"Hi." I say, smiling back at him.

"You wanna show me these photos?" He says.

I smile as I take his hand and drag him over to the couch. I get the laptop and scoot up close to him as we look through them.

Zoe took so many good ones, I have a hard time picking. Adam, however, is decisive as ever, and picks one from the several that I narrowed it down to. I zoom in on the one he picked. The white fence and the maple tree are glowing in the background and we are pulling a titanic pose: Adam behind me, arms spread wide, holding mine out in front of him, and I am cracking up. I remember it was a genuine laugh, as Adam had just whispered in my ear one of our old inside jokes. It's a great picture. The only thing is ... such a pose, of course, puts my typically bracelet clad arms on full display. Zoe, being the type of person that she is, did not take the liberty of editing out the visible scarring on either arm.

I stare at it a little longer, trying to decide if I'm okay with this photo going out to everyone I know.

"That one gonna work?" He says.

My smile twitches, "Of course it is. This is great."

I close my laptop and give him a peck. I've got to start treating my scars like they're not a big deal.

I stand and hold out my hands to him. He takes them and stands, pulling me into a deeper kiss. I get the overwhelming urge to push him back on the couch and ... I pull away, dizzy from the kiss. These thoughts are dangerous.

"Well, darling," I swallow, "I should probably get going on these invites. Now that we have a good picture."

He closes his eyes and lets out a steady breath from his nose.

I kiss it.

When he opens his eyes, they have a certain intensity to them. They convey every bit of desire he has for me.

Smiling a little, I back away from him, turning to go to my room. He follows me there but stops in the doorway.

I go over to my mirror and shake out my hair.

Adam watches me with careful eyes as I begin sliding off each of my bangles onto my dresser.

"I wish you didn't feel like you have to wear those." He says softly. It catches me off guard.

I lower my bare arms to my sides, purposefully resisting the urge to fold them over my chest.

"I don't."

He frowns.

Because we both know me better than that.

I turn away from him and traipse over to my bed, slightly angry with him for knowing. "Goodnight, Adam."

He stares at me a moment longer with unsmiling eyes. He doesn't appear angry back, just perhaps frustrated in his subdued sort of way.

He comes over to the bed and sits, watching me.

He opens his mouth to say something, but then his eyes fall to my freshly bare arms and widen.

"Good *grief,* Rae, what is this??"

He grasps my wrists and scans the new scratches. Some have scabbed over, but some still look fresh.

I jerk them away from him.

"Oh my word, Adam, it was Grace's *cat.*"

The muscles in his face relax. He's clearly relieved, which infuriates me.

"Sheesh, what'd you do, hold her under water?"

I squint, "You have no idea. Please flip the light switch when you go."

I don't know why I'm being so snappy with him. The last thing I want to do is start fighting again, but the feeling that's escaping up through the surface is such a deep, intrinsic hurt that's been throbbing dully inside me for a long time now … some mixture of shame for my scars, my past, and just being so sick of not having him in my bed with me at night.

I want nothing more … *need* nothing more … than for him to take me in his arms and remind me that I'm his flawless girl. I feel hideous … like no one *really* believes in my growth.

He shakes his head, "Lacey Rae …"

"Also, if you could stop doubting me already, that would be solid."

"Baby," He says softly, "I don't —"

"You know what? Don't even act like you weren't just assuming I did that to myself. Like it hasn't been over a year since I — whatever."

He is silent.

"Are you ever going to trust me? That I'm a perfectly fine, stable human being? Because anything less than that is entirely unhelpful and not welcome here. I need to spend my life with someone who believes in me, Adam, not someone who carefully approaches me like I might break at any given moment. Otherwise I'm never gonna be able to … I'll never *really* …"

"Rae, honey." He moves close to me and pulls me into his arms. He knows to take these comments with a grain of salt.

I stay there, just resting against his chest. Neither of us say anything, because both of us know …

We miss making love. I miss the security it gives me. I'm snappy when I feel bad about my wrists … and he's what makes that go away.

He keeps his arms wrapped around me for a few more minutes, then he pulls away a little.

His eyes lock with mine, unsmiling ... wanting. He kisses me gently, as if asking permission.

I don't withhold it from him. Slowly, the kiss intensifies.

My body feels rhythmic with his ... as if all our senses are perfectly in tune with each other.

But I pull away.

"We can't," I breathe.

His eyes search mine, longing for me to say it's okay. But I don't.

He squeezes me one last time, kisses my hair, and shifts like he's going to leave.

"No." I say, tightening my grip on his arm.

"Rae ..."

"Stay."

"I can't."

"You can," I say, "Please."

I know I'm asking a lot of him ... but I need this. Being the one to stop us is hard for me and I need to take it in baby steps, like Kaya said. After all, I think we can be in the same bed sleeping together without *sleeping* together.

He wavers. Then settles back onto the bed with me.

"Thank you," I say, kissing his cheek.

He lifts the blanket beside him up for me to crawl in and I do, sidling closely up against him.

My eyes feel heavy. I fall asleep quickly.

But faintly I recall in the middle of the night ...

Stirring.

Eyes fluttering open.

Adam's lips on mine.

The warmth of his chest pressed against me.
Wandering fingertips.
His breath against my neck.

27

Grace - Saturday

My phone beeps loudly at 6:58 a.m., warning me that something has triggered my nanny cam in the art room. At first, as I wipe the sleep from my eyes, I panic that someone has gotten into my house. As my senses return, I remember that I didn't lock up the art room before I left the house. I groan. I'm sure everything is fine — Amity just probably snuck in. But just to be safe, I go ahead and text Rae and ask her to check on the house for me. I curl back into my warm spot in the bed and try to go back to sleep, but then I remember last night's events. The reality of it all sinks in and forcibly takes away any sleep I may have had left.

I sigh and kick the covers back, sauntering out to the kitchen for some tea. I find a note on the table, hastily scribbled in my mother's writing.

Got called into work early. Sorry to leave like this. Here's some money for a cab to the mechanic. Text me when you're home safe.

I roll my eyes. Of course she got called into work. That's nothing new.

It's all the same to me I suppose. Yesterday felt so long anyways, I doubt I'd have the energy to deal with my mother this morning.

The only thing that surprises me is the last sentence of her note. She's never said anything like that before. I assume it's only a result of her guilt from our conversation last night.

My mother is pretty hands-off, but she's not ignorant to believe that what I said had no validity. She's also not so heartless as to not feel any guilt for it.

Most teenagers would've been glad to have such a permissive mother — but that childhood 'perk' was a complete waste on me. I was always home at a reasonable hour, never let boys into my house while she was gone, and I certainly never used her money for anything indulgent. In fact, it would appear as though I was more responsible as a young teenager than as a young adult.

I take one more pregnancy test before I call the cab, but it's still positive — the second line is more prominent on the screen than it had been the night before.

***

I settle in the driver seat of my car, sighing. My bank is now $234.00 lighter, all thanks to some bad spark plugs.

On top of that, I tried to get a hold of Terrence again for the ride back home, but I guess he wasn't available today, so the cost of a ride from Montpelier to Gevali turned out to be more than my mother gave me. Why does everything have to be so expensive?

As I turn the key to start the engine, my phone vibrates with a text from Rae.

I open it, gasping at the pictures attached ... Paint everywhere, an angry Amity, and some very bloodied up arms. I call her immediately.

"Are you okay?" I say, the second she picks up.

"Yeah," She laughs, "It's no big deal."

"No big deal?" I say, "Are you kidding? I owe you big. Your poor arms!"

"Your poor *floor.*" She says, "I tried to clean it as best I could, but ... blue is a potent color ..."

"Oh my goodness, Rae. Forget the floor. I'm so sorry I'm just now seeing this. I've had a ... really crazy past couple of days."

"Oh yeah, I was gonna ask you. Is everything okay? When you said you were at Corinne's, I was like, umm, okay, something's up."

"Oh boy ..." I sigh, "I honestly don't know where to begin, Rae. So many things are 'up' right now, I'm about to lose it."

"Uh oh. Do you want to talk about it?"

I shake my head, nothing short of exasperated. "I mean, I don't even know how to *begin* condensing this. I met up with Hadley yesterday and you were *right.* Chick had no idea about me and Jayden. Pretty cool gal, actually – she likes books and stuff. So since that whole thing went so well, I felt compelled to call Jayden and tell him to eff off –"

"What?!" She says excitedly.

"Yeah." I say, not missing a beat. "So then my car broke down on the way to Montpelier to see mom who told me to come to the clinic to take another pregnancy test because she didn't think the first test was accurate or whatever. Then I accidentally ended up in a cab with *Liam* of all people. So that was weird. Then my mom and I kinda had a huge fight—which just made me feel worse—and long story short, turns out she was right about the accuracy thing. I'm pregnant."

"Whoa, whoa, whoa, *what?*" Rae says.

Saying the last two words felt so foreign on my lips ... like an issue that couldn't *possibly* be mine. I hadn't let myself think about it much until now ... but vocalizing my new reality induced something similar to panic.

"Are you serious?" Rae says.

"I ... I am." I say, almost not even believing myself.

"Grace ... I ... What can I do?"

I frown, "I honestly don't know just yet."

I don't like what I'm feeling right now — a dark emotion I can't describe. I just want to ignore it ... to push it away.

"Listen," I say, "I'm gonna let you go. I need to get home real quick and assess this paint damage. I promise we'll talk later."

"We better," Rae says, a hint of concern in her tone.

* * *

I stare blithely at the deep, oval-shaped splatter of blue on the floor of my art room. Amity circles around my feet, purring loudly.

I squint down at her, quietly muttering, "Should've gotten a dog."

It's about lunch time, but I don't have the energy to make food. Instead, I close Amity out of the art room and take a seat in front of my easel by the window. I set up a fresh canvas and squeeze some paint blobs onto a clean palate. I don't bother to line the floor with newspapers ... it's ruined anyway.

My palate holds several shades of blue and purple paint, all dark and somber. I figure if my soul had a color right now, it'd probably be a mixture of these.

At first, I paint gentle strokes ... letting my wrist glide without intention. Then I set down the paintbrush, not satisfied with it's work. I dip my bare fingers into the cold substance, smearing swirls of color onto the canvas. They blend into a blackish hue, which turns out to be much more satisfying.

I allow myself to get lost in my painting, attempting a visual of my emotions, but then, as always, my mind interrupts:

Perhaps this color is so appealing to me right now because it is a dark, empty void of a color ... the way I wish my uterus was right now.

Pinching my brow together, I immediately scold my train of thought. Why on earth would I ever consider such a thought?

My gentle paint swirls turn sharp and jagged.

It's because my mother brought it up as an option.

She *knows* how I feel about abortion. How I've *always* felt about it — and yet, she still mentioned it as if it's no big deal. I guess I shouldn't be surprised. She's never been opposed to them, and as far as I know, she even helps administer them occasionally. God knows how Grandma Jackie would feel if she knew *that,* seeing how religious she was. The blessed woman is probably turning somersaults in her grave over our whole conversation last night.

My whole canvas is a dark, blackish-blue now. I lean back to look at it, and my shoulders soften. It's not that I was considering *aborting* the baby ... just that I was considering the peace I'd have if it was never there in the first place.

Somehow, even *that* thought makes me hate myself.

A tear threatens to escape down my cheek as I squeeze a fleshy-colored pink onto my palate. How could I be so heartless? I don't wish any harm on this innocent thing inside me. It's a human being ... a little tiny *life.*

As I paint, my mind teeter-totters between the peace I would feel if it were just me, myself, and I, and feeling incredibly cruel and guilty for wishing a tiny baby out of existence.

When I stand back to view my painting a second time, I'm a mixture of horrified and in awe of what I created. There in the middle of the blackness — a little pinkish form floating ... a helpless fetus grasping at nothing.

***

I sat down and cried and cried.

What on earth do I do?

I don't want any helpless little being to be filled with these bad vibes, or even the slightest idea that they're not wanted, but I also don't know if I'm ready for all this. I *know* I'm not. How in the world will I afford it? We certainly can't survive off my lowly income.

In a moment of weakness and a loss of ideas, I pull out my phone and begin a google search: "How to be at peace with an unwanted pregnancy".

What comes up, as I shouldn't be surprised, is several articles on how to prevent unwanted pregnancies ... you know, *before* it's an issue. But as I scroll down, I see an article that says, "God's voice on unwanted pregnancies and abortion".

Intrigued, I tap the article.

"If you're reading these words, this is most likely a very hard time for you," It reads, "Your emotions will feel conflicting, as is totally normal. My goal is not to make a decision for you, as your life is *your own.* All I hope to achieve is to help you consider some things you may not have thought of before. If you *have* considered them, awesome! You've done all the research you can, and should feel free to carry on ... but if you *haven't,* there's no harm in a little subjective reading, right? If nothing else, you'll gain a new perspective that you're welcome to take on as your own or throw in the trash. The choice is *yours.*"

I read on to discover that the author is a woman who had an abortion of her own. She continues to explain what you will experience at the clinic if you choose to go, which terrifies me.

Then she leaves you with some scriptures. She doesn't write out what they say — she simply says that she personally wishes that she had read the scriptures first, before making her final decision.

The scriptures are Jeremiah 1:5 and Proverbs 31:8. I toss my phone aside and locate Grandma Jackie's Bible. I flip through the rainbow of pages to the passage in Jeremiah, which reads,

Before I formed you in the womb I knew you, and before you were born I set you apart.

I close my eyes, soaking in the words. Although my baby is no bigger than a poppy seed right now, God knows them. I've been wondering if they would have my hazel eyes, or Jayden's light grey ones, but God already knows.

Holding my breath, I flip to the next scripture in Proverbs, which reads,

Open your mouth for the speechless, in the cause of all who are appointed to die.

I read over the passage again and again, trying to make sense of how it applies, but it all feels blurry to me right now.

My body feels an invisible pull into the couch. I want to sink into the cushions and tune out everything but the same three songs, just as I had done last night. I'm tired of overthinking things and caring too much. I'm tired of being hurt and feeling so much when I'd rather just feel nothing at all.

But I know at this point, with so much going on, I won't be able to feel or think of nothing. If I lay here and let the couch swallow me up, my coping mechanism will be futile. I will end up grief-stricken over the things I have no control over. What I really need is to distract myself... to *do* something that'll help me forget.

So instead, I pull out my phone and tap out a simple message.

To: Liam

Sent: 10/12/19

Time: 3:04 pm

"So where is this dinner taking place tonight?"

28

Rae - Early Sunday...

My eyes flutter open, trading darkness for darkness. There's not a hint of daylight outside my window. I glance over at my clock, which indicates the time is 2:04 a.m. Adam is sleeping soundly next to me, his chest rising and falling beneath the covers, his skin emanating warmth. I smile at his slightly parted lips, marveling at what a beautiful sleeper he is. But my appreciation is cut short. Our clothes are tossed into a pile on the floor — my hair a knotted mess from where his fingers tangled tenderly through it.

I frown.

We were doing so good.

I'd been so insistent on him staying with me last night. Between our fighting and my persistent insecurity about my scars, it felt necessary for him to stay with me—like I'd never be able to sleep otherwise. I didn't ask him to make love to me, but at that moment I felt so marred and unlovable ... so unworthy of anyone's affection. I needed his love to feel okay, and Adam has always known what I need.

I bury my face in my hands, wondering why this is so hard for me. I've always been one to make goals for myself and see them through — why is this any different?

I can't just blame *him* for what happened. I knew what I was doing …

I *knew.*

29

Grace - Saturday

Gravel crunches beneath the rubber of my tires as I turn into a parking spot. The Crosses live way out in the country apparently — something I wasn't expecting — but even more surprising is the size of the beautiful house in front of me. It stands two stories high with a warm glow peeking out the windows.

I tread lightly on the wooden deck leading up to their door, pausing for a moment on the welcome mat.

This is stupid ... I think to myself, *I shouldn't have come.*

The cold wins over my doubts and I tap my freezing knuckles against the door. I can hear laughter on the other side.

After a moment, it swings open, and I am greeted by an ornately dressed woman with honey-colored skin and long black hair. She smiles widely at me, bringing her hands together and doing a little bow, the way we do in yoga class. Taking in her lovely features and the little red mark between her brows, I briefly wonder if I have come to the wrong address.

"Welcome, welcome!" The woman says with an accented voice, "Please, come in out of the cold!"

"Thank you," I smile, rubbing warmth into my cold arms, "Are you … Mrs. Cross?"

"Yes, I am," she smiles proudly, "Call me Dhara."

"Nice to meet you," I say, doing the little bow thing back.

That seems to make her super happy.

"Come this way," she says, whisking me into a big room to the left.

There's a huge, ornate fireplace crackling against the wall and a high ceiling showcasing a lovely chandelier. The home has rich features, like the huge decorative rug on the floor and the sectional outlining the room, but the whole set up is still cozy.

"Your friend is here!" Dhara calls, and Liam looks up from where he sits on the sectional. He'd been talking with an older woman next to him who looked to be somewhere in her eighties, but appeared to be an elegantly aged version of Dhara.

"Grace," He says, striding over to me with a wide grin, "You came after all. Didn't feel right about your accusations, huh?"

I'm about to squint and say something snarky, but something about his mother being there stops me.

I clear my throat instead, "I was hoping to meet your sister."

"Ahh, yes. We'll get there. But first I have to introduce you to the most precious woman alive."

He places his hand on the small of my back before I can question him any further and leads me toward the woman he'd been talking to.

"Nanni, this is Grace. Grace – Nanni."

The old woman looks up at me.

"Hi, Nanni," I say, tucking a lock of hair behind my ear.

For whatever reason, this makes her chuckle, and she nods at Liam.

Liam smiles in a satisfied sort of way and then leads me away to another area of the house.

"What did I say?"

"Nothing wrong," He says.

"Well why did she laugh then?"

"Nanni isn't a woman of many words," Liam smiles, "but also, her actual name is Aisha."

"What?" I say, "Why'd you tell me it was Nanni?"

"Because it is. Nanni is Hindi for 'Grandma', and she's my Grandma."

I shove him, "So I just said 'Hi, Grandma?'"

He laughs, "You did. And she loved it. Trust me, she has so many unofficial grandchildren."

We come to a grand staircase and he starts to go up.

"Where are we going?"

"To Sakura's room," He looks at me as if to say '*obviously*'.

I cross my arms and follow. This ought to be good.

We enter a room that is decorated with all things pink, rose gold, and Paris. There are decorative Eiffel towers, and the whole thing is very classy — not young and girly like one might expect.

There in the middle of the bed is the girl from the Café, on her stomach, immersed in something on her laptop. Liam knocks lightly on the side of the door, getting her attention.

"Sakura, this is Grace. Will you please tell her that you're my sister?"

The girl looks back and forth between me and Liam and bursts out laughing, "Oh, you're the girl from the Café!"

I feel my face flush. He was seriously telling the truth?

Sakura shakes her head, smiling, "Yeah … Liam is my lil' bro. Sorry for the confusion."

"Um, *older* brother, dork. I'm not gonna keep having this argument with you."

"I was here first." She shoots back good-naturedly, "Therefore, you're the 'youngest' child."

"You were *adopted* first." He protests, "I'm still older!"

"Whatever. If two years mean that much to you, you can have the title."

Liam rolls his eyes, "This is irrelevant. Long story short, the kissy thing you do threw her off."

Sakura laughs, "Just wait until she meets Dad."

Even as they banter, there's an obvious familial love between the two.

I try to keep my expression pleasant, but inside, my brain is trying to piece together this puzzle: Indian mother, Japanese sister (whose room looks like Paris), and then Liam ... whom I can't quite figure out.

Liam ... whose skin is a lovely mixed shade of dark and light.

Liam ... who was telling the truth.

* * *

"Believe me now?" He chides as we head downstairs.

I roll my eyes.

"Say you believe me." He pokes my ribs.

"What? About your sister? Fine ... I believe you."

Liam throws up his hands, "Then why are you still being so salty? I didn't cheat on anyone by writing you that note. I'm completely in the clear."

I pause to consider. I guess in *theory* he's right. The whole 'buying me a cinnamon-bun apology' was maybe even *sweet.*

But it doesn't matter. I can't afford to think like that anymore.

"Hey, I should really get going." I say, "Sorry to crash your family thing."

"What? What do you mean?" He chuckles, "I *invited* you."

"I know," I squeeze my arms together, "I just ..."

Am pregnant. I'm sorry I came here Liam, but stop charming me. You don't want me. Not all of me.

Dhara appears in front of me with a piping hot plate of something that smells delicious, "Come try my *Gatte Ki Sabzi.* You'll love it!"

She disappears into the dining room and I glance at Liam, "Her what?"

He laughs, "It's basically like spicy dumplings. Very flavorful. Have you ever tried Indian food?"

I shake my head.

"Oh my, we have to fix this. You haven't lived until you've tried mom's cooking."

I smile the slightest bit.

"But first," He says, "I'm gonna need an apology. And you know what? I won't even ask for a thank-you for the cinnamon bun I bought you. Since I'm a gentleman."

I raise an eyebrow, "Oh yeah? You need an apology?"

"For the mean message on my phone." He smiles smugly.

I roll my eyes, "Oh come on, it wasn't that bad."

He raises his eyebrows. He whips out his phone and dials his voicemail, quickly setting it to speakerphone.

"Liam, this is Grace." My voice bites out from the phone, "We met a few days ago in the Café, and you gave me your number. I just wanted to say how highly inappropriate that was, seeing as though you have a girlfriend — who I would be more than happy to contact for you about this, by the way. Please do not use this number to call me back, and for goodness sake, quit handing out your number to random — "

"Okay, okay," I hold up a hand, hoping the whole dining room hadn't heard my snappy tone, "I'm sorry ..."

"I mean," He shrugs, "you're welcome to tell Sakura on me if you want to."

I purse my lips in frustration, "I thought ... well, you know what I thought."

"Yeahhh," He admits, "I'm just being an ass. Come get some of my mama's cookin'."

I glance toward the door, and then back at the dining room. I really should leave ... but the smells wafting through the house are all too enticing. That, and this family certainly has me intrigued. How did this mismatched group of people come to be?

"Well ..." I say, "I guess I could stay for a few bites."

* * *

I suddenly found myself squeezed between Liam and Sakura, and overwhelmed with the tableful of delicious exotic food.

It quickly became clear why Sakura had said, "Just wait until she meets dad." When he came through the door (I am guessing from work) He kissed each of his family's cheeks, one on each side, just as Sakura had done in the coffee shop. It was really a rather European thing to do.

I felt the siblings staring at me as I observed their father, who introduced himself to me as "Brent Cross". His accent was purely American.

What *is* this family's ethnicity?

"I'm sorry, what was your name sweetheart?" Brent says as he piles some veggies onto his plate.

"It's Grace." I smile.

"But what's your *full* name?"

"Oh boy," Liam says between bites, "Here we go."

Unsure of what Liam means, I tell Brent, "Gracelynn Brielle Rains."

"Ah, that's a beautiful name. Very versatile."

Liam shakes his head, "Dad studies the meaning of names. It's like, his hobby."

"Oh yeah?" I smile.

I learned what 'the study of names' is actually called once. Read about it in a book — if only I could think of it! I search my brain, trying to locate the name, and then it surfaces.

"Onomatology, right?"

Brent's eyes widen as he looks at his family members, "Oh, I like her. I like her a lot!"

Sakura nudges me and whispers, "No one ever knows what dad's hobby is called. Major points."

I smile at that, enjoying Brent's excitement, "So what does my name mean?"

"Well let's see now ... 'Gracelynn' means favor or blessing, or since you go by 'Grace', your name could be interpreted to mean simple elegance or refined. 'Brielle' appropriately means 'God is my Strength', and then the meaning 'Rains' would piggyback off the word 'rain', which you obviously don't need a definition for."

I slow my chewing, "Really? I mean ... wow ... I've always known what Grace means, and obviously my last name ... but my middle name? Is it really 'God is my strength'?"

"It is," He smiles, "See? *She* appreciates my studies."

"Totally!" I enthuse, "That's pretty awesome you know all that off the top of your head."

He straightens in his seat, and something about having made him feel important feels good to me.

"Well, let's see here," He says, pointing to Dhara, "My lovely wife's name means 'Earth', and then Liam's name means 'Protector', or 'strong-willed warrior'. 'Sakura' means 'Cherry Blossom', and her middle name — "

"Don't say it," Sakura interrupts, "It's lame."

"Her middle name is 'Naoki', and it means 'honest tree'," Brent blurts.

Liam snorts and Sakura buries her face.

The rest of the table bursts out laughing.

"Oh come on," Brent nudges her playfully, "It's not *that* bad."

Sakura's smiling now, "Why didn't you guys change my name when you had the chance?"

"Because it's a perfectly lovely name." Dhara says affectionately.

My mind shoots back to all the times Rae and I have heard the exact same sentences from *our* mothers. What is it about mothers and insisting on the loveliness of our names?

I take a piece of bread, "So why the study of names, may I ask?"

Brent sits back in his chair, "Well, Grace, it honestly started for me where every good thing in life starts: The Word."

I see Nanni stiffen, but Brent keeps on with passion.

"From the very beginning — in Genesis — God is already naming things right off the bat. He gives the sky it's name ... the light, and the darkness too. Later, God says he calls all the *stars* by name even — can you imagine?"

I brighten because I know the scripture he's talking about. It's the first scripture I ever read in Grandma Jackie's Bible.

"He also calls *us* by name, you know. So no one can tell me that names aren't important to God. And anything important to the man upstairs is important to me." He takes a satisfied bite of his soup, smiling despite Nanni's pointed reaction.

"What about you, dear?" Dhara says to me, eyes flicking briefly to her husband and then her mother, "Is there anything you enjoy doing?"

I swallow my last bite of food as every head turns to me.

"Well," I smile, "You could definitely say my passion is natural medicine. Like, healing through herbal mixtures and essential oils. I love making natural products too. Soaps, candles, lotions — things like that."

This piques her interest, "*Really* now?"

"Yes ma'am. I've also recently taken up yoga. I'm not very good yet, but I really enjoy it."

Dhara's eyes sparkle, "What rare qualities in someone of your age."

I tell them about *Hyssop N' Sage* and a few things involved in my work.

"An entrepreneur!" Brent claps, "You know, Liam is a bit of an entrepreneur himself. Why don't you go show her?"

Liam shakes his head, "Nah, I don't think she wants to see that."

"See what?" I say.

"His shop." Sakura supplies.

"You have your own shop?" I say, eyeing Liam.

"I mean, you can see if you want to." He says.

Dhara begins collecting our plates for washing.

"Do you need any help?" I ask, standing.

"Oh no," She smiles, "You go right along."

I shouldn't go with Liam. I shouldn't care that he has a business of his own. I should leave and never think about him again. But that's not what I do. When he puts on his shoes and invites me outside with him, I go.

* * *

"It's a super long walk," Liam says, nodding to a nearby building, "As you can tell."

I pull my sweater snug against my torso, "That's your shop?"

"My house, actually. My shop is attached around the back."

As we near the front door, I glance back at his Parent's place. It's a comfortable walking distance, but still enough for him to have his own space.

"You like being this close to your parents?" I say as he jiggles the doorknob.

"Family is very important to me," He nods, "And their property is beautiful, don't you think?"

I glance around at the prairie and the rolling hills in the distance, "It is ... you guys are totally secluded out here."

"Our own little sanctuary," He says as he pushes the door open. "My parents own all of the land out here. I was actually settled into an apartment in the city when they offered to let me build on the land and set up my shop here. I couldn't resist."

He flips on the light switch, illuminating the cozy little space inside. The place is much smaller than his parents grand abode, and there aren't any decorative touches to speak of, but I can tell he seems to like it that way.

I follow him to the back of the house where he opens up what appears to be a garage door. It leads into a big room with concrete floors and metal cabinets. There are also strange looking tools and machinery I've never seen before, and a workbench with lots of drawers attached to it in the corner.

"Any guesses?" He grins at me.

"Ummm ..." I say, scanning the tidy room for clues, "Not yet ..."

He grabs my arm like an excited child and pulls me closer to one of the cabinets.

He takes a set of keys from his pocket and unlocks it, revealing rows of thin metal drawers inside.

I peek over his shoulder as he gently pulls one out. Inside, in little velvet-lined cubbies, twenty or so sparkling gemstones glint as they hit the light. My eyes widen at the beauty of them.

"You're a jeweler." I say.

"In my spare time," He smiles. "I collect all of my materials myself from various places — antique shops, estate sales — things like that."

I marvel as he takes out another drawer. It holds an abundance of pearls — all shapes, sizes, and colors.

"The ladies must really love you," I tease, "You know what they say is a girl's best friend."

"Diamonds," He supplies, taking out a gorgeous blue gem, "Although I'm really not sure why. There are far more valuable, far more *rare* gemstones out there. Tanzanite, for example."

He places the gem in my hand nestled in its little protective case.

"That's what this is?" I say, enchanted by the iridescent stone.

"Mm-hmm," He nods, "If I were to make a necklace out of that particular stone, I could easily charge anywhere between five hundred and three thousand dollars."

My eyes widen and I quickly hand it back to him, "Expensive things make me nervous. I don't own anything that expensive, except for maybe my car."

He smiles, accepting the gem, "I bet you will one day, if your man is worth his salt."

"Oh man," I snort, feeling heat creep into my cheeks, "Yep, I was right. All the ladies love you. Saying things like that."

I imagine Liam whispering sweet nothings to each girl he brings to his shop. Thoroughly enchanting them with his jewels, making them giggle at the idea of a future with him.

He laughs, "Actually, I'll have you know that most of my clients are *men,* thank you very much. So the *ladies* love the smart *men* who choose to trust me with their jewelry needs."

He places each drawer carefully back in its place and locks the cabinet.

"Wanna see something *really* cool though?" He says.

I nod, and he directs me to another section of his shop - a huge safe I hadn't noticed before. He twists the combination lock until it clicks open, and there within the vault lies some of the biggest crystals I've ever seen. A royal looking purple amethyst, some rough, crystalline gems I couldn't name if I tried ... all gorgeous and grand.

"Oh my ..." I breathe.

"Did you know," He says, presenting a small tray of polished stones, "Very much like names, every gemstone has a specific meaning assigned to it?"

My eyes fall helplessly over the beautiful stones, "I've always known that about *birth*stones, but I don't know much beyond that. Honestly, I'm not even sure what mine is."

"Oh yeah?" He says, "What's your birthday?"

"April twenty-fifth."

He selects a sparkling, clear gem from his tray and hands it to me, "Then your birthstone is a diamond."

"Aww ... That's a bummer," I say, turning the gem over in my hand, "We just got done saying how diamonds are so common ... why couldn't it have been the Tanza ... Tanza?"

"Tanzanite." He smiles, "But hey, diamonds are still a classic. Sure, they're pretty common, but they're still a precious gem. They symbolize purity and eternal love."

I smile, shaking my head at the little gem, "It's not that I'd rather my birthstone be more expensive or anything, just something with a little more color."

He chuckles at this, "Fair enough."

I hand the gem back to him and he places it carefully where it belongs. He closes the safe, pulls a stool from under his work bench and sits.

"So what got you into this?" I wonder aloud, "How'd you know you wanted to make jewelry?"

"My mother loves making jewelry. When she lived in India, she used to sell what she made at the market, and I guess she sort of passed that love down to me. It was one of my favorite things to do together when I was little — stringing beads. It's sort of therapeutic."

I smile, "That's so sweet. I hope my child loves what I do."

For a brief moment, I panic, fearing I've called myself out. Then I realize that's a totally natural thing to say, even if you aren't pregnant.

"That's important to me too," Liam smiles.

A few beats pass between us.

"So what do you think?" He says, leaning forward on his palms.

"About your shop?" I say, glancing around the space. It looks so ordinary, with all the plain looking cabinets and workspaces. You'd never be able to guess at the explosion of colors and sparkle that lies within them all.

"About everything." He says, eyes intent on me, "You've met my family, experienced my mom's cooking ... you looked so damn thoughtful throughout the whole thing, now you've got me wondering what you're thinking up there."

I laugh, "*Thoughtful,* huh? Well thank you, I think."

He smiles, waiting for me to continue.

"Let's see ... your mother's cooking is awesome. Definitely a good introduction to Indian food for me. Um, beyond that, I think I have more *questions* about your family than fully developed thoughts."

He nods, "Right. Totally understandable. Shoot."

"Ha," I say, trying to decide what to ask first, "Okay, I can't quite figure out the official nationality of your family ... literally each of you are your own separate thing."

He bursts out laughing. It's a warm sound ... like taking a sip of hot cocoa.

"Can't argue there." He agrees.

I lean against the wall comfortably, "So what exactly is your dad, then? I mean ... not that it really matters, but now I'm just curious. He's American, isn't he?"

"Well, nobody is 100% anything, you know." Liam says, "Everybody is made up of all kinds of nationalities, even if it's just a small percentage. But to answer your question, my dad would be considered primarily American."

"Okay," I nod, "I'm with you. So what's with the cheek-kissing thing your family does? I've always known that to be more of a European thing."

"And you're correct." He says, "My dad loves, and I mean *loves* to travel. His parents used to take him traveling all over the world when he was little, and when he was old enough, he joined the Peace Corps. Spent two years of his time with them in Albania, took a short break, and then spent another two years with them in India, which is where he met mom."

"Wow," I say, "Suddenly I feel really unaccomplished in life."

"Right?" He laughs, "I always do too. But to make a long story short, my dad was just enamored with his time in Europe. The area, the people, their customs and etiquette ... everything. According to my Grandma on *his* side of the family, he came home from that trip doing the cheek-kiss greeting thing all the time. Both Sakura and I have grown-up watching him do it. She was quick to adapt it herself, but my mother and I, not so much."

I nod, "Okay, so why didn't you guys adapt it?"

He shrugs, "Mostly because Sakura's a daddy's girl, but it's also just a personality difference too. There's a lot of things that my mother does differently from my dad."

"I think I noticed a little bit of that," I say, recalling the tension at the table when Brent mentioned the Bible, "With her being native of India, I bet she has a different religion from him entirely, doesn't she?"

"Right again," Liam smiles, "She's a Buddhist. That's sort of a tension point between the two of them. Well, more so between dad and Nanni. But what can you do? I mean, we all live together, so we're forced to make peace with our differences somehow or another. That's why dad is so big on individuality and owning who you are — what your name means and all that."

I smile, "I really like that. Why is it less of a tension point for your mom, though? Is she less religious than Nanni?"

"Oh no," Liam says, "She is very much a devoted Buddhist. She just loves my father. I guess she chooses to focus on the similarities of their beliefs rather than the differences."

"*Similarities?*" I say, "Between Buddhism and Christianity?"

He laughs, "At first, that seems crazy ... But think about it. Both Christianity and Buddhism value putting love and kindness first, being humble, and the importance of forgiveness, right? The two religions agree on foundational principles, So that's what mom chooses to focus on. Nanni can't see past how different they are, though."

I nod, eyeing him for a moment, "And what do you believe?"

"Eh … I veer more on my dad's side than my mom's."

"So you're a Christian?" I smile.

"Yeah," He shrugs, "You could say that. It's weird though, right?"

"Of course not, why would it be weird for you to be a Christian?"

"No, not that," He specifies, "It's weird that my family is half Christian and half Buddhist, but the majority of the state is Catholic …"

"Oh," I consider this, "Yeah, I guess that is sort of strange."

I'd never thought about it before, but what are the odds that most of the state *is* Catholic, and yet my circles have mainly been either non-religious, or recently, Christians?

Liam smiles. I could be mistaken, but I think I see him flick his eyes briefly to the watch on his wrist.

His polite time check snaps me back into the now. What am I still doing here?

"Oh goodness, it's gotta be getting late," I say. "Thank you for the tour and for inviting me tonight, but I should get going."

"Oh, okay." He says standing, "Let me walk you out to your car."

"No," I say, "That's okay. No need to get you cold if you don't have to be."

He smiles sideways at me, "Okay, then. Have a good night, Grace."

"Thanks," I say, giving him a churchly side hug, "You too."

I open the door to leave, greeted by a gust of cold air. As I make my way back to the car, I silently berate myself for staying as long as I did. For wanting so badly to forget my current situation.

For letting myself hope.

30

Rae - Sunday

My hair is still messy from the night before as I sip my coffee. Adam slipped away early this morning to help some friends move into their new apartment, while I took the opportunity to relish in some weekend sleeping-in.

I haven't decided how I want to go about handling what happened last night yet ... Instead, my mind is occupied thinking about Grace.

She's really pregnant.

Shouldn't she be scheduling a doctor visit soon? And who will accompany her if Jayden is out of the question?

I didn't like the way she sounded yesterday on the phone ... like someone who feels empty inside. As someone who knows exactly what that feels like and what it can do to a person, I refuse to let anyone else feel that way if at all possible. I pull out my phone and dial her.

"Hello?" comes a groggy voice.

"Grace, damn, did I wake you up? I'm sorry."

A sniff, "No. Can't wake someone who never fell asleep."

My lips part, "You haven't gone to bed yet?"

"Mm-mm."

"Well, are you okay?" I shake my head, "Hell, of course you're not. You know what? Just sit tight. I'm coming over."

"Rae ... you don't have to-"

"I'm coming."

* * *

I let myself into the house and immediately Amity is at my feet. She's circling my legs with her twisting tail and purring loudly.

I shake my head, "Girl, I swear ... you have a split personality."

She runs over to her food bowl, which is totally empty.

I frown, going over to fill it up. *Grace usually feeds Amity around seven ...*

I hear the worst retching sound coming from her bedroom. Wincing, I proceed down the hall.

The retching has stopped, but I knock lightly on her door before opening it a crack.

"Grace?"

"You can come in." Is her stuffy reply.

I open the door and try for a smile, but truth be told, I have *never* seen my best friend looking like this. Her nose is red and her eyes are puffy. She holds a puke bucket in her hand and her blanket tightly to her body.

"Sorry I'm gross," she says. "I'm not sick... I'm just... well, I guess this is life now. Morning sickness ... nose clogged from crying."

"Girl, you don't owe me an explanation for anything." I say, going over to her, "You've been to hell and back."

She rolls her eyes, "Understatement. Those random bouts of nausea after the first test was negative are starting to make sense now."

I sit down on the bed, eyeing her puke bucket, "You need me to take that for you?"

"Rae, no. Please. You don't have to take care of me like this."

I squint at her, "What's it gonna take for me to get you to sleep?"

She laughs, "I've been asking myself that all night."

I shake my head, "Lay down. Now."

"Rae —"

"Stop," I say seriously, "I'm not gonna let you do this to yourself."

She looks at me, shocked. I've never spoken to her like this.

To my surprise, she listens. She sets her bowl on the side table and settles under her covers.

"Now just try to relax ..." I say, lightly grabbing the bowl from her table, "Please try to sleep."

With that, I quietly slip from the room and into the bathroom to dump out her bowl. It's a task I couldn't ordinarily stomach, but some sort of maternal instinct kicks in and I find that I don't care all that much.

I see something on the counter — one of her essential oils. It's lavender ... which is supposed to be the sleep one I think.

I take the tiny bottle into her room and eye the little device on her nightstand. I try to figure out how to work it, since she told me once that diffusing oils helps her sleep. I open the lid, sprinkle a few drops into the existing water, and press the button. To my delight, the machine powers on and begins steaming a dreamy scent into the air. I tighten the lid on the bottle and set it down, peeking over at Grace, who is already fast asleep.

My shoulders soften. Her lips are parted because her nose won't breathe right and she just looks so damn beat.

I've never been good with saying the right words to a person who's grieving, but hell if I don't know how to take care of one.

* * *

While Grace slept, I tried to help out with little odd jobs. Things that'd be easy to neglect when you've got a lot on your plate, like watering plants, doing dishes, folding laundry, and so on. I even gave my family physician a call to see if they had any openings today for a prenatal exam, just in case Grace felt up to it.

Around two p.m., Grace's door creaked open. She sauntered out to the seat next to me at the table, looking disheveled but *rested.*

"Hey beautiful," I say, "How you feeling?"

She nods, "Pretty good. Better."

"Good," I smile, scooting my chair back, "I made you lunch. Or breakfast I guess. Whichever."

I go over to the fridge and take out the sandwich I prepared. I place it in front of her on the table, but she just stares at it. After a few seconds, her face begins to crumple and she covers her face.

"Oh, Rae … I don't deserve this."

Some instinctual part of me moves my arms around her. I squeeze her gently, shaking my head, "Are you kidding me? If anyone deserves this sandwich, it's you."

Her shoulders shake, and for a minute I think I've made the crying worse, until she removes her hands from her face and I see that she's laughing. Her tear-streaked face is mingled with an unfitting expression of joy.

She rubs her nose on her sleeve and stares at the plate, "Thank you for this. I didn't know what I needed, but this was it."

I sit back in the seat next to her, smiling a little. "You know, I remember a pretty impressionable point in my life where I didn't know what I needed either ... but you did, Grace. Without hardly even knowing me, you had my back."

I think back to the first time Grace invited me to go to the gym with her — one of her New Year's resolutions. I didn't want to ... but the idea of having a friend at my new school was enticing enough to get me out of my bed where I usually took refuge. It was during these gym visits that I really learned my passion for physical training, so even in that regard, I have Grace to thank.

She smiles at me, "Remember that one smoothie we made at your mom's house after a gym sesh? It had a weird ingredient ..."

"Ricotta," I laugh.

"Yes!" She says, "And it was flipping delicious?"

"It was better than it had any right to be. I have never, ever liked ricotta in any other format."

She belly laughs — such a warm sound that makes me happy.

"I needed someone to remind me how to take care of myself," I shake my head, "How to make healthy food and lifestyle choices ... and you did that for me Grace. I can't thank you enough for that."

Grace's eyes get teary, "Oh, stop it ... You're gonna get me going again."

I can't help but smile to myself. Somehow, some way, I said the right words this time.

***

We hang out for awhile after she eats. We make a couple containers of bath salts and laugh about things that have nothing to do with her current situation. I'm not as into making things like this as she and my mom are, but I wanted to make sure we were doing something *she* would enjoy. Something she'd feel is productive.

"So I made a phone call while you were out," I say as we seal the last container.

"Yeah?"

"My family physician said she could get you in for a prenatal exam today if you feel up to it. The opening is in about an hour, so I'd just need to call and let her know."

Grace nods, "Oh ... yeah, I need to do that."

She glances down at her grey sweats and fitted T-shirt, then over at the mirror at her tousled hair.

"Oh ..."

I smile, grabbing her brush from the dresser and pulling a hair tie from my wrist, "What'll it be, boss?"

She smiles, "I don't know, surprise me."

I go over to the couch and she sits on the floor between my knees. As I gently brush through her tangles and pull her hair into a loose braid, she is silent. I've always needed to talk through my emotions, but Grace needs silence to sort things out. So I don't interrupt, because I know she's already sifting through a lot of noise in there. I imagine she's trying to untangle every loose string of her thoughts and organize them into boxes.

"Gorgeous," I announce, holding up a hand mirror.

She smiles into it.

As I call to confirm the appointment, Grace sweeps on a little mascara, looking nothing like a girl who's been up crying all night. She keeps on her cozy clothes at my encouragement, looking flawless regardless.

"Doesn't take much for you," I tell her as we head out the door.

She rolls her eyes, seeming a bit more like herself.

***

The clinic is chilly inside.

Why are they always so damn cold?

Grace grips a plastic cup of green tea as we wait for her name to be called. I can tell she's deep in thought, the way her eyes are trained intently on the wall across from us.

"What's going on in there?" I say, giving her back a rub.

She shakes her head, snapping out of her trance. "Oh, nothing. Just thinking about last night."

I nod attentively.

"I could use a distraction, actually," She says with resolve, "Tell me something about your life. Your class progress, or something."

I wince, "Class progress isn't one of my finer topics at the moment. I was supposed to meet up with this savvy student-tutor, but we haven't been able to yet, and the test is coming up fast."

"Ooh," Grace frowns, "I'm sorry."

"But forget about that," I say, "I have way more interesting updates."

She turns with interest.

"Do you remember Sam?" I smile.

"Ross?"

"Yes."

"Of course I remember Sam. What about him?"

"I ran into him the other day at the gym."

"You're kidding," She smiles, "How is he?"

"The same. But a man all over. We met up with Rosie too."

"Really?? Gosh I miss her."

"Me too," I smile, "But no worries, I asked her to be a bridesmaid."

"Yeah? Oh wow, I'm excited now! We *need* to get together soon. Sam too. He can come shopping with us or something like we used to make him."

I wince, "Ehhh, not so sure about that."

Grace's smile drops, "Oh no, it's not awkward for you guys, is it?"

"No," I frown, "Not at all actually. It's just ... I think our little run-in struck a nerve with Adam."

"Ohhh," She says, "I guess I never really took him for a jealous guy."

"Well, me either," I say, "But you know how I felt about telling Adam *everything* when we got engaged? You know, 'no secrets from my future husband' kind of thing? Well, I didn't spare any details when it came to Sam ... so."

Grace winces, "Ooh. Yeah, I can understand that. He probably pictures you two in bed whenever he hears that name.

My face twists, "Eww no. Don't say that. Sam and I were just kids. It's not like it was any good."

"Doesn't matter," Grace says, "You know how our minds distort things. And you're the love of Adam's life. Anything you do is nothing short of a beautiful, flawless act. His mind is gonna create that virgin-sex into the most passionate, lustful-looking thing there ever was."

I frown.

"I mean, you can't tell me your mind doesn't do that when he mentions Lexi," She adds.

It does.

I shake my head, trying to clear the visual, "That's beside the point. I didn't tell you the craziest part about all this yet."

Grace raises a brow.

"Sam is with Rosie now," I say.

"*What?*"

"Yes!"

"How did that transpire??"

"Long, adorable story." I smile, "You should ask Rosie when you see her."

"I will," She smiles back.

After a few seconds her face pales.

"What's wrong?" I say.

"The wedding ... I'll be around eight months pregnant for it."

"That's okay," I say quickly. "We haven't ordered dresses yet or anything. Even if we had, it wouldn't be a problem to get you another."

Her lips quiver, "You and your sister and Rosie are gonna look like goddesses and I'm gonna look like a whale."

"Nooo," I console, "You're gonna be adorable. Don't think like that."

She presses her fingers to the bridge of her nose, "I need another distraction. A good one."

With Grace on the verge of tears, I start to panic. I don't have anything else ...

Think. Think. Think. The wedding – yeah. We were talking about the wed – Oh! I know!

"Adam and I aren't really having sex right now," I blurt.

Her hand drops, "Wait, what?"

I instantly regret it. I should've kept that one sacred.

"Are you guys fighting?"

"Well, no, not presently," I say. "Don't laugh at me, but I did some Bible reading about it. I just don't really feel right about it anymore."

She frowns, "Why would I laugh at you?"

"I don't know ..." I consider, "I guess I just assume people will laugh when they hear *me* talking about trying to lead a more biblical life. With my past and everything."

She shakes her head, "Who cares what anyone else thinks? I think it's wonderful. And what's important is that you feel like you're doing the right thing. That's between you and God."

I stare at my friend for a moment, wondering how we got here. A month ago, the two of us wouldn't even know how to have a conversation like this. About spiritual edification, I mean. But here we are: two girls who have been enlightened and worked with ... and I just can't help but feel so much joy.

"I would honestly like to do the same thing with my next relationship," Grace continues, "It's just ... a better way to live. Has Adam been supportive so far?"

"So far, so good," I blush, recalling our rendezvous last night.

"That's so sweet," Grace smiles, "I love you two together. Plus, think about how special your wedding night will be. To have waited all this time — it'll be like the first time again."

"That's the goal," I smile back, "I'm not gonna lie though ... it's a hard goal to keep up."

"Well I can imagine," She says. "How long have you guys been at it?"

"Hmm, I guess it's been about two weeks since I first mentioned it," I say, "We had the conversation shortly before I ran into Samuel, actually ... so you can imagine how Adam might've correlated the two.

She looks confused, "What do you mean? Correlated you guys not having sex with you accidentally running into your ex?"

I go on to explain the whole photography mishap.

"So yeah ..." I say, "the way it must've looked from his perspective is like, first I appear uninterested in having sex anymore, and then it looks like I'm sneaking around with my ex. Obviously that wasn't the case, but after he explained his perspective to me, I understand how it looked."

"Damn ..." Grace says, "That's rough ...you guys are all good now though, right?"

"Yeah," I nod, "We're all good. Sam is just a sensitive subject as of right now."

Our conversation is halted by the appearance of a nurse, "Gracelynn Rains?"

***

"The worst of it's over," The doctor smiles at Grace, whose body has been fully violated.

They took her vitals, blood pressure, measured her weight, examined her breasts, and completed a pelvic exam, and now Grace looks tired again.

"Looks like we won't be able to hear a heartbeat just yet. That's more of a week nine perk. However, I *can* tell you that your due date should be about June third."

Grace nods, trying for a smile.

"Let's go ahead and get you out of that robe. Then you can head to the front for scheduling. Let's see you back in another three weeks so we can hear that heartbeat!"

The doctor shakes our hands and closes the door behind her.

"I guess," Grace says in a small voice as she slips off the robe, "I need to tell Jayden."

31

Grace - Sunday

"Well hello, beautiful!" Aunt Kim waves at me through my laptop screen.

"Hey," I smile.

"Let me see it, let me see it!" She says.

I blush through my smile, holding up the little sonogram up for her to see.

"Awwww," She coos, "Look at that ... not even a little bean yet. So precious."

I had called Aunt Kim to tell her the news on the way home. Turns out she'd been exactly the person I needed to talk to. While everyone else appeared somber and concerned at my news, Aunt Kim beamed with excitement and demanded a video call to see her great-niece or nephew.

"There's not much to see yet," I'd laughed, "We're barely a month in."

She didn't care.

Her enthusiasm was refreshing. Especially since she knew the situation with Jayden. She just chose to treat it like a joyous occasion nonetheless, not mentioning the father unless I did. Every first pregnancy deserves at least *someone* being happy for you.

"So how do you feel?" She smiles.

I shake my head, a smile still on my face, "Bloated. And nervous."

"Well hush that negativity, you look amazing," She beams, "And you should *feel* amazing too."

My smile falters, "Well … it's a lot to take in. And I still need to tell Jayden …"

"Ah," She nods, eyes closed, "There's that name. I was wondering when I'd hear it."

I look down at the picture, shaking my head, "I know this probably sounds weird … but I'm not scared that he might not be receptive to the news. I think I'm actually kinda scared that he'll be *open* to it. Like, want a role in our lives."

Kim nods, "I hear you. Well listen, there's not a thing in the world wrong with raising a child on your own. It'll be a little harder of course, but you gotta do what's best for you and this baby according to *your* judgment."

"Yeah …" *And it's not Jayden.*

"Have you considered what you'll do if he *does* show an interest?"

I frown.

Of course I have.

In fact, when I think about life with his baby, I imagine Jayden as the loving father I always thought he'd be.

But that's not how it will be.

The Jayden that I once knew is not the Jayden that exists now.

Unfortunately, no matter how much I wish I could cut this new Jayden out completely, I can't just keep his own baby from him.

"I have ..." I tell her, "But that's what I'm afraid of. What if he only wants to be half-committed? Occasionally showing up for our child, but mostly being a bad example when he does? To be honest, I just ... don't want him involved ... but if he decides he *has* to be. I'm going to have some clearly outlined expectations ready for him. None of this half-in, half-out nonsense."

"Understandable," She sighs. "Well ... Just know, no matter how it turns out, I'm rooting for you, Grace. You're an overcomer, and so incredibly strong."

I cradle my head in my hands, feeling the stress of this Jayden conversation already.

"Listen, honey," Aunt Kim says, "*Whatever* happens, I want you to do something for yourself."

"What's that?" I say.

She leans in, "Start enjoying *life* again. Don't deprive yourself *one more minute* of joy over this. What's done is done, so try to find a way to enjoy each little moment for what it is. Your body is going through something beautiful and amazing right now. Don't miss it because of someone else's bad attitude."

I smile a little, feeling the warmth in my eyes, "Thanks, Aunt Kim. I think I may be getting there."

* * *

My finger hovers over Jayden's name in my contacts for what feels like forever. Finally, I swallow hard and hit the 'call' button.

Two rings ... four rings ... I almost think he won't pick up. And then,

"Hello?"

My mouth goes dry.

"Hello?" he says again.

"It's me, Jayden." I say.

Silence.

"I'm sorry to call you like this," I say, instantly regretting the apology. "Look, I need you to come over. Or meet me in town somewhere."

He sighs, "Grace ... I can't."

I bite my tongue, hating his instant dismissal.

"Why not?" I say tightly.

"Let me get this straight," He says. "I show up at your place, lay my heart on the table and apologize for everything ... setting aside my pride and my manhood and my whole *life* pretty much. And you respond by sending Hadley over to cut my dick off. *Now* you want to meet up — just like that? What makes you think I'm ready to get back together?

At first, I'm surprised. Then I'm disgusted. Is he really trying to turn this around?

"It's not like that," I say firmly, "At *all.* I just need to tell you something."

"Tell me." He says.

"In person, Jayden."

He sighs, "Grace ... I'm right in the middle of something. Can it wait?"

I inhale deeply and slowly breathe it out, tamping down the volume of my words, "It's important."

He exhales, "Fine. I'll be at your house in ten minutes."

The phone clicks.

I thought he was right in the middle of something.

* * *

I'm praying the whole ten minutes it takes Jayden to get here. I only realize it's been that long when I hear a knock at the door.

I give the sonogram in my hand one last affectionate glance before carefully folding it into my pocket.

I go over to the door, grateful that I look much more put-together than the last time we met. I open it to reveal the unsmiling, yet devilishly handsome man behind it. Weird how my stomach produces no flutters this time.

His cologne wafts up my nostrils as he strides past me, but it makes me feel queasy more than anything else. He sits wordlessly on my couch and stares at me expectantly. I go to join him, though allowing a good four feet between our bodies.

"Well?" He says, "Let's hear it."

My fingers fiddle with the glossy paper in my pocket. I've got to rip this off like a Band-Aid.

"There's no graceful way to tell you this, Jayden. I'm just gonna go for it." I breathe, "I'm pregnant. You and I are."

A few beats of excruciating silence pass. Then his eyes narrow at me.

"You're playing."

My jaw tightens, "No, Jayden. I wouldn't lie about this."

"Yes you are," He stands, running his fingers through his hair and pacing, "Either that or you've been messing around with someone else on the rebound, because there is *no way*."

"Quit casting blame," I say firmly, taking out the sonogram. "I had my first prenatal exam today and they confirmed it. The due date is June third."

He snatches the picture from my hands and squints at it. "That's not a baby. Quit trying to pull some shit."

Furious now, I snatch the picture back, "The baby is too little, Jayden. That dark spot in the picture is the fertilized egg. That's all you'll be able to see this far along."

He stares at me with an expression some might call angry, but I know he's just stressed. Something in his face softens and he looks as though he might fall apart.

"Grace ..." He says, gently now.

He searches my face, and I can tell he's trying to draw from the relationship we *had,* not the one we have. I wish he wouldn't.

"I can't ... I can't do this." He says, almost sadly.

"I'm not asking you to." I say, keeping my composure.

"Can I ... just see the picture again?"

Oh no ... Lord, please don't let him stay.

I swallow hard and stiffly hand over the picture of his baby. Or rather, the egg that is *becoming* his baby at this very moment.

He stares at it for a few minutes, his Adam's apple bobbing.

I can't take it anymore.

"Listen to me, Jayden. You are either all in, or all out. You hear me? There is no halfway loving this child. You can't do him or her the way you did me. I won't let you."

Something in his face shifts back to the way it was before:

Angry.

"You know what, Grace? If *that's* how it's gonna be ... If this little *black spot* is what you're trying to pass off as a baby, then there is none." Jayden says with resolve, "Get rid of it."

The bite in his tone surprises me — though I don't know why at this point.

"I'm not going to." I say, struggling to keep calm.

"Grace, I get a say in this." He says, "Do what I said."

That does it.

"How *dare* you," I scream at him, "You and I are *not* a thing, and I will *not* do what you say!"

He shakes his head, "Either get rid of it or find a way to deal with it yourself."

"You are the most unfeeling human being I've ever met!" I spit.

"Better than you! Lying like a whore, trying *everything* to get me back!"

What??

"*You* are the *last* person I want back in my life! No less this baby's."

"Well good, because you're on your own, Grace."

"Fine!" I say, tears threatening. My anger chokes them down. "I told you about this because it was the right thing to do. *Not* because I wanted any part of you ever again!"

Jayden stands, "I'm sorry, Grace. Just know I tried."

"You did *not!*" I shout.

I watch as he storms out of my house, slamming the door behind him. I'm left in absolute silence.

I don't cry.

In fact, I'm a little ... *relieved.*

At last. He's gone.

"No more Jayden," I stroke my tummy protectively. "Just you and me."

I stopped feeling afraid of my pregnancy shortly after my doctor visit ... after the little guy's presence became more real.

It's a feeling I would've never expected to have considering how unprepared I feel for motherhood ... but seeing that little human developing inside of me for the first time stirred up an emotion inside of me that I can't quite put to words.

I thought about my painting of the baby and the scripture I read about God forming the little darling Himself. Staring at my ultrasound a day later, the scripture had a brand-new meaning for me. *My* art is made with paint and a canvas, but *God's* art is made of breath and life. It made me feel like an important instrument of His artwork. Like He chose me to help create this little masterpiece. He already knows the baby and has given it a purpose … and knowing *that* helped me to be at peace with bringing it into the world.

Instead of feeling afraid, I actually found a little *comfort* in my new situation. Me and this tiny human are a team now. The only thing standing in the way of our happy life was Jayden. Now that he's out of the picture, maybe I can try this happy thing one more time.

32

Rae - Monday

Okay, I breathe, *Accountability. That's what this is for. I'll never meet my goal if I don't remain accountable.*

I saunter up to Kaya's table at Aroma Mocha. I spent a good thirty minutes psyching myself up to make the phone call, and another thirty minutes convincing myself that I'm doing the right thing.

"Thanks for meeting me so last minute," I say, pulling out a chair.

"Don't mention it!" Kaya smiles, "I reserve my Mondays for you girls."

"Do you really?" I say, "All of Monday?"

"Mm-hmm," She nods, "Saturdays are my time with the Lord, and then Monday I reserve for meet-ups with you guys, so you actually called on the perfect day."

"That's so awesome ..." I say, "And then you host A&B on Wednesdays. How do you make time for all that?"

She shrugs, "It's not always easy, but the Lord makes a way. We didn't meet up to talk about me though, did we? What's going on with *you?*"

I sigh, lowering my gaze, "Well, let's see … How do I want to start this."

She waits patiently.

"I feel like for any goal you make, whether it's trying to eat healthier or maintain a specific weight, you either have an app, a trainer, or a friend to hold you accountable until you learn the methods and the self discipline to maintain it on your own. That's the only way you'll successfully meet your goals."

Kaya nods.

"Well … you know the goals I made for myself recently … for me and Adam." I sigh, "I can't seem to get my grip on them. We were doing really good. Adam was super receptive to it and has been wonderful. But I think the thing that trips us up is my own … like … I don't know, I guess insecurity?"

I try to find more words to explain, but I feel like I've explained all there is to it. I have an insecurity problem. That's the fact of the matter.

She nods, "Well, first of all, Rae, I just want to say I am so proud of you. What you just described is the essence of Christianity. We're not made to do things on our own, but to carry each other in love when necessary. And the only way we can do that is if we're honest with each other — *especially* about struggles with sins. Otherwise we can't pray for each other as intimately as we should … otherwise, I never would've thought to share with you that I've struggled with this same thing in the past."

"Really?" I say, "With the one guy you told me about?"

She shakes her head, "More recently than that I'm afraid."

"What?" I fail to hide my surprise

She chuckles, "I'm thirty-four now, and still not married. I'm okay with that now, because I'm not sure that marriage is what God has in store for me. But when I first hit the big three-oh ... man ... did that do a number on me. I started feeling all those feelings you're describing ... but in the sense that I was getting old. I sought out people to prove it to me otherwise — that made me feel young and beautiful."

"Yes," I say, surprised, "You understand then ..."

"I do," she says, "and I struggled for two, long years. I didn't just pick up any guy with wandering eyes. I still had standards for myself. But the point is, I was looking for security in other human beings, which will never lead to real fulfillment. The sex didn't feel *empty* necessarily, it was just that no amount of it could keep me feeling secure in myself. I'd need it again and again, routinely, to prove that I wasn't getting — oh I don't know, old and boring I guess?"

This makes me laugh.

"I'm serious," She smiles, "This was a problem for me. Rest assured, I understand where you're coming from."

"Wow ... I never would've thought that you ..." I trail off, worried I'll say the wrong words, but she just nods.

"And that's what we gain by choosing to be transparent with each other. All of us have more in common than we think, if we'd just *choose* to show our humanity a little bit."

I let that sink in.

"So how'd you, like, pull yourself out of it?"

"Well," she sighs, "Lots of crying. I decided that I didn't like who I was becoming ... *totally* reliant on someone else to feel my worth. I prayed and prayed, asking God to fix the broken person I'd become ... and then something amazing happened."

A pause.

"It's like He just ... whispered the words in my heart, and He said, '*Find your identity in Me.*'"

My heart thuds.

"Turns out," she says, "There are a *ton* of scriptures where God lays out for us *exactly* who we are in Him. He uses words like, called, chosen, adopted, and forgiven ... just to name a few. I began studying them deeply. Picking one thing per day to focus on, and slowly I began finding my security, just in reading about the personal identity *God* has given me. He reminded me of exactly who I am — not broken, not reliant on people, but healed, free, and strengthened."

My shoulders relax, "Could you share those scriptures with me?"

She smiles, "Absolutely. In fact ..."

She reaches into her purse and pulls out her notebook. She opens the cover and pulls out a single page, looking over it with an affectionate smile before handing it to me, "You can keep this."

I scan the scripture-filled page. On the top, she's written: *Identity in Christ.*

"Are you sure?" I say, "Do you have another one?"

She shakes her head, "Those scriptures are pretty much written on my heart at this point. My lessons have been learned, so now it's your turn."

"Wow," I smile, "Thanks, Kaya. I really appreciate this."

"You're welcome," She smiles.

I fold the paper and slide it in my pocket.

"Rae," Kaya says.

"Hm?"

"I really believe that you can do this."

"Thanks," I smile.

"It's important that you do," She says, a little more seriously. "This journey for you isn't just about being abstinent for the next seven months ... it's about finding lasting security in your Identity through Christ. *That* journey is going to last *far* into your marriage."

I nod, holding her gaze.

"Hear me when I say that your insecurities *won't* go away just because you got married. It's going to take a little more on *your* end to be where you want to be."

"I believe that," I say.

"And I believe you're ready for it." Kaya smiles, "On your own, you have what it takes to beat this, but you said that Adam has been super supportive too, right? So that just makes this all the more possible."

I smile, "Yes, he has been, but sometimes I wonder if I'm asking too much of him. This is a goal *I've* made for us completely on my own ... not *we,* yet I'm asking him to just be all in. Is that ... fair of me? He's just one man."

I meant the last part to be funny, but Kaya is all seriousness.

"I want to ask you something."

"Okay," I shift.

"If there was ever to come a time that Adam *wasn't* willing to do this with you, something that clearly means a lot to you, is he someone you're willing to give up?"

Her question, so blunt, surprises me.

"Because this is the hardest part about being faithful to God. If He tells you that you have to give Adam up, you have to be willing to listen."

"I mean ..." I say, "I don't think that ..."

I don't find my words, so Kaya continues, "Just try to understand that He will never ask you to do something that is not in your best interest, even if you don't understand it at the time. If God tells you to do that, He already has something better lined up for you, or at a bare minimum, is saving you from a situation that'll continually hurt you in the future."

I nod, taking in her words.

"Not that I think this is the case for you and Adam," she smiles, "It's just important once in awhile to do a little self-check. 'If I want God's peace and guidance, am I willing to listen to His leadership over my life? Or am I making something else more important?' That was the thing that tripped me up the most in embracing my identity ..."

Identity in Christ

I Am...

- Lavished in Love (1st John 3:1)
- His Daughter (1st John 3:2)
- Known (1st Corinthians 8:3)
- Holy & Blameless (Ephesians 1:4)
- Predestined for Adoption (Ephesians 1:5)
- Chosen - Appointed (John 15:16)
- God's special possession - Called out of darkness (1st Peter 2:9)
- Accepted (Romans 15:7)
- One in Spirit (1st Corinthians 6:17)
- No longer a slave to sin (Romans 6:6)
- Part of the body (1st Corinthians 12:27)
- A temple for God's Spirit to live in (1st Corinthians 6:9)
- Triumphant (2nd Corinthians 2:14)
- Blessed (Ephesians 1:3)
- Bold - Confident - Able to approach God with anything (Ephesians 3:12)
- A Light in Christ (Ephesians 5:8)
- Guarded in Peace (Philippians 4:7)
- Complete (Colossian 2:10)
- God's Handiwork (Ephesians 2:10)
- Redeemed - Forgiven (Ephesians 1:7)
- Created in His image (Genesis 1:27)
- A Friend of Jesus (John 15:15)

- A Conqueror (Romans 8:37)
- Fearfully and Wonderfully Made (Psalm 139:14)
- A New Creation (2nd Corinthians 5:17)
- Free (Romans 8:2)

* * *

From: Claire

Sent: 10/14/19

Time: 12:27 pm

Hey, I don't think I'm gonna be able to meet up this afternoon – I'm sorry :(I'm studying like crazy for midterms.

I frown. What does she think *I'm* doing?

The test is in just *three* days, and so far, the only part I'll understand is the part that covers our last lesson *(and that's only because I have her notes).*

I find myself in a familiar state: sitting on my yellow rug trying to make sense of the red-inked papers spread out around me. They're nothing but gibberish.

I pop a couple of stress gummies. They're delicious, but unfortunately not very powerful.

Maybe I just need to call Adam … see if he can walk me through it. But once again, I'm met with the idea of him realizing how inept I am with math, and I just can't bring myself to tell him.

I let out an exasperated sigh, just as Grace's face lights up my phone. I welcome the distraction.

"Hey there," I say.

"Hey," She sounds tired, "What are you doing?"

"Just… stressing over math. What about you?"

She sighs, "I told Jayden."

My jaw slacks. I set down my pen.

"And?"

"He flipped out."

"Oh," I frown, "How bad?"

"Bad," she says, "He accused me of lying, sleeping around, and get this: trying to get back with him. All in the same ten seconds."

I laugh humorlessly, "You're *kidding."*

"Nope ..."

To think we adopted him into our friend group for so long.

"So ... now what?"

"Well," she takes a breath, "Now I figure it out."

I wince.

"I'm actually not like ... *devastated* at his reaction," she continues, "Maybe a little *shocked. E*ven after everything, I'm still surprised that this is ... the new *him.* But I'm not devastated. If this really is the new him, I'm glad he decided to back out of this one. I don't want him around us."

I nod, "I don't blame you."

"The only trouble now is ... I'm not sure *what* I'm going to do. I have to be real with myself and accept that I can't do this on my own ..."

"You'll have help, though," I smile, "Believe me, the baby is gonna love his or her Auntie Rae."

She chuckles, "I know, you and Adam will be awesome. It's just that ... I don't know. I have to consider picking up another job ... affording daycare. My dream was always to stay home with my children and raise them until they're school-age, but that's not even an option here."

"Well," I say, "You *do* have options though, even if staying home with them isn't one. I don't want this to come off the wrong way ... I totally support your decisions ... but have you thought about adoption?"

There's silence for a minute and I worry that I've offended her.

"I'd be lying if I said it's never crossed my mind." she says finally. "I feel so guilty for that though. The baby would never know me … or maybe it would and hate me for deciding I don't want it."

"You're not aborting it, Grace …" *I knew better than to suggest that.* "You're not saying you don't want it. You'd simply be deciding that you can't provide the best possible care for your child on your own, and that you're doing this so that they can have a better life. Out of love."

I can see her shaking her head, "But a little child isn't going to think like that. Those are mature, grown-up thoughts. All they're going to think is, 'Mommy didn't want me, and I don't know why'."

I purse my lips, "That's not true for every child …"

"I mean, I'm a grown adult and *I* feel bitter toward mine for doing far less,"

I shift my phone to the other ear, "Okay. Maybe adoption isn't the move, and that's totally okay. In fact, I think the relationship you've had with Corinne will be an amazing tool for *you* as a mom. From your experience with her, *you* know the kind of love and belonging your baby will need to feel from you — the perfect balance of independence, and moral support — and I have no doubt you'll do an amazing job of providing it."

I can see her smiling, "Thanks, Rae."

"I mean it," I say, "I can't wait to see you shine as a mom, whether that's eight months from now, or years in the future when you feel more prepared. Just know that you *do* have options, and you shouldn't feel bad for considering them. To do that is human."

She sighs, "Yeah … I guess you're right …"

"Love you, Gracie," I smile, "Chin up."

She laughs, "Love you, Rae. Good luck with math."

I glance over the papers spread out around me.

"Thanks . . . I need it."

33

Grace - Monday

I slip my shoes off by the door and do the little bow thing to Nancy behind the check-in desk. I haven't been to yoga in almost a month now, and truth be told, I've missed it.

I usually don't mind the fragrance of synthetic frankincense wafting through the sanctuary, but today it smells sickeningly sweet. I think I might throw up. I focus on my breathing to keep the nausea down and imagine the little human inside my stomach rubbing against me affectionately.

"Grace!" Calls the instructor, "I haven't seen you in weeks. How've you been sweetheart?"

I nod, "Hanging in there."

Betty's arms are gesturing wildly to two other ladies on the far end of the room. I can only assume she's telling another ex story, which makes me smile.

I'm busy unrolling my mat when all the ladies, including Betty, suddenly gather at the entrance of the room. They're all making a fuss over someone. Words of adoration like *handsome,* and *'our boy',* are thrown around.

I look up to see who is receiving all of these *masculine* words of praise, only to be met with the face belonging to none other than Liam Cross. He's not looking at me, though. He's greeting each older lady by name and passing out strong hugs.

Finally, he sees me, but he doesn't look surprised. He simply smiles and goes to place his mat next to mine.

"This spot taken?" He says.

I shake my head from my place on the mat, "You do yoga?"

"My mother does from time to time. This would be a first for me. Well, I guess a second."

I glance over at the group of adoring old ladies, who are still gathered at the doorway, "How do they all know you so well?"

He smiles, "For one thing, because of my mother. But also because I came to last Monday's session."

"Why did you —"

"Alright ladies," The instructor says, pausing for a smile, "and *Liam.* We're gonna go ahead and get started."

I close my mouth, deciding to put all of my focus into the session. But as the instructor begins guiding us through, I can't help but peek over at him. His muscles flex throughout each pose — veins rippling through his tan skin. I never thought a man doing yoga could be ... attractive, but Liam is the essence of strength.

When the session is over and he is rolling up his mat, a little chuckle escapes my throat.

"What?" He says, smiling.

I shrug. The laughter makes my heart warm.

"What're you laughing at?"

"You." I say, shaking my head.

He places a hand on his chest, looking exaggeratingly surprised.

"Moi?"

"You're very persistent, you know that?" I smile, "I can't believe you came to do yoga with me. Jayden would've *never* –"

I stop short.

Liam studies me. His face looks as though he's resolved not to ask.

"What?" He says, redirecting, "Can't a man enjoy a little yoga?"

"Of course he can," I say, smiling again, "But what's your excuse for coming here for the first time a few days ago? You were trying to find me. Admit it. 'Cause you're too mysterious to send a text."

"You think I'm mysterious, huh?" He smiles.

I open my mouth and then close it, while playfully punching his arm. How'd he get me to say that?

He laughs, "I put the pieces together … you said you do yoga. There's only one yoga place in Gevali, and only two sessions per week. And before you go getting too excited, I only know that because of my mother."

"So," I jest, "You figured I'd have to be at one of them."

He shrugs, "I took my chances."

He tucks his mat under his arm and stands, "It was good to see you again."

"You too," I say, not expecting him to start walking toward the door.

"Wait," I call without thinking.

He turns, "Hm?"

"Um," I say, standing, "What are you doing now?"

He glances at his watch, "Well, my client canceled this morning, so I was gonna go check out the Maple Festival."

"Oh," I smile, "I didn't know they did that this time of year. I thought it was only in April."

He switches his mat to his left arm, "The big one in Saint Albans is in April. I'm talking about the little one on Maine Street that Mr. Cane is throwing this year."

"*Mr. Cane* is throwing his own Maple Festival?"

"Yeah," Liam smiles, "Is that not the cutest thing you ever heard?"

I nod and stand there awkwardly for a second.

"Do you ... wanna come?"

I shouldn't.

But then I think about what Aunt Kim had said ... *"Start enjoying* life *again. Don't deprive yourself* one more minute *of joy over this. What's done is done, so try to find a way to enjoy each little moment for what it is.*

"Yeah." I smile.

***

We took his car. A little grey Elantra with heated seats like Persia's.

The car ride isn't long, but it'll be too quiet if I say nothing at all, so I turn toward him and attempt small talk, "So you said one of your clients canceled on you this morning, right?"

"Mm-hmm." He nods.

"What kind of jewelry are you making for them?"

He smiles, "None, actually. Jewelry making is just my side hustle, remember? I actually have my Bachelor in Interpretation, so that's my full time gig."

I eye him with interest, "What do you do with that?"

His eyes are trained on the road, "Are you asking what I *do* with it, or what I'd *like* to do with it?"

"Why not both?"

His fingers grip and ungrip the wheel. "Well," He says, "The dream is to be a world traveling translator, but the *reality* is that I teach foreign languages to people one-on-one. Some local, some over video call, but all in the U.S. so far."

"Languag*es?*" I marvel, "As in plural?"

He nods, "English, Hindi, and Italian."

I think of his voicemail, and how he has it recorded in two languages.

"No way," I smile, "I wanna hear you say something."

He laughs, "Okay, what do you want to hear?"

"I dunno. Surprise me."

"Ah, okay, well let's see ... how about '*yah ek raaj hai*'."

"Whoa," I clap my hands together, "What'd you say?"

"It's a secret." He grins.

"You're not gonna tell me??"

He shakes his head, trying to suppress his smile.

"Come on," I punch his arm and we swerve a little.

"Hey!" He laughs, "Quit assaulting the driver."

"Tell me then!"

"I can't!" He says.

I squint at him, "I'm gonna Google Translate it."

He laughs, "Good luck with the spelling."

I cross my arms.

"Growing up, my mother spoke Hindi to us, and my father spoke English to us, so my sister and I picked up both. Later, my dad taught us the bits of Italian he learned when he went to Albania, and I pursued it further on my own. I guess I realized I have a knack for picking up languages."

"I'll say ..." I peek out my window, "Do you think you'll learn any more?"

"Maybe," He says, "Though it's not my focus right now."

We scour the crowded little strip for a parking spot, having to settle for a parallel space. If I'd been driving, I'd have butchered a parallel parking job. Maybe even parked far, far away to avoid the space altogether, but Liam pulled into the spot with ease.

Across the walkway hangs a banner with an orange painted leaf: *Cane's Gevali Maple Fest.*

It's exactly like the annual festival in Saint Albans, only miniature. The sun is shining on several little food stands, all promoting maple flavored products: maple coffee, fudge, ice cream, pancakes, nuts, butter, and even maple-glazed carrots. There's a talented young boy strumming effortlessly on his guitar on the sidewalk, and a little grassy area with games like Cornhole and life-size Jenga. Signs on either side of the road promise a scheduled tour of Mr. Cane's maple farm, where he will walk guests through his maple syrup process 'From Tree to Bottle', and a special stop at his gift shop afterwards.

In a rocking chair on someone's patio sits Mr. Cane himself. He waves hello to Liam and Me.

"Hey, Mr. Cane!" I say, "Quite the event you've put on for us here."

"Oh, yes," He smiles. "I usually go out to the annual festival… sell my maple treats there, you know, but I won't be able to make it this year."

Liam frowns, "Why won't you be able to?"

"Oh," He says sadly, "Patricia's family will be coming up from Pennsylvania for a visit. They miss her like I do."

Mr. Cane's wife passed away a little over a year ago now. The old man has been just pitiful without her. But Patricia's family always loved Mr. Cane like their blood kin, so they still visit regularly.

"They'll be happy to see you," I say, offering a smile.

"So you just decided to host a festival of your own since you couldn't make it?" Liam says, "Pretty savvy of you, I'd say."

"You know how I love it so!" His wrinkled face brightens, "The music, the children, the food ... it makes me young again."

My heart melts.

"Oh, would you listen to me carrying on?" He leans in, handing us two maple flavored candies from his pocket, "You two go on and have a good time."

"Thank you, Mr. Cane." I smile, accepting the candies.

"That man is a saint." Liam says when we're out of earshot.

"Mm-hmm. He offered to let my best friend have her wedding on his Maple farm free of charge."

"I rest my case!" He throws up his hands.

We continue walking down the strip, trying one item from each food stand. So far, the ice cream is my favorite, but Liam likes the maple nuts. You'd think having so much maple at one time would make us feel sick of the flavor, but Mr. Cane's homemade syrup is not the same as the store-bought kind. It's rich and fresh and never gets old. When we get our maple coffees, we decide to find a sunny picnic table to sit for awhile. At this moment, my heart feels so happy and carefree.

"So," Liam says, sipping his coffee, "I'm curious, what made you want to come with me today?"

"Well," I say, "I figured since we keep randomly showing up in each other's lives, we may as well pause to say hello. Get to know each other a little bit."

"Fair enough," He smiles, "Though you definitely know more about me than I know about you."

I grip my warm cup, "How do you figure?"

He shrugs, "You've *met* my family already. I don't even know your mom's *name*. Plus, you do this thing where you like to ask more questions than you answer."

I smile, staring down into my coffee.

"See?" He says, "Look at you. *You* even know you're doing it."

"I just like listening. I'd rather learn about someone else's heart than hear my own for the millionth time that day – you know?"

He nods, "I do."

"Plus, I just like figuring people out. Getting to know their quirks and passions and fears. I'd rather have one conversation that skips to the deep stuff than three conversations about the surface-level stuff."

"'What are you going to school for'," Liam says in a posh accent.

"Exactly!" I say, "Like, you don't really learn anything about anyone that way."

His brown eyes stare into mine, "I think you just like to figure people out before they figure you out."

I hold his gaze for a moment and then quickly look away. I don't know what to say to that besides maybe 'and what have *you* figured out?', but that would be far too intimate of a question. And I don't quite think I'm ready for the answer.

I clear my throat, "Her name is Corrine, by the way."

"Who?" He says.

"My mom. You said you don't know her name."

"Oh," He laughs, "I got you."

A few yards away from us, a child erupts into tears as his Jenga tower topples to the ground, pulling our attention from the conversation. As his mother comes to console him, I use the opportune distraction to swallow down the feelings Liam stirred up inside me.

Crisis averted.

When the child is consoled, Liam gets up and goes over to him, smiling.

"What happened, buddy?" He says, stooping down to help rebuild the Jenga pieces, "Did your tower fall down?"

The boy, who can't be more than three, nods with big, teary eyes.

"Well you know what the good part is?" Liam says, "No matter how many times this thing falls down, you can always build it back up again — and I bet next time, you'll get it even higher than before."

The child smiles and wipes his nose on his sleeve. He bends to pick up a piece and helps Liam reassemble the tower.

I can't help but smile myself, watching the two of them. *So Liam is good with kids.*

The child's mother mouths a 'Thank-you' to Liam as he begins to play the game with the boy.

As I watch them, I consider what kind of a mother *I'll* be in a short while. A good one, no doubt ... but no mother can play the role of mom *and* dad efficiently. A good father would add so much to the baby's life, and I want to give it what I never had.

I think of what Rae said the other day about possibly putting my baby up for adoption, and I realize the opportunity I have in front of me. *Liam* was adopted. I can just ask *him,* an actual adoptee, how the whole process made him feel. But I'd have to word it just right. I don't want it to be *too* personal of a question.

When he comes back from his Jenga game, I give him a smile.

"That was really sweet of you," I say.

His smile lines crease as he shrugs, "I love little kids. Life is so simple for them."

"It is ..." I nod, "Beautifully simple."

A few beats pass between us as we watch the child walk away hand in hand with his mother.

"So ..." I start, "I have a *really* deep question for you."

He chuckles, "Hit me with it."

"Okay. How do I say it ... I guess I'm wondering, how did you *feel* about your adoptive situation? Like, more specifically, toward your birth mom?"

He stares at me for a second, "Are you writing a book or something?"

I laugh, "No, I'm way more of a reader than a writer. Sorry if that's too personal – you don't have to answer."

"I mean, no, it's not," He says, "Just oddly specific."

I blush.

"That's not necessarily a bad thing," He grins at me, "Honestly, I don't think much about my birth mom. Dhara's been my mother for as long as I can remember."

"So you were adopted pretty young then?" I say.

"Not as young as Sakura. She was adopted as a newborn from a family in Japan who *knew* they couldn't keep her. So mom and dad were actually in correspondence with that family while they were pregnant. My birth mom took a little more time to decide if she wanted to keep me, so she put me up for adoption when I was a year and a half. And I didn't get adopted till I was almost four."

"Oh ..." I frown.

"Given, if she'd decided to do what Sakura's parents did when they were pregnant, I probably would've gotten adopted a lot faster. You know, since the demand for newborns is greater than the demand for kids. But I'm not mad that it happened the way it did. I hardly remember the children's home I was in, and if my mom had chosen a family ahead of time to adopt me at birth, it wouldn't have been my current family."

"So you don't know much about your mom then ..." I say, thinking of the little bean inside me, "Do you ever ... wonder about her?"

"Not really any more. I sort of romanticized the idea of meeting her when I was thirteen or so. I thought maybe it'd reveal some new and magical thing about myself if I knew her. But then my parents told me what they knew of her personally, and that was enough for me."

I rub my arms to keep warm, "How did they know her?"

Liam looks off into the grassy area, "I guess she confided in my caregiver at the children's home when she was putting me up for adoption. Said that I was the result of a terribly abusive situation, and as much as she's tried to figure out a way to keep me, 'I deserved a life far better than she could give me'. My caregiver passed that bit along to my parents."

My heart sinks, "It sounds like she wanted to keep you. She tried for a little while, right?"

"Probably just an excuse," He says, "I bet that I looked too much like my father for her liking. I can't see an ounce of myself in the pictures I've seen of her."

I frown, my heart feeling heavy, "You know what she looks like?"

"My parents showed me the headline of her arrest. She was strung out on drugs. Tried to rob someplace."

"No ..."

"Yep. A real winner. She's pale and blonde — nothing like me."

"Wow," I shake my head, "I'm so sorry to hear that."

"Don't be," He shrugs, "I pretty much lost interest in my blood relatives after learning that."

"I can imagine. I mean, your real family is so wonderful – why even focus on the others?"

He smiles, "My 'real family' is right. Everyone always insists my *blood relatives* are my 'real family', but I'm nothing like them."

"You're not," I agree, feeling defensive of him, "You're talented and friendly, and like your dad emphasizes, you're your *own person.* Just imagine if Dhara and Brent *hadn't* been your parents. Who knows if you would have discovered your passion for making jewelry or teaching different languages without their influence? Your life would probably be completely different from the way it is now."

He laughs at this, "Well thank you for that vote of confidence. And you're right. It would be."

I smile.

We get up and throw our coffee cups away, making the unspoken decision to walk through some of the gardens.

"So now you know all about my family," Liam says, "Let's hear about yours.

"Ah," I say, "There isn't much to tell."

"Don't do that to me," He pokes me, "Not after I told you all that."

I laugh, "Well, I mean it though. I'm not just being difficult. My mom and I don't get along too well. My dad is MIA. I feel like that's a common theme among the young women in my life. Your birth mom ... my mom ..." I almost add myself into the mix before I think better of it.

"Why don't you and your mom get along?" He says frowning.

I shrug, "I dunno, we just never see eye to eye. For one thing, our beliefs about medicinal practices couldn't be more different, as you so intuitively pointed out in our taxicab ride."

"That's too bad." He says quietly.

"I mean, not really," I frown, "I get along fine."

"Yeah, but ... she's like, the only family you have."

"That's not true," my brows pinch, "I have my Aunt Kim, and we're super close."

"Sorry," He says, "I just feel like ... medicinal beliefs are a totally surmountable issue."

I stop walking. "You don't really know the whole story though. What you have with Dhara is way more than what I had growing up."

He throws up his hands, "You're right, you're right. I'm sorry. I didn't mean to press."

"My mother and I hardly ever saw each other..." I add, "We *still* hardly see each other."

He shrugs, "Maybe you should change that."

"*Me?* Why should *I* be the one to —"

"Because you're different from her." He says, smiling slightly at me, "Don't give back to people what they give you themselves. Show them who *you* are."

I stare at him for a few seconds, "I feel like you're doing some sort of reverse psychology on me."

He smiles, "No. I'm just telling you what I see. You're someone who doles out love without ever worrying if it'll be reciprocated. That's *you.*"

I blush. But how could he see that? Given our interactions, I would think he'd see a girl with her walls put up ... a spirited girl, at best, because of the bold voicemail I left him.

Just then, my phone notifies me that something has triggered my nanny cam. I pocket my phone with a groan. How do I keep forgetting to close that door?

I turn to Liam, "So that was my nanny cam I set up for my cat. The last time it went off, she destroyed my house and my best friend's arms."

He chuckles, "Wait, what?"

I shake my head, "Long story. Basically, I probably need to go check out the situation."

He frowns, "Your nanny cam doesn't send the image to your phone?"

"That part of the cam broke," I say, pulling out my phone, "It can see motion and record and everything, which alerts my phone, but I can't pull up what the camera is seeing."

He raises a brow.

I laugh, "I'm not lying. Here, look."

I show him the phone screen, which says:

Something has triggered your NannyCam2.0!

(Security Detection Setting: Motion Sensing)

Error Code 404: No Picture Available.

"I feel like that's totally fixable," He says, examining the message, "Maybe I can take a look at it sometime."

I pocket my phone, "That'd be great, honestly. So I don't keep having to run around after this crazy cat."

"Why don't you bring it by the house tomorrow around five? The cam, I mean. I bet mom would make dinner again if you want."

I think of Dhara's delicious dumpling recipe and my mouth waters. But then I hesitate. He is, in a subtle way, asking me out a second time. It'd be almost cruel of me to continue this charade of appearing perfectly available, when I am a walking package deal.

"I don't know," I say, "As lovely as that sounds, I wouldn't want to inconvenience your parents."

He smirks, "Are you kidding? Between you doing yoga and knowing what it's called to study names, my parents love you. Having your own business in the natural medicine industry was just the icing on the cake for them."

I smile involuntarily, "Are you sure?"

"Oh yeah ..." He says, "You hit the nail on the head."

I look down, "Wow, they barely even know me."

He shrugs, "They don't need to. It doesn't take a genius to recognize a quality girl."

I smile, wrapping my arms around myself. The air is suddenly shivery again.

"Thank you, Liam, I'll definitely think about it. And thank you for today, too. This was lovely."

We exchange formal goodbyes, and I proceed to my car — except for the fact that I didn't drive here. We carpooled.

I turn around, holding my arms out, "Well, guess I can't leave without a car."

He chuckles, "I guess not. Let's get you home then."

As we walk, I can't help but smile. Sure, if you last-minute invite yourself to go somewhere, it probably doesn't count as a date. But he'd been a perfect gentleman. He'd done just about everything but send me home with his jacket.

34

Rae - Monday

When I get home from work, I review the one trig lesson that I *do* understand so that it's fresh in my mind for the test: Trigonometric identities.

"Identity" ... That reminds me.

I set my homework page aside and carefully unfold Kaya's paper from my pocket. As I scan it over, I realize that this test I'm stressing over is something I can pray about. After all, one of the main reasons I began this spiritual journey to begin with was so I could enjoy having a 'helper'.

But then I frown.

I haven't done well on this 'spiritual journey'. Just four days ago, I messed up. I undid all my hard work in striving for abstinence. Would God even help me if I asked now? Perhaps Claire is so busy all of the sudden *because* of how I messed up. She seemed to appear out of the blue when I'd suggested abstaining to Adam, and then when I gave in, she altogether disappeared.

These things that God says about my identity through Christ ... These things are for people who are giving their *all* to loving

God and obeying his commandments. How could I be 'giving my all' if I was so quick to give in?

That's not true, I hear Kaya's voice saying, *God is looking for people who are genuinely doing their* best. *His promises are for* them.

A memory scripture comes to mind from when I was a little girl. I remember I had lied to my dad about a Hershey's bar I swiped from the store. At the end of the day, he asked me if there was anything I wanted to tell him. Now, in my adulthood, it's clear that he knew the whole time what I'd done — but I'd already eaten the candy, so I shook my head. Ten minutes later, eaten up by guilt, I came forward and told him what I did. He just shook his head and asked me if that was the right thing to do. I shook my head again, and said I was sorry.

He asked me how I was gonna make it right, since stealing is a sin. I asked him if he would drive me back to the store so that I could pay for it. He agreed, but he also said that I needed to apologize to God. The scripture he gave me was 1st John 1:9, which says,

If we confess our sins, he is faithful and just to forgive us our sins, and to cleanse us from all unrighteousness.

"If you do that, Lacey Lue," He said, using his special nickname for me, "You can start all over like it never happened. Just remember to do better next time."

God probably liked me a lot better when I was little. My heart was so pure. But the memory reminds me of what I need to do now. Then I can start trying my best again, and He'll come when I need him. My identity in Christ will be true.

I set down the paper and sit on my knees.

Lord, you know what happened. You saw.

I bow my head.

I don't want to be someone you're disappointed in. I'm sorry for what happened. I need your strength to keep this up for seven more months. To you, that's just a blip in time, but for me, it feels like forever. I've become reliant on and attached to a sin. I'm asking you to cleanse me from it – purify me – so that I may start my efforts again. Give me the words to talk to Adam about it, so that we both *might make you proud.*

Just then, I remember something Kaya read in A&B last week. It was in James ... but where in James? Chapter 4, maybe? I locate my Bible and turn there. I scan the page for what I'm looking for, and my lips part as I find it in verses 6-8:

He gives us more grace. That is why scripture says: "God opposes the proud but shows favor to the humble. Submit yourselves, then, to God. Resist the devil, and he will flee from you. Come near to God and he will come near to you. Wash your hands, you sinners, and purify your hearts, you double-minded.

Then in verse ten, it says,

Humble yourselves before the Lord, and he will lift you up.

I place a hand on my heart, which is beating fast.

Thud. Thud. Thud.

God just replied to me. He literally just spoke words into my life. Hopeful ones ... approving ones.

I jump when the door opens, snapping me out of my Jesus moment. Adam appears.

"Hey, lovely," He says, eyeing the Bible in my lap, "What're you doing?"

"Nothing," I say quickly, "I mean, that's not true. Studying. What are you doing here?"

He looks puzzled, "Coming to see you? It's been four whole days. I've missed you."

"Oh, right," I say, combing a hand through my hair.

He laughs, "'Oh right'? Did you not miss *me?*"

"Of course I did," I go over and wrap my arms around his torso, "Sorry,"

He pulls me back to look at him, and shakes his head with a handsome smile, "It's like you think I don't know you. What's wrong, Lacey Rae?"

I look up at him and take a deep breath. It's time for the 'make it right' part …

"Adam, I want to talk about what happened …"

He looks past me and at the Bible I left on the table, "I thought you might."

"I'm not blaming you," I say quickly, "What happened was mostly my fault. I'm just trying to hold myself accountable … get back on track, you know?"

He sighs, pulling out a chair at the table, "Yes, Rae. I know."

Why do I feel like he's getting sick of this conversation?

"What's wrong?" I say.

"Nothing," He says, sitting. "This is just … interesting to me. I support it, I guess. I just … I don't know. I guess I just didn't expect this from you. You caught me completely off guard with this."

Oh no … please be willing, Adam.

"What do you mean, 'you didn't expect this from me'?"

"Well," He says, "When I met you, you weren't all into this stuff. The prayer and Bible reading. You … well … you'd been with a *couple* other people. I knew I wasn't marrying a straight-laced Sue."

I'm taken aback. I've only ever been with two other guys. Samuel, and although I'm not proud of it, someone I met at a club. It was a one-night stand during my nineteenth year, which

I regretted. But I never thought when I told Adam about it he'd throw it back in my face later.

"Well, Adam, that's really unfair of you to say, and quite frankly, pretty hurtful."

"I didn't mean it to be hurtful," He says.

"Well how'd you mean it then?"

He backtracks, "I don't know … I just … I don't …"

I wait while he tries to find his words.

He doesn't.

I think back to the conversation I had with Kaya.

If Adam isn't willing to do this with you, something that clearly means a lot to you. Is he someone you're willing to give up?

Am I willing to listen to God's leadership over my life, or am I making something else more important?

I sigh, "Look, Adam. I don't know how to tell you this. I don't *want* to tell you this."

A tear trickles down my face, "But if you can't be okay with doing this for my sake … if you place *that* much value on sex, that my feelings on it are overridden, then I don't see how we can … well … I don't think we should —"

His expression falls, "Don't, Rae. Please don't."

Another tear falls, "You're giving me no choice, Adam."

He stands, taking my face in his hands, "Listen to me, okay? Nothing, and I mean *nothing* is worth us fighting like this. We never have before, and we shouldn't start now."

At first I think he's talking about God. That He is not worth investing in if He's coming between us like this, but then, as an answer to my prayer, he clarifies:

"If it means that much to you, we will try to do it again. I just … want you to be happy."

I shake my head, feeling such relief, "Adam ... don't mistake me ... you *do* make me happy. And the things we do ... *God knows* I miss them. It's just that ... I've become reliant on them. I pretty much *depend* on you for my security. I'm trying to rewire my brain to not need it to *that* extent. I'm also not *just* doing this for religious reasons, but also because it'll take a load of pressure off of you — to *constantly* be reassuring me in that way."

He sighs, "Well I assure you, I don't mind."

This makes me chuckle. "I *know* you don't mind ... but Adam, damn it, I'm *really* trying to do things right with you." My smile drops, "I've made so many mistakes in the past ... as you so acutely pointed out. But I let myself make them because I didn't really care about those people or how we turned out. Not in the way I care about you. I want my *forever* partner to be someone God is rooting for me to have too. So that we can have the most successful marriage possible. It's because I love you ... *so* much."

He frowns, "I'm sorry I said those things earlier. About your past. I didn't mean for it to sound the way it did."

I give him a half smile, "I forgive you. I just ... don't think you understand how hard it is for *me* too. I'm not just trying to take something from you or change who I am on you last minute. I think the *truth* is that this is who I've been the whole time. I've just been lost in the chaos of everything, and recently rediscovered myself."

He's still frowning as he plays with a lock of my hair, twisting it between his index and thumb.

"Is that ... something that you can accept?" I say, praying with each word, "Going forward, knowing that this is me?"

He is silent for two agonizing minutes, searching my face and considering. I know he won't speak unless he really means it, because that's who *he* is.

"Rae... I love you," He starts slowly.

My heart beats loudly, preparing to be hurt.

"I think it'd be ignorant of me to assume that you'll never make changes in your life, especially ones that you feel will be edifying. Because the one thing about you that has never changed — one of your *core* principles -—is that you're constantly striving to be a better version of yourself."

He closes the space between us, "And I love that about you. You *will* achieve greatness in this life, and I want to be a part of that. Forever."

Fresh tears pour down my cheeks, and my face crumples into his chest. I stay there for a few minutes, ugly crying while he holds me. I'd been holding them in — pent up emotions in preparation for whatever he might say. Now that I have my answer, the barrier that'd been holding everything back breaks.

He strokes my hair while I shudder into his chest, breathing in his comforting spiced scent. I feel so loved and accepted.

"Thank you, Adam," I say, steadying my breath as we pull away, "I don't think it'll be easy for either of us... but I *do* feel like we can do it, especially if we're *both* striving for it."

Adam exhales through his nose, "All I can promise you is trying my best. This religion thing — I support you in it ... but it's just not something I'm ready to delve back into right now. I respect your wishes for us and your goals, and I will try to give you everything I can ... but it's more about that for me than it is religion right now."

I nod, understanding that it's fair. I can't expect Adam to experience conviction at the same time I do, since it's such a personal thing. As Adam pointed out, life is full of seasons — we make many changes throughout life. He may not stay in this season of unfaith forever, but I can't rush his process. His willingness to respect and cherish me is more than enough right now.

"Adam," I say, my voice strong and my heart full of love, "All I ever want from you is your best."

Maybe someday, we'll talk about how that's all God ever wants from him too. I'll get to share with him what I've learned and watch him grow.

He kisses my cheek, sweetly, "I love you, Lacey Rae."

I smile, "I love *you,* Adam Compton."

* * *

After our conversation, I wanted nothing more than to snuggle up in a pile of blankets and watch a movie with him. Something mindless that I don't have to think much about. But I realize, with a frown, that I need to spend every spare minute studying ... gaining *some* understanding for this upcoming test.

I also don't want to tell Adam to just go home after all that, and deep down, I *know* he can help me with the homework, But I feel a strong need to hide my math struggles from him. He's going to think I'm so inept.

"Something's still wrong?" He says at the expression on my face.

I look up at him, thinking of the scriptures I read earlier on pride. At that moment, they'd been reassuring me that God was pleased that I humbled myself before him and confessed my sin. It was Him saying He'd lift me up for it ... but could he really be pleased at my humility if I was being prideful about something right now? Maybe *Adam* is the answer to my prayer for help, and I just have to swallow my pride to see it.

"I ... well, I'm *really* stressing out about a test I have coming up in two days."

"Yeah?" He says, "What subject?"

I hesitate. I could get out of this right now - say some subject I'm great at. But I don't. That's not what this is about.

"Trigonometry," I say.

His face lights up, "Oh, trig is fun!"

"No it is not," I whine, "Trig is the devil."

He laughs, "Good grief, Rae, it's not that bad. Go get your stuff and I'll help you."

I sigh, bringing Adam my red-inked stack of papers. I don't want to show him, but I have to.

"I just ... have *no* passion for this subject." I say, defensive already, "It has nothing to do with my degree."

He considers this for a moment as he looks over the papers. If he's shocked at my inability, he gives nothing away.

"Really though, you don't *have* to be passionate about this specific subject," He says, "You just have to want the end goal badly enough. Your passion for that should drive you to make it through the shitty parts of the process."

I smile at that. He's not wrong.

He continues to look over the papers, and just knowing his mathematical eyes are instantly finding every error I've made is intimidating.

"Look," I say, "I'm gonna be real with you. I didn't want to show you this ... I don't want you thinking I'm ... I don't know ... incompetent."

His eyes find mine, and they are smiling, "Incompetent? Rae ... come on. I know there are plenty of things you're good at. Math just ... isn't one of them. And that's okay."

I laugh genuinely, "My skills are meant to *complement* yours, right? Not compete with them."

"Exactly," He smiles, reviewing the paper one last time.

I already feel better about showing him. If he can accept my strange new goals, why wouldn't he accept my struggle with math?

After he gets an idea of what we're learning in class, we sit down and work slowly, page by page, until I start to understand a little.

Adam doesn't look at me like he loves me any less than before. Instead he goes full-on teacher mode, explaining multiple different ways of solving things and letting me in on little tricks. The whole time, he's so enthusiastic. Enthralled in his favorite subject, and I can't help but smile. I'm out of my element, but he's totally in his, and I don't regret asking for his help. I find myself amazed that he could teach me in three hours what my professor couldn't teach me in two months.

35

Grace - Tuesday

Okay, I'm settling this once and for all.

I go over to my bookshelf and pull out a notebook.

I lay it flat on my desk and poise my pen.

Let's see ... *I* went up to *him* in the beginning with the cinnamon buns. That was *my* effort. Then *he* invited me to dinner. So that was *his* effort.

But neither of those things really count, do they? Because neither of those efforts were made out of genuine interest for each other. I just wanted some cinnamon buns, and he just wanted to clear his name.

I scribble those two out on my page.

Okay, after that ... I made the decision to actually *go* to dinner at his parents house, so that counts as my effort. Then, *he* made the decision to show up at yoga, just to find me, so that definitely was *his* effort. After that, *I* decided to extend our day together and invited myself along to the maple festival (maybe a little too much effort on my part). But then, *he* invited me *back* to his house to potentially fix my nanny cam — so where does that leave us? I hold up my list and squint at it:

My Effort	**His Effort**
~~Cinnamon Buns~~	~~Dinner Invite~~
Dinner Acceptance	Yoga
Maple Festival	Nanny Cam

I groan. We are dead even.

I've been trying to weigh this all afternoon, determined to figure out if Liam likes me or not. It certainly *seems* that way, but I could just be overthinking it.

For as long as I can remember, making comparison lists has been my way of having order. Seeing my thoughts put into charts on paper usually helps me make sense of things, but *this* comparison list is just frustrating. How is it that our efforts have been completely equal? Does that mean we're both giving off vibes that we're interested?

Like clockwork, my alarm goes off at 4:30 with the description: "Liam's House?"

I sigh. If I go, that'll be one more 'effort' to write down on my side of the columns. But if I don't, we're both still stuck in this awful "equal" cycle.

I go into the art room, grab my nanny cam from its place, then my keys from their hook by the door.

Just this one last effort on my part — I decide. After this, if he invites me to do something else with him, that'll settle it. He likes me. From there, I'll decide what to do.

***

I feel a mild sense of déjà vu as the gravel crunches beneath my tires. Liam's car is not parked in front of his house, so I pull out my phone and shoot him a text.

Sent: 10/15/19

Time: 5:01 pm

"Sooo... you comin'? I'm here. Nanny cam in-hand."

I wait a few minutes, but no reply, so I unbuckle my seatbelt and head up his parents' porch. I knock, and in just moments Dhara opens the door. Her face lights up when she sees me.

"Hey, Dhara,"

"Grace!" She says in her gentle way, "What a lovely surprise!"

"Oh no, Liam didn't tell you I was coming? I hope I'm not intruding."

"Nonsense!" She steps aside, "Come in."

I do, and am instantly greeted by a delicious smell — something savory cooking in the kitchen.

"What are you making? It smells delicious,"

"Thank you," She says, "It's called Rajma. Perfect for a cold night like this."

She opens the lid of the pot for me to see. From what I can tell, it's mostly beans swirling in a thick gravy of some kind, and she's got a pot of rice on the stove as well — the ultimate Indian comfort food.

"It's not quite ready yet, but how about a cup of tea while we wait?" She says, "You do like tea, don't you?"

"I love tea," I brighten, following her to the pantry, "Sometimes I make blends of different kinds for my clients ..."

I stop short when I see a wall of apothecary jars that'd put my tea collection to shame. Each jar is sealed with cork and has been meticulously labeled.

"Oh my ..." I say, lips parted.

Dhara laughs, "My husband tells me it's a bit much, so I'm glad someone appreciates it."

"Are you kidding?" I say, brushing my fingers over several jars, "This is exactly enough – one of everything!"

"Not quite," She smiles, "But I'm getting there. What would you like?"

I feel like a kid in a candy store.

"I'm a sucker for Tulsi tea, but I hardly ever have any. Do you think that'd be good with rosehips and hibiscus?"

"I think that'd be a lovely combination," Dhara says, selecting the jars, "In fact, I think I'll have a cup of the same thing. Sounds quite tranquil."

As she combines and expertly steeps the tea, the front door opens and Brent appears.

"Mmm, something smells good in here!" He inhales deeply.

Dhara spins around at his voice and runs over to embrace him. He kisses her sweetly, massaging his fingers down her spine. Their love for each other is so evident, but I'm not used to seeing that ... from like, anyone, really. I blush and check my phone, which has a text from Liam.

Sent: 10/15/19

Time: 5:31 pm

"Way to let a man know lol. Last I knew you were 'thinking' about it. On my way over now – sorry."

Oh. I guess that *is* what I left him with.

"Is that Grace I see?" Brent says, smiling widely.

"Hey," I smile back.

He opens his arms for a hug like we're old friends. I find the gesture endearing, but I'm positive my body is stiff when I receive the hug. How strange it is to be hugged by a man who is twice my age who has no intentions towards me ... just genuine, fatherly-friendship.

"We were just about to have a cup of tea while we wait on dinner," Dhara says to her husband, "Would you like a cup?"

"None for me, *Shahad,* but you two go right ahead."

She smiles profusely at the word he had called her — I suppose it's a Hindi term of endearment.

The tea is steeped perfectly now, and Dhara goes over to pour us a cup.

"You guys make such a great couple," I say after Brent leaves, "I'm so happy for you two."

Dhara smiles, handing me a cup, "Brent has always been very good to me. I'm so lucky to have found him. Well, he found *me* really."

"Liam was telling me about that," I say, blowing the steam from my tea. "Brent was in the Peace Corps?"

"Yes," she says, taking a seat, "Brent was working closely with my family. My *Pita,* or 'father' as we say here in America, had just passed away. So my *Ma,* myself, and my two sisters were trying to make life work on our own. Each one of us are artisans and crafters. We would work together to make jewelry, pots, and clothing, and then sell them in the marketplace. But when Brent came along, he gave us the opportunity to learn how to be teachers. My two sisters loved learning, but I never found my passion for teaching the way they did. I wanted to keep creating art. *Ma* and I could tell that Brent took a special interest in me for some reason. He would teach me different things and tell me about

America in a way he didn't with the other two. Long story short, after spending a year together, we fell in love and agreed to be married. He loved my art and told me that I would be free to keep creating it with him in America. From there, it was just a matter of legal formalities. My sisters stayed and taught at the new school that was built in my town, but my *Ma* wanted to leave too. Staying there reminded her too much of our *Pita*."

"Wow," I say, "So she came with you?"

"Well," she says, "Becoming a legal citizen was a long process for myself, and it was even longer for Ma, but it's all sorted now. I'm grateful we're together."

"That's an incredible story," I smile, "I bet you miss your sisters sometimes though."

"Yes," she says, "But I know they're happy. They write often."

A gust of cold air seeps in as the door opens and Liam hurries in. My heart thuds.

"Hey," He smiles at us, "I'm really sorry, but something came up with a buddy of mine last minute and I'm gonna have to hurry off again. I should have enough time to fix your nanny cam, though, if you can tell me where it is."

"Oh," I say, "It's in my car."

"Great," He says, reopening the door, "I'll be right back then."

Dhara chuckles from the doorway, "That crazy child of mine. Always on the move."

I smile down at my tea, swallowing my disappointment. I guess we're having dinner without him.

"So what does Brent do now that he's not in the Peace Corps?" I say.

Dhara smiles, "When Brent's parents passed, he inherited this land and his family's business. Both things have been a huge blessing because they've allowed us to adopt our two children."

I nod, considering my baby, "I really love that you guys chose to do that."

Dhara shakes her head, "Honestly, Liam very much chose *us.* In fact, I — well … I don't know if he'd appreciate me showing you this … but I'm going to anyway." She winks.

She pulls out her phone and begins to type something in. I see that it's a website for a children's home. She taps a section labeled "Archives – I've been adopted!"

Under that section are about thirty "introductory videos" of children, and she scrolls until she finds an adorable little boy with brown hair and too-big-for-him glasses. It's titled: Liam.

She taps the video and hands it to me, and suddenly the little boy comes to life.

"Hi Liam," An adult woman says.

"Hi!" He says back in a tiny, enthusiastic voice.

"Oh my …" I say, covering my mouth. I almost can't take the cuteness.

"What's your favorite color, Liam?" The woman says.

"Ummm," He ponders, unable to sit still, "Red. But I like cars better than red."

"Nice," the woman says encouragingly, "And what would you like to have in a potential family?"

The adorable little boy is quiet. He looks confused.

"Would you like a mommy, a daddy, or both?" The woman clarifies.

"Oh! Both!! And maybe a sister." He says, pushing his glasses closer to his face.

I stop the video there, feeling utterly in love with this child, but also feeling slightly intrusive of Liam's personal life.

"When we saw that, we knew," Dhara says, taking the phone with a smile. "We'd been wanting a little boy to complete our clan, and there he was."

"He's unbelievably precious," I say. "I had no idea he wore glasses."

"I wish he still would," Dhara says, stirring the Rajma, "He still has a pair I think but he prefers his contacts now."

I gently place my cup in the sink as the door opens again.

Liam enters with my nanny cam and strides over to me.

"Should be fixed," He smiles, "Simple wiring issue."

"Wow," I say, trying not to imagine him with too-big glasses, "I've been dealing with that error code for so long now, and it was that simple? Thank you so much!"

He shrugs, "Not a problem."

"Liam, *mera beta,* will you at least have some dinner before you go?"

"I'd love some," Liam says kissing her cheek, "But it'll have to wait until I get back. My buddy's car is in a ditch and he needs help pulling it out."

Dhara looks concerned, "If you're taking the truck, please be careful."

"I will, mom," He smiles at her, charming as ever. Then he turns to me, his handsome face apologetic, "I'm sorry about this. Let's do a rain check. What are you doing Thursday morning?"

My heart plummets. There it is ... the fourth "effort" on his part. That makes us even once again. This alluring man *does* like me.

"Oh, um, I'm not sure yet," I say, "Can I let you know closer to time?"

He smiles, "As long as you actually *do* let me know this time."

"Sorry," I blush, "I thought I had ..."

"Don't worry about it," He affirms, "I'll see you later."

With that, he grabs his keys and heads for the door.

I look down at the nanny cam in my hands as Dhara calls the rest of the family into the dining room.

"Hey Nanni," I say, giving her a hug, "Hey Sakura."

Sakura smiles, "Hey."

We all pile around the table with piping hot bowls of Rajma over rice. The food is abundant and the chatter is bountiful. The conversation flows with ease, as if these people have known me forever. Although I am participating in it, it's also as though I'm watching it happen from afar: Brent jokes with me, Sakura laughs at something Nanni said, Dhara is beaming with joy at her family around the dinner table, and the whole thing has its own, special kind of beauty. It is foreign, yet comforting, to see a *whole* loving family gathered around a table for dinner — one that has two parents ... a mom *and* a dad. To add to that beauty, these people are really a family by *choice* rather than by blood. They *choose* to be together, to love each other, and accept their differences.

It makes me think of my own mother and the life we had together. No round table discussions ... no heart-to-heart talks about life ... no loving father figure to speak of. I've never even experienced that with Rae's family, since her dad is constantly doing military work. It all makes me wonder if maybe Liam was right. Maybe I *should* reach out to my mom. I doubt we could come close to having what this family does ... but we won't even scratch the surface if I don't try.

36

Rae - Wednesday

I hurry into the doors of the A&B building.

I'm late and it's already started, but Grace waves me over to the empty seat next to her, my mom, and sister.

"What did I miss?" I whisper to her.

Grace holds a paper in her hands.

"Kaya passed out these little home Bible-study sheets. It's on someone named Job in the Bible," She whispers back.

"Ladies," Kaya says, "I want you to raise a hand, if you've *ever* felt like the devil is just picking away at you slowly, whether it's a string of little annoying things, a couple of really big things, or maybe even a mixture of both?"

Grace leans over and whispers, "Can I raise both hands?"

I laugh under my breath and throw my hand up with her.

"Nice," Kaya nods, "Now everyone look around the room and notice that every. single. person. has a hand up."

It's true.

We've multiplied in numbers over the month, so now there are about eighty women in the room, each with a hand up.

Kaya's expression goes sad, "So why aren't we *talking* about this, you guys? Look at all the collective knowledge in this room. All the experiences that are so different, but so similar. If only each of us understood that we could be the source of inspiration for another girl … her reason to keep going, and to feel like she's not alone."

"It's important that we're transparent with each other. It's how we grow and develop into our full potential in Christ." She says, and I feel like she's talking directly to me. Praising me even, without calling me out, for our discussion last week.

"I'm pretty open with you guys about my life," She continues, "Most of you know that I lost my parents too soon … that I've struggled with my earthly relationships … and that most recently, I've been diagnosed with cancer."

"But let me tell you how I'm feeling about all of those things. I'm feeling *honored.* Not because it doesn't suck … it absolutely does, and sometimes it's *hard*. But I want you to consider this: For Satan to be attacking you so hard, just one thing after another, he must see you as a pretty threatening target."

She pauses for us to fully consider what she said.

"By 'threatening target', I mean someone who is growing in their faith … someone who is threatening the risk of *spreading* their faith with others and the joy it brings. And boy, does that scare Satan. Satan *will* do everything in his power to keep you from doing that. Because we all know his goal: to make sure no one knows the joy of the Lord."

Several people nod in agreement.

"So if discouraging you and tearing you down with hit after hit is the quickest way to quiet you down about the Lord, or worse, make you feel like God isn't as present in your life or as gracious and loving as you thought, you can *bet* Satan is going to do just that. His attacks will come in the most personal, most intimate ways possible. And throughout those attacks, we have to remember that *God* has enough faith in *us* to say to Satan, "*My* beautiful daughter isn't going to give in. Try what you will, but she loves me, and she will be strong even through your attacks."

I think of the story in the book of Job ... a perfect example of what she's saying.

"God even gives us the gift of extra strength throughout these trials so that we are able to combat Satan. The key is, we just have to know how to access it and utilize it ... and how do we do that?"

She pauses.

"Through fervent prayers, so that God can step forward and fight these battles for us."

My pen is flying as I write in my notebook.

"The quickest way to discouragement is when we try to do it all on our own. When we don't draw from the extra bits of strength God is gifting us with — we give up on asking God for it, and as a result, we end up battling Satan all on our *own*. Well, my friends, we're merely humans. Satan is a *divine force* ... and it takes one divine force to combat another. We *need* to give it to God."

She takes a seat, "So next time you feel like it's just one thing after another ... I challenge you to alter your way of thinking. Feel *honored* that you have grown to be a spiritual threat. Feel *honored* that God has placed his faith right back in *you*, and told Satan about his confidence in *you*. But most of all, please don't give up ... pain and suffering are amazing instruments of growth. If you're going through something, your character is being beautifully refined in how you choose to handle it. When it's all said and done, you'll be left with a story that'll inspire others. That'll help them keep going. *But,"* she smiles, "You *have* to *share* those stories in order for that last part to be effective. So now, before you go, I'd like to encourage you to be transparent with each other. *Ask* one another what's going on in life, and, here's the clincher, *actually share* what's going on. I don't want to hear any 'I'm fine, how 'bout you' being exchanged in this room."

We laugh and Kaya dismisses the session.

I turn towards Grace, "I feel like that spoke straight into my soul,"

"No kidding," She says, eyes wide, "The part about Satan slowly picking away at you? That was ridiculously relevant."

I frown, "Update me, boo. What's going on?"

She sighs, "I have a huge update, but I don't think I can cover it all here."

"Listen," I smile, "I'm thinking after I take this test tomorrow, you and I need to just *go* somewhere. Take some time away — a couple days, to just talk, catch up, and relax for once."

She nods, "I hope you're serious, because I'm all in. I need a vacation."

"Fall break slash early bachelorette trip, you feel me?" I wink.

"Hell yeah," she laughs, gesturing to her stomach, "Before I get large."

I give her a shove, lowering my voice, "Stop — baby bumps are adorable, and you know it."

She giggles.

"Ladies," Kaya comes up to us, gathering both of us in a squeeze.

"Kaya," Grace says, taking her hand, "I had no idea you've been dealing with cancer. I'm sorry to hear that."

Kaya winks, "It's alright. I'm honored, remember? Actually, I came over here to give you guys an update since I know Rae's been praying. I have an appointment to get all the cancer removed in a few months. I'm asking people to pray for the procedure, because if all goes well, this trial will be a thing of the past for me."

"Absolutely, that's amazing news." I say.

"It's going to go perfectly," Grace smiles.

Kaya smiles back at Grace, "I also wanted to check in and see how your situation is going ... the one we prayed about."

"Oh goodness," Grace sighs, "It's been a rollercoaster. The conversation we prayed about went beautifully, but now I've got a whole new set of problems to worry about. Much bigger than emotional conflicts."

"Oh no," Kaya frowns, "Well how can we change our prayer for you this week?"

Grace shoves her hands in her pockets, clearly debating. She looks at me, and I know she's wondering if she should give this "transparency" thing a try. I nod encouragingly.

"Well," she starts, "I actually found out this week that I'm pregnant. With my ex's baby. And he is 100% not interested."

Kaya's lips part, her expression one of concern, "Oh, Grace ..."

The two of them break off into the far end of the corner and after a few details are exchanged, Kaya begins praying for her. I can see tears on Grace's cheeks.

"Lacey," My mom says, turning my attention to her.

"Hey mom," I smile back.

"How are you, honey? I heard from your father yesterday. He said he's going to try his hardest to be at your wedding, but you know how it is. He never knows ..."

"I know," I say, "Let him know it's okay if he can't."

Mom smiles at me, placing an affectionate hand on my cheek, "You're a good girl."

***

From: Adam

Sent: 10/16/19

Time: 7:23 pm

"When your Bible study group is over, come to the pizzeria – I've already got us a table. I have to tell you something."

I bite my lip as I pull up to the pizzeria. His tone was so serious, I worry something is wrong.

Has he decided he can't accept my goals for abstinence? That he doesn't think I'm worth it after all?

My worries melt when I see him at our corner table, smiling at me.

"Hey gorgeous," He says when I approach.

A steaming hot plate of our favorite dish is waiting for me.

"What's all this about?" I say, sliding in next to him, "Don't make me wait anymore."

He shrugs, "I just want you to know I met with Sam today."

"Sam?" I say, not fully registering. Then I almost spit my drink, "Ross?"

"Yeah."

"What? Why? Or *how?"*

"I ran into him in town," He says. "Recognized him from your profile picture a few years back. Decided to introduce myself."

Oh no.

'Introduce himself' how? With his fists?

My face must convey my horror because Adam laughs.

"Oh my goodness, Rae, relax. We just talked. Decided to get a coffee. He's a cool dude."

I stare at him for a few minutes, "He's a cool dude?"

"Yeah," He nods, "We're cool."

"You're … cool? Just like that …"

"Yeah," Adam shrugs, "I like him. He's coming to our wedding since you asked Rosie to be a bridesmaid."

I pause, unable to process. All that drama, and then, "we're cool"? Men are so weird. I decide to just accept it for what it is and be grateful.

"Did you meet her too?" I ask.

"No, just Sam today. Apparently he's into rock climbing like we are. Been to a lot of places we've been."

I knew that about Sam, but I say nothing.

I simply smile at my husband-to-be as he tells me about his day, feeling blessed.

37

Grace - Thursday

She's not home, but I'm not surprised.

I expected to spend a few hours here on my own, especially since I showed up unannounced.

I smile when the floor creaks in familiar places on the way to her bedroom. I remember when I was younger, I'd crawl into her bed at night when she wasn't home and breathe in her lovely scent. I'd snuggle in her blankets and pretend she was holding me. Then it always felt like magic in the morning when I woke up in my own bed — a nice fairy must have transported me there in the night.

I push open her bedroom door and crawl into her unmade bed. I wrap her soft, blue blankets around me and hold her pillow close, breathing in vanilla mint. I don't know why I've always found her scent joy-inspiring; I don't really associate it with a happy memory. I guess now I just associate it with childhood. A simpler time.

If I send her a text, she'll ignore it.

I call her instead.

"Corinne," she answers.

"Hey mom,"

"Grace?"

"Yeah," I smile, because *who else?*

"Are you okay?"

"Yeah, I'm okay. I'm at the house."

"The house?"

"Our house." I say.

"Oh. You *are?*"

"Yeah," I laugh.

She's silent.

"Come home, mama."

"Grace … I'm … I'm right in the middle of –"

"I wanna see you," I say, "Please?"

She sighs, sounding a bit flustered, "Baby, I can't just … I've got to …"

I wait.

"Oh, screw it. I'm coming, Grace. Give me about an hour."

She hangs up the phone in that abrupt way of hers, but then again, she's never taken off work for me before. Maybe she only is now because I caught her off guard, but whatever the reason, for now, I am grateful.

I suppose it is a collection of things that really drove me to come here today. Between Liam's prodding, his beautiful family, and last night's A&B session, I couldn't justify doing anything else with my day. My talk with Kaya had gone in a different direction than I thought it would. We ended up talking long after everyone left, and I admitted something to her that I really don't think I'd admitted to myself yet:

"I think I'm struggling to forgive them both," I told her, speaking of Jayden and my mother, "I never really thought that was an issue for me until someone suggested making amends with her after all these years, and the animosity that I felt … the pure attitude of 'why should I', surprised me."

"Right," Kaya nodded with understanding, "Because it didn't feel like yourself."

"Exactly," I said, "I have always, *always* been a peacemaker. Never resentful like that."

"That's because it *isn't you,*" She says. "While I do believe — given your circumstances — that your feelings are valid, you *yourself* are not a resentful person. That's all Satan … trying to make those emotions feel natural."

I nodded, feeling frustrated, "I feel like he's making it so difficult for me. Forgiveness is, like, a core value of mine. Why is it so hard to move on *this* time?

Kaya's expression softened, "Forgiveness is hard. Plain and simple. The most important command God gives us is to love one another. And personally, I've always thought the second most important thing is to forgive one another. Of course, the quickest way Satan can keep us from doing those things is by getting us to harbor a grudge. But take religion entirely out of it for a moment. Even if you're not concerned with being forgiven by God or anything like that, simply forgiving someone is really one of the greatest kindnesses you can give *yourself.* Holding a grudge allows that person to continue *taking* from you … your joy, your good mood, you name it. You spend precious time focused on what they've robbed you of, whereas forgiving them allows your mind to take a step back and *heal.* You don't have to be their best friend after you've forgiven them, but at least you've taken *back* your freedom to feel joyful rather than dwell on *them.*"

I nodded, agreeing whole heartedly with her words.

"In the case of your mother, though," she continued, "Man ... I don't know, Grace. Forgiving and then cutting out an ex-boyfriend is one thing, but ... your *mother* is another. I guess ... I just really wish I'd gotten the chance to make things right with *my* mom before she died."

That's what really moved me to make the drive. My mom and I may have never had a connection, but if she were taken from me tomorrow? What sort of regrets would I have? What kind of relationship could we *potentially* have if we just put everything behind us and agreed to start over?

***

"I would carry you to bed, but you're all grown up now," My mother says from the doorway.

I don't remember falling asleep, but her voice is what I wake up to.

I sit up from where I lay and smile at her. She stares back at me with an unfamiliar expression of sadness. It's subtle, but it's there.

She places her hand on her heart with a heavy breath.

"I used to believe a fairy magically took me to bed each night," I say, "Some kind, distant relative of the tooth fairy."

I also used to think that maybe you *were a fairy, and that's why I didn't see you much.* It all added up in my six-year old mind ... my mother's delicate beauty, her limited contact with me ... a human.

I pat the bed next to me. She hangs up her coat and joins me.

"What's this all about? Is everything okay?"

I shrug, not sure how to start, "Yeah, everything's fine."

"And you're feeling alright? Kim told me you had your first prenatal exam."

I nod, remembering the sonogram in my pocket, "You can't really see much yet, but here it is."

She looks over the picture, and something in her expression shifts, "I remember when I got mine, and you were nothing but a little speck."

I soften, taking a deep breath, "Were you scared?"

With her eyes glued to the picture, she whispers, "I was terrified."

I wait for her to continue.

"My mother … Your Grandma Jackie … She was very hard on me. When I got up the nerve to tell her what happened, she suddenly became super involved in my life, and not in a good way. Told me who I could and couldn't hang out with, monitored my phone, and instilled a strict curfew. She never for a moment let me consider not having you, saying things like 'If you think you're old enough to make adult decisions like that, you're old enough to deal with the consequences'. Not to say that I didn't want to have you myself … from the moment I first saw your little face … or I guess the outline of it on the sonogram, I knew I *had* to be your mom. It's just that I was scared—terrified, really—that I wouldn't make a good mother so young. Especially when I was still under my *own* mother's roof … her rules. Trying to raise a child when you have *zero* independence of your own …"

She shakes her head, and a tear streaks down her cheek. It surprises me. I've never heard her say any of this before.

"I promised myself I'd never do that to you," she says, "That you would have the freedom to make your own decisions. But after your last visit … after you said those things … I'm afraid all I've ever done is hurt you with that mindset. I'd been trying to give you something your grandmother *never* gave me, but instead I deprived you of a basic need. I'm just ... so sorry, Grace."

Shocked as I am, I wrap my arms around her. Salty tears streak down my own face.

"Mom, I forgive you. You were doing what you thought was best for me."

"My beautiful baby girl," Her lips quiver, "My Gracelynn Brielle. I gave you the most beautiful name I could think of. It broke my *heart* leaving you in someone else's care each day, but working every shift I could get was the only way we could afford to move out. I knew your grandmother didn't deserve to pay for my decisions ... that it wasn't fair for her to support us forever."

She wipes the black drips from her cheeks, "When you came over and your test was positive, though this may be selfish of me, I felt an opportunity. A chance to be the mother I wish I'd had, who asks what *you* need instead of blowing up. But I also felt like what I'd been scared of all these years had come true: that I wasn't good enough a mother to keep you from repeating my mistakes. It's not because raising you wasn't a delight, but raising you on my *own* was *hard work,* and I missed so many precious moments. I didn't get to hear your first word, for example. Your caretaker, Tia, did."

My mother chokes, hardly able to get her words out, "And you know what it was? It was *her* name."

My heart sinks. I have very little memory of my old caretaker at the daycare, but I can imagine how devastating it would be for my child to recognize her before they ever recognized me.

"By the time I was finally making good enough money to spend some time with you ... you were all grown up, and as independent as I raised you to be. You didn't need me anymore. All I'd ever known at that point was how to work, so I immersed myself in it … a welcome distraction from all my miserable years of failing my mom and failing you."

"Mom," I shake my head, tears dripping, "We can put all that behind us. Forget what I needed then. What I need *now* is *you.* I've felt so alone and I'm *scared.* I need my mom."

She looks at me with red-rimmed eyes, her face a gracefully aged mirror of my own, "Gracelynn … I love you so much. I'm here for you baby. Whatever you need."

I smile, wiping a sleeve under my nose.

She wraps her arms around me and I melt into her chest. For the first time, I find not just joy, but genuine comfort in her vanilla mint scent.

38

Rae - Thursday

From: Grace

Sent: 10/17/19

Time: 7:54 am

"A little ocean therapy anyone? Available the day after tomorrow for booking ;)"

[Link - tap to view]

I tap the link attached to her message and am greeted with an adorable, bright little condo right on the beach of Ocean City, Maryland. I'm instantly enamored.

"Alright, class. Phones up!" Mr. Algray announces, jolting my attention.

Anxiety thuds through my chest as I tuck my phone away.

As the teacher passes out test papers, I force myself to repeat the formulas that I've learned in my head. Each time I feel doubtful that I've studied enough, I try to make the voice in my head louder that's repeating "You got this," over and over again.

Mr. Algray passes a page to me, and I stare down at it with blurred vision. For a moment, my mind won't process the complex problem before me. It only repeats, "Oh no, oh no, oh no."

But then, I force myself to concentrate and begin to dissect it, starting with what I *do* know.

To my surprise, when I do this, I slowly begin to recall information naturally. I hear Adam's voice in my head, explaining what the problem is, and my pencil flies accordingly.

Before long, I've solved each problem, amazed at what I just did. My brain hurts from remembering, but a strong sense of pride overrules it. I'm done. It's finally over.

With a smile, I march my paper to the front and place it lightly on Mr. Algray's desk. He gives me a nod and I head for the door, feeling almost *giddy.*

When I get to my car, feeling the freedom of fall break settle over me, I pull out my phone and flip through the pictures one more time: Brightly colored walls, cute little kitchen, ocean views, and affordable ... I nod with approval.

To: Grace

Sent: 10/17/19

Time: 8:42 am

"How fast can you pack?"

39

Grace - Thursday

My mother gives me one last squeeze before I head for my car.

"Can you call me when you get home? You forgot to the last time I asked."

I smile, "Yeah, mom, I can."

"I love you, baby. Be safe."

After our chat this morning, we turned on the TV to watch an episode of ANTM together and promptly fell asleep due to the sporadic tears.

Mom wasn't in bed still when I woke up, and I almost wondered if I'd dreamed it all. Then I worried that the heart-to-heart talk had freaked her out and she fled back to her safe place: Work.

But all my fears dissipated as she appeared in the doorway clad in sweats and bearing a huge bowl of fruit salad.

I smiled, sitting up in bed as she passed me a fork.

"I took the day off work," she said, stabbing a grape, "What do you want to do?"

I stared at her, completely unfamiliar with this version of mom, but happy that she's willing to try. I wanted to take baby steps in this new territory; rushing into spilling secrets to each other and giggling at some inside joke would be far too big a leap. I want our relationship to feel natural — not forced — so I picked something I know we both love.

"Why don't you read your book, mom? I brought my own."

She eyed a book on her dresser. It's the one I recognized from her post on Facebook over a month ago when she'd said she couldn't *wait* to finally read it. Yet there it sat, still wrapped in it's factory plastic.

"Is that what *you* want to do?" she said.

I nodded, "I just want to relax, honestly. I feel like I've lived a year in just three weeks."

At that, her face seemed to regain a little bit of it's youthful color.

We sat and chewed in silence, but it was a comfortable silence. It was nice simply enjoying each other's company and not feeling the need to force out a discussion. It's a strange little companionship we have, but it works for *us*.

Before I left, she assured me I would have financial help with the baby, and to not let that be a reason I consider not having him or her. I told her that wasn't necessary ... that I didn't want to burden her like that.

She shook her head, looking me squarely in the face, "You need to spend time with your baby, Grace. Trust me. Let them know how loved they are by you, because that doesn't have a price."

My face softened, wanting to cry all over again.

"Plus," she added, "I've never had a grandchild to spoil before. Don't take that away from me."

I shook my head, gave her a big squeeze, and felt the most relieved I have in a long time.

When I arrive home, I let mom know, then check the unread text from Rae. I smile when I read it, tapping the call button right away.

"Hey!" She says, upbeat as ever.

"I take it the test went well?"

"Nailed it," she says, "In the bag. Over."

"You go girl!"

She laughs, "So, how fast can you pack?"

"Are you for real?" I smile.

"Yes, Grace, I don't kid. We need some catch-up time, some R&R, and a bachelorette trip."

I laugh, "I guess I should get in some bikini time before I can't anymore."

"Oh please," she says, "None of that in our positivity bubble. You're going to be big, beautiful and nothing less. And I wanna see those bikinis all the more when you're rocking a bump."

I look over at my suitcase, smiling, "If you're paying, I'll go."

"Then I'm booking right now," she says, "We leave tomorrow morning."

40

Rae - Thursday

Flashbacks of high school flicker before my eyes as I wander through the halls of the school Adam teaches, but I shove the broken memories associated with my school years aside. That was then — this is *now,* and I'm growing every day.

I find Adam's classroom and peer in the rectangular window. My heart lifts when I see him in his element, somehow making high school math an enthusiastic endeavor.

It takes him about five minutes to glance over at me, only because about ten little faces found me first and continued to stare. When he sees me, I smile my biggest and offer a little wave. He smiles too as he excuses himself for a moment.

He steps out into the hall with me, shutting the door behind him.

"What's up? Everything okay?"

I'm practically bouncing, unable to remove my smile, "I couldn't wait to tell you. I did it, Adam. The test is over."

"And you feel good about it?" He smiles.

I nod enthusiastically.

He picks me up at the waist and spins me around, "I *knew* you could. I'm *so* proud of you."

"It's because of you," I say, "Without your help it would've been a lost cause."

He tucks a lock of hair behind my ear, "That's not true. You put in the hard work to retain it all. I didn't take the test for you."

I shrug, still smiling, "I'm sure the prayers didn't hurt anything either."

He smiles, "I'm sure they didn't."

An eruption of laughter fills the air suddenly from behind the classroom door.

Adam frowns, "I'd better go see what's going on."

"Okay," I chuckle.

He turns to go.

"Oh hey —" I say before he turns the handle, "Grace and I want to take a quick girls' trip to the beach. It'd be for a day or two and we want to leave tomorrow. You don't have anything planned for us, do you?"

He turns and smiles at me, "You know, your spontaneity is one of the first things that I fell for. You're good, baby girl. Have a fun time."

I give him a quick peck on the cheek and let him tend to his class.

As I turn on my heel, I allow the excitement of a road trip settle over me.

* * *

I send Grace a text, letting her know I'm picking her up at eight o'clock tomorrow, and then my manager to make adjustments to my work schedule. Then I begin my packing.

On this trip, I want to focus on feeling *good.* I decide right now that if I start to feel any insecurities creeping in, I'm going to pray about it and shove them from my mind completely. I also want to push myself to feel this way — good overall — without the use of any bracelets on my wrists. It will be difficult, but I'm ready to set this goal for myself ... to remember my identity in Christ and *it's* importance rather than my physical identity.

In the spirit of feeling good, I recall a pair of swim shorts that I absolutely love ... but *where* are they?

Living in Vermont, I don't pull out the swimsuits that often anyways ... but this particular pair of shorts is one I haven't seen in years. They're a beautiful olive green color, and with the luscious way they hug my hips, there's no way I would've gotten rid of them, so I begin my search; They've got to be *somewhere.*

Forty minutes later, with clothes strewn across my floor, I locate the shorts tucked in the back of my closet. *Victory.*

I pull them out from their place, but a shoe box topples out onto the floor along with it. It's contents spill onto the floor: Twenty or so pages of small, blocky handwriting.

When I realize what they are, I stop in my tracks.

My old love letters from Sam.

I slowly stoop down to pick one up.

"I hope there never comes a time that I'm not your everything the way you are mine. Lacey Rae Brooks, I –"

I stop reading, heat rising to my cheeks. It doesn't feel right.

Even to simply *see* words like that about me that aren't from Adam feels unnatural and wrong.

I eye the other pages on the floor. If Adam ever found these, how would he feel?

I shake my head, unwilling to risk it. I scoop them up and toss them in my suitcase along with a lighter, shooting Grace one last text before zipping my bag.

Sent: 10/18/19

Time: 2:03 pm

"Got any Jayden memorabilia to burn? I say we spare nothing."

41

Grace - Friday

Morning sunlight spills into our car, giving Rae and me the opportunity to pull out our sunglasses. I've dressed for comfort — a soft t-shirt and leggings with a flannel around my waist, and big, fabulous red sunglasses. Rae looks effortlessly, adorably athletic as always, wearing shorts, a fitted Nike tank, a snazzy pair of Ray-Ban, and to my surprise ... *no* bracelets. She doesn't mention it though, so neither do I.

We stopped in town to fill the gas tank and grab a road snack. And now with the essential "road-trip cappuccinos" in-hand (decaf for me), we're ready to *leave* Gevali.

We kiss it goodbye from our windows, hearts beating expectantly as the GPS says, "In nine hours, you will arrive at your destination: Ocean City, Maryland."

Rae smiles, rolling back the sunroof. With a swipe of her hand, she turns the volume on our music *way* up and throws a hand up in the outside wind.

I laugh, and it feels good. I throw up a hand with her and we belt the lyrics to Sheryl Crow's, *"Soak up the Sun"*.

We jam out for hours, nothing but shameless dancing, sun-soaked wind in our hair, and trying to sing louder than the volume of our music, which never quite happens despite our best efforts. When our voices are hoarse and ears ringing, we decide to take a break from music.

"Okay, now that we got that out of our systems," She says, breathless.

I laugh, "It was much needed."

Rae takes a swig of her water bottle, "So update me. Tell me all the things you wanted to tell me at A&B, but couldn't."

"Oh man," I sigh, "I feel like I had a lot to tell you then ... but even more has happened *since* then."

She smiles, "Well, we've got seven straight hours of time, so tell away."

I take a deep breath, "Okay, let's see ... I went to see my mom the day before yesterday."

"Yeah?" Her expression is empathetic.

"It wasn't bad actually," I say, since we've both come to associate me seeing my mom with an unhappy Grace, "After some prodding from Kaya and ... a couple other people, I felt compelled to see if we could mend our relationship a little ... or rather begin to form one at all."

Rae looks unsure, "So what happened?"

"Well, I showed up at her house, but she wasn't there. So I called her and asked her to come home from work. She actually *did*."

Ray raises her brows.

"Right? Then we got to talking ... and the surprising part is, *she* pretty much led the conversation, which makes me think it must have been on her heart too. But before I could say anything about why I came, she was already apologizing for everything and giving me these thorough explanations for the decisions she made as a young mom."

"What?" Rae says, amazed, "She just delved in like that?"

"Well, I showed her the sonogram, and I guess seeing it reminded her of looking at *my* picture years ago. She apologized for being so absent ... explained that working all the time was really her only choice to support us. And by the time she didn't have to be so diligent, I was already grown and gone."

Rae frowns, "Oh my gosh, that's really kind of sad."

"I know right? She was *crying*, Rae. I have *never* seen my mother cry like that. So of course, being the emotional wreck you know and love, I started crying too and we had this big conversation about how it could be different from here on out. How I need her *now*, and we can put all that stuff behind us."

"You're kidding," Rae smiles, "Wow, I am *so* happy for you."

I shake my head, "I almost can't believe it ... I have a *mom* all of a sudden."

She shakes hers in disbelief, "God is so good … that's incredible. So how did this transpire? I understand Kaya, but who are these other people you said prodded you?"

"Wellllll," I say, "That's the rest of what I have to update you on. Big time."

She raises a brow.

"Do you … remember Liam?"

She squints "Liam?"

I nod, but she still doesn't know.

"From Aroma Mocha?"

It takes her a few more seconds, then her mouth drops, "Cinnamon bun guy??"

I laugh sheepishly, "Yesss ... cinnamon bun guy. His name is Liam Cross."

"Don't tell me you've been hanging out with *cinnamon bun* guy. Doesn't he have a girlfriend?"

I chuckle, "No, he doesn't. And that's actually a long, funny story too ..."

I go on to tell her about my snappy (righteous, at the time) phone call to him, getting stuck in a cab together on the way to Oakland, and spitefully accepting his dinner invitation just to prove I was right and he was wrong (about his own sister).

"It just sort of developed from there," I blush, "His family is just ... absolutely lovely. They're all so different but still so unified ... together by choice. It warmed me to see a fully functioning family where each member loves the other. And they were so welcoming to me, Rae."

I continue to gush about Liam's jewelry shop, how he's trilingual, how his mom loves tea, how his father is a Christian and Liam veers more towards his father's religion than his mother's, and the details of our unofficial "dates". I only realize that it sounds like I'm completely in love when Rae points it out with a skeptical eye.

"Dang, girl. You better be careful. The way you're braggin' on him makes you sound a little smitten."

"Smitten?" I say, flabbergasted, "Heavens *no.* Certainly not *smitten.*"

"You sure?" She says, "You're all red."

"Focus on the road," I smile, blushing all the more.

She chuckles, but after a few minutes her smile fades.

"Grace ... I love you. I want you to be happy ... but I really want you to tread lightly on this. You *just* broke up with Jayden ... and, well ..."

"I'm pregnant," I say for her, frowning.

She purses her lips, "How do you know he's the kind of guy to take that lightly? What if he's the hopelessly jealous type?"

I stare out my window, "I guess I don't..."

"It sounds like to me, before you proceed any further, a conversation needs to be had letting him in on that little detail."

"Well," I say defensively, "I *want* to tell him. I mean, it's not fair for me to keep doing whatever we're doing without telling him. I can't just have him over there thinking he's got a great thing going and that I'm totally available when I'm clearly a package deal. But what if I'm reading too much into this, and he's not even interested like that? I don't want to freak him out by all the sudden being like, 'Hey, I'm pregnant. Just so you know.' when he's not even into me. Then it'll be awkward forever."

Rae snorts at me, "Well, based off what you told me, it sounds like he's definitely interested. I don't think letting him know about the pregnancy is totally irrelevant at this point. I just ... want you to proceed with caution. Don't rush into anything."

I smile at her, "I mean, just to ease your conscience here, I'm not trying to instantly delve into a relationship or anything. To me, this conversation would be like ... a pre-*pre* dating step ... to see if we even *can* proceed with *maybe* liking each other. If he says he's not interested, I can just move on from this and quit obsessing. But if he's willing to give it a try ... knowing my baggage and all that I come with ... well, then there's *that.*"

Rae laughs, "There *is* that. I love you, you crazy, wild girl."

"*You're* one to talk," I say, jabbing her.

She flips on her turn signal and passes a car that doesn't know the "five miles over" rule.

"So," she says more seriously, "Have you had some time to think about what you're gonna do with ..."

She nods at my belly.

I frown, "Yeah … I have."

She waits for me to continue, "And?"

"Well," I say, sipping my almost-gone cappuccino, "I mentioned Liam and his sister are adopted and all that … but I didn't mention something Dhara showed me."

Rae waits as I type out the website on my phone. When it loads, I tap the *"I've Been Adopted!"* section and find Liam's video.

I pass it to her and she glances between the road and the video, her face falling as the adorable brown-haired, bespectacled boy showed the camera his favorite truck.

"His mom showed you this?"

"Yeah," I say, pausing the video "That scored him his adoption with the Crosses."

She holds a hand to her heart, "He was so precious."

"I know …" I say, "After I saw that video … I don't know, I just can't imagine seeing *my own* sweet baby in one of those videos, listing off his or her favorite things, trying to make them sound really good, so that maybe someone will adopt them. A family that'll love him for those favorite things."

Talking about it forms a lump in my throat, but I swallow it down.

"I also had the chance to talk to Liam and how he felt about his mother after the adoption. He has very little interest in her now. I just can't do it, Rae. I need to love my baby."

She nods, "And that's totally your call. It's yours, and I support you."

I take in a deep breath, feeling a surprising amount of relief after getting everything off my chest.

"How about we listen to some more music?" Rae says, cueing the radio, "I know was a *lot* to share, Now let's shake it all off and get ready for the beach."

I couldn't agree more. She cranks the volume and we jam for another couple hours.

42

Rae - Friday

"You have arrived," My GPS announces as I pull into our new address for the weekend. Excitement flutters in my heart.

The house is adorable on the outside with light blue paint, white shutters, potted plants spilling over the railing of the front patio, and a happy golden pineapple on the door to knock with.

We step out onto the pavement, stretch our legs, take one look at each other, and squeal, dashing into the house. The kitchen is just as adorable as the picture hinted, and the decor screams beach house, but the real showstopper is the *back* patio. The sliding glass door opens to a gorgeous beachscape. We can see, hear, and even feel the gentle mist from the North Atlantic.

After we have dinner and settle in, I step out onto the porch again and breathe in the salty air. Even though it's night, it's still warmer here than in Vermont. Stars sprinkle out over the calm ocean. It seems to be beckoning me toward it.

Grace steps out onto the porch too.

I glance at her, adventure in my gaze, "You up for a late-night walk?"

She perks up a little, "Always,"

I grab two apple ales from the cooler we brought and toss her one.

"Bring the stuff."

* * *

We stumble out onto the beach, laughing that Grace's flip-flops already broke. The soft sand hisses and shifts beneath our feet.

I carry my shoebox, while Grace carries a sizable shoulder bag filled with many more things — *four years* worth of things to be exact. The beach is vacant, which gives us no excuse to back out of our plan: Burn every. last. thing.

"Sand can't burn … can it?"

"No, silly," I affirm.

We walk a good half mile down the endless strip of beach.

When we reach a spot that *feels* right, we set our things down. I brought a lighter, but no sticks to start it with, so I wedge my entire shoebox into the sand and nod to Grace. She smiles and cues our music. Sean Kingston's *"Fire Burning"* echoes faintly down the beach as I flick the lighter and hold it to the box. A little quicker than I thought it would, the whole thing ignites.

The orangish yellow flames reflect in Grace's eyes. She's smiling.

In her graceful sort of way, she rummages in her bag and pulls out some paper. There are lines of boyish handwriting on it. With a look of resolve, she tosses it into the fire and I cheer.

"*Hell* yeah!"

With each thing she tosses, she becomes looser — more joyful and light, like she's lifting a weight off her shoulders.

When she tosses the last thing ... a necklace he gave her with *'forever'* inscribed on the front, she's a whole new Grace. Or rather, she's back to her original self ... beautiful, whimsical, and free.

Something catches the corner of my eye and I turn to see what it is. Far down the beach, there are two sets of lights. *Flashlights,* I realize, as they begin to move in closer.

"Shit,"

"What?" Grace says, still euphoric.

"Patrollers. We gotta put this out."

Grace's eyes widen as she spots them too.

I kneel down in the sand and quickly begin to smother the fire with it. Grace joins me with a sense of urgency as the flashlights inch down the beach.

When we're sure it's out, we make a run for it, leaving a suspiciously large heap of sand behind us.

As we run, wind blowing through our hair, helpless laughter bubbles out of Grace's chest.

I look over at my friend and feel only joy. Our lives may not be perfect, but moments like these make it all worth it.

* * *

On Saturday, we decided to have our morning drinks on the beach — green tea for her and coffee for me. Later we'll slather ourselves in tanning lotion and enjoy the sun, but on this blissful morning we agree to be intentional about spending time with God. Earlier I told Grace about my meeting with Kaya and how she reserves her whole Saturday for time with Him. It reminded her of the printout study Kaya passed out on Job, and she suggested spending time with Him

ourselves this morning.

So she lays on her belly on the towel we spread out, thoughtfully writing on the paper, while I start my second ever Pinterest board — one that doesn't have anything to do with fitness and nutrition. The ocean waves cleanse my soul as I pin my favorite scriptures to the new board.

"Do you regret last night?" Grace says, out of the blue.

I raise a brow, "Burning stuff?"

"Yeah."

"No," I say, "Why would I?"

"Well, because Sam was a big chunk of your life."

I furrow my brow and shake my head, "Those letters aren't something I'd feel comfortable bringing into my marriage. When we get married, I want it to be a clean slate for both of us, you know? Nothing of the past matters at that point. From then on it's just me and him, because *that's* the start of our life together."

She smiles, "I like that."

I take a sip of my coffee, "Why do you ask? Do you regret it?"

She shakes her head, "No … not really. But I do feel some sort of … I don't know, *loss,* I guess. It's like I put a huge piece of me to rest for good, which naturally generates some feelings of loss, but it's also freeing at the same time."

I smile at my friend, playing with a tendril of her hair, "Everything's a process, Grace. This is just a part of it."

43

Grace

Two months later ...

I play the recording that I took on my phone again – my baby's heartbeat rushes through the speakers and my mom grins widely on the computer screen.

"Awww, my precious grandbaby."

I've already shown her my most recent sonogram. I can actually see the profile of my little love now and his or her tiny fingers.

"Corinne," A voice says on her end of the video call, "We need you back on the floor."

"Okay," she says.

When the person leaves, she rolls her eyes, "I wish they would give me a minute."

I smile. I've noticed I've been doing that a lot more lately.

"I know you have to go," I say, "But what are you doing tonight? I could use some help with nursery shopping.

"Oh, honey," She smiles apologetically, "I really want to, but it's just ... well ... I have something."

I roll my eyes, "That clinic would fall apart without you."

"Well," she blushes, "It's not that actually … it's just, well, it's silly really."

I raise a brow, "What is it then?"

She blushes more.

"Mom?" I push.

"Well, it's sort of like a date thing."

My mouth drops open, "*What?* You're going on a *date?*"

She shushes me, glancing around, "Keep it down."

My still-open mouth smiles, "With *who?*"

"Just a guy I met …" she says, "It's not a big deal."

"It *is* a big deal. You haven't dated in years."

She winks, "As far as *you* know, that is."

My eyes widen.

She laughs, "I'm just kidding. You're right."

"So how long have you been seeing him?" I waggle my brows.

She fidgets with a loose strand on her scrubs, "I don't know … I guess a couple months now."

"*Mom!*" I say, giddy for her.

"Okay, okay," she says, smiling, "Enough of that talk. I gotta get going."

I chuckle, "Go get 'em tiger."

I've never seen my mom so shy. It's honestly adorable.

My stomach growls angrily even though I just had a snack. It seems like my stomach is a bottomless pit lately, especially when it comes to my latest craving: olives.

I slide off of my bed and eye my reflection in the mirror. Everything on me looks like the same old Grace except for my belly, which is just beginning to show the slightest bit. If I wear loose clothing, you still can't tell.

For about the fifth time this week, I think of Liam – how I left him hanging. I never got back with him about that Thursday … never told him what I meant to. And the sad part is, I don't really even know *why* I didn't.

It started with being far too busy when I got home from Maryland. My clients were submitting orders left and right the previous week and I had a lot of catching up to do. But after that, I'm not sure what it was. Maybe I was just scared … every time I went to text him, I could feel myself chickening out. Making up a reason *not* to.

Back in Maryland, Rae agreed that it seemed like he liked me, but now with so much time passed, there's no telling if he's still interested.

But I'll never know for sure if I don't go talk to him.

I lift my shirt up to feel my belly, which is starting to become slightly firm. I don't have much time … if I'm going to do it, I need to do it soon.

The truth is, I've *missed* Liam's company. Since Rae pointed out how fresh everything with Jayden was, I tried to back off … give myself some space. But the thing is, I don't think space is what I need anymore. I think what I need is to get this off my chest.

To: Liam

Sent: 12/19/19

Time: 12:26 pm

"I know this is way late … but … you down for that rain check now?"

---

* * *

It's practically a blizzard outside by 5 p.m., but it's nothing Persia and her tire-chains can't handle. As I make my way to

Liam's house, I wonder if maybe it's fate that his whole family is on vacation ... everyone *but* him because of work. If he'd been able to go with them, maybe this conversation would never have happened. I'd have missed my chance and I'd never really know if there was something

in store for us.

Just in case, I pray as I drive. For God's will mostly, but I'm careful to add my desires as well.

The snow assaults my face as I make the familiar pilgrimage to the Crosses front door. He opens it for me immediately and ushers me in. My teeth are chattering as he hands me something warm: A steaming cup of hot cocoa.

I smile down at the mini marshmallows and look up at him for the first time. Side grin, chestnut brown eyes, neatly spiked hair ... yes. This is the man I've missed.

"Hiya," He says.

I can smell his fresh spearmint scent mixed with something much stronger: wood smoke. I can hear a crackling fire going in the living room.

"Did you make us a fire?" I say, excited.

"Fires are a winter essential," He says, nodding to the living room.

We make ourselves comfy on the couches in front of the fireplace and I sip my cocoa, not sure where to start. It's surprisingly not awkward. Just ... much anticipated.

"So they left you behind, huh?" I say, peeking at him over my glasses, "In this big empty house?"

"Yeaaahh," He says, "What kind of family are they, anyway?"

"A beautiful one," I say, "I love them so much."

He chuckles, "I'm glad to hear that."

"I was gonna tell you," I say, setting down my cup, "I um ... took your advice."

He leans forward on his palms, "What advice is that?"

"To make up with my mom ..."

"Yeah?" He says, gazing intently, "How'd that go?"

"Amazingly," I smile down at my knees, "She's ... well, *we're* like family again."

He smiles, "See? I told you that you needed to take that first step."

"Yeah ..." I say, clearing my throat.

How do I start this??

"I guess ... I also wanted to apologize to you for something."

He raises a brow, sipping his cocoa.

"I'm sorry I kind of blew you off on our rain check a couple months ago ..." I say, "I didn't mean to."

He laughs, "I was starting to think you're just really bad at getting back with people."

I shake my head, "No. Honestly, this is going to sound really weird, but I was trying to be fair to you."

"Fair to me?" He inquires, "How do you mean?"

"Well ..." I start, taking a deep breath, "Hanging out with you was really fun. *Surprisingly* so. But ... I have to admit ... I wasn't being completely honest with you."

He nods and waits for me to find my words.

"See ... around the time I met you, I had just gone through a horrible breakup. I mean, *horrible.* My ex had cheated on me after years of dating."

Liam purses his lips, "I know."

"I — wait, what?" I eye him curiously now, "You know? What do you mean?"

He frowns, "I mean, just by the way you went off on me in the car and that message you left me beforehand ... it wasn't hard to guess you'd been through something like that yourself. Recently."

"Oh," I blush.

"And usually I wouldn't pursue someone who treated me the way you did," He smiles, "But having picked up on that ... I don't know, I guess it was easy for me to give you a pass. Here was this beautiful, *spirited* girl who'd been terribly wronged somehow... it didn't seem fair."

My heart flutters.

Beautiful.

Spirited.

But then I frown, "Am I a pity-friend?"

He smiles, amused, "A what?"

"Someone you show interest in because you feel sorry for them. For being broken."

He shifts, "Well that's certainly not true. In fact, I remember feeling intrigued by you."

He pauses for a moment, making eye contact with me, "I still *am* intrigued by you."

My tongue feels dry all of the sudden, because there's my answer. He *is* still interested. That makes this conversation all the more vital.

"Liam ..." I say, wringing my hands. I resist the urge to scoot close to him.

I can't. Not yet.

"I won't keep pretending that liking me is a simple decision ..." I say, "Or rather, I can't keep letting *you* think that."

He sets down his cup and looks at me inquisitively, "What do you mean?"

"I'm not ..." *Ugh.* "Well, I'm not just totally available."

His face falls, "You're back with your ex?"

"No, no," I say, holding up a hand, "*Definitely* not. It's just that ... I now have baggage from that relationship that I'll have to carry with me ... for literally *ever.* I don't think it's fair of me to ask you to accept it."

He leans forward, "Grace ... I don't want you to worry about that. If I'm going to date *you,"* My heart flutters again at the mention, "I'm going to date *all* of you. Not just the pretty parts. If you've built up some walls, rightfully so, then that's okay. You'll have to learn what it's like to be with someone who actually cares about you enough to take them down slowly ... at your pace."

I'm taken aback by his bluntness. If there was a shadow of doubt in my mind about his interest, there's absolutely none now. But then, my countenance falls. I feel a lump forming.

"Liam, that's really, *really* sweet of you ... but you're still not getting it. I'm not just some complicated girl inside who needs gentle care to be okay ... I'm ..."

I take a deep breath and swallow the lump in my throat. Just rip it off like a Band-Aid.

"I'm pregnant."

His eyes widen for a moment and then resume back to normal. If I'd blinked, I'd have missed it — this glitch in his otherwise careful composure. His Adam's apple bobs and he sits back in his chair, frowning. The silence seems to last forever as he rubs his hand across the light stubble of his chin and stares into the fireplace.

I squeeze my eyes shut, unable to take it anymore, "Please say something."

He breathes heavily out of his nose and makes me sit in silence a few more minutes — nothing but the crackle of the fire to keep me.

"You're pregnant," He repeats slowly.

I nod, feeling miserable. I'd just started to experience joy again. Now I can feel it draining from me.

"And it's your ex's?" He says.

My brows pinch, "I haven't been sleeping around since then if that's what you're asking."

He shakes his head, "It's not. I'm trying to gauge how deeply into our lives your ex would be."

My heart stops. Is he saying that "we" are still an option?

I shake my head, "Uh, yeah, don't worry about him. He's not interested."

"In you or in his baby?" Liam says.

"Both of us," I say, swallowing the lump hard.

"Hm," he rumbles, sitting back in his chair again. He gifts me with another minute of silence. Then I hear him mumble something under his breath:

"I suppose it wouldn't be the end of the world."

I lean in, sure I've misheard, "What'd you say?"

His eyes meet mine, thinking carefully, "I'm not sure this is something I've ever told you about myself, but something I've always wanted to do — always *thought* I'd do — is adopt. You know, as like, a way to give back what my parents did for me and Sakura."

I nod, tongue feeling dry again.

"Now of course, I thought that would be *years* in the future. And maybe it still is. Who can really say? God's plans are not my plans."

I wait, hoping he means what I think he does.

"But something I've always held fast to is this: Why would you bring more babies into the world, when there are already so many babies already in it who need to be loved? Not to say I don't want one of my own someday. I definitely want at least one. But that's beside the point. I guess what I'm saying is … I'm not totally opposed to this. You and me, I mean. I'm willing to give it a shot."

My eyes widen and my heart caves. I feel the tears filling eyes.

"That's not to say it'll for sure work out," He clarifies, "I'm not saying I'm completely ready for this … I guess I'm just saying … let's see how it goes?"

I nod, tears streaming. Without thinking, I crawl into his chair.

He stiffens for a second, but as I rest my head on his shoulder, he softens, wrapping his arms gently around me. My crying is silent, but I still can't say words. Gently, he strokes my hair. We stay like this for a few minutes until the fresh tears stop.

"You're gonna be okay, Grace." He says.

I smile, fully aware of my snotty-nosed self.

I wipe the snot on my sleeve and pull myself from his shoulder. I look into those deep brown eyes, associating his words with his face.

I know for a fact my face is not as pleasing of a view: Red, puffy, wet — but even knowing that, I can't help but get lost in that sea of chocolate-colored irises with the little golden flecks.

My eyes flick down to his lips, noticing the lower lip is fuller than the top … beautifully sculpted, really. When my eyes meet his again, his warm gaze is intent.

He doesn't look at me like he wants to devour me … like I am a sexy piece of meat. His eyes don't hold the intensity of sexual desire, like Jayden's always had. Instead they are soft and caring.

He tucks a lock of hair behind my ear and slowly brings his face close to mine. I can feel the warmth of his breath. But while everything Jayden did could only be described as "taking", Liam *waits* for me to complete the gesture ... to give my permission.

I bring my fingertips to his jaw, feeling it for the first time. In a slow, relishing movement, I close my eyes and touch my lips lightly to his.

He brings his hand to the back of my neck and gently presses us closer, a deep rumble reverberating in his chest.

Usually, this is the part where the kiss gets indelicate, clothes get thrown, and bodies collide - but here and now, for Liam and I, it's where this kiss ends.

As we pull apart, searching each other's faces, we smile.

Because of the simplicity of the kiss, the pure lack of romance (thanks to my snot), and because this might just be the start of something new.

44

Rae

I position myself at the starting line, flexing my fingers in and out of my palms. I mentally count down from three before kicking off the dirt behind me and dashing into a full sprint. I run *hard,* not stopping when my lungs begin to burn, trying to keep pace with my legs. I push my body to its limit, leaving my doubts far, far behind me.

Just a little farther, I tell myself, amazed at how fast I can go, and I keep this up until my mind is clear of anything other than the ache in my stomach.

When I finally stop, my body is shining with exertion. I walk over to my bag and pull out my water, collapsing onto the grass after the first three swallows. I lay there, staring up at the sky, thinking about absolutely nothing, and it is wonderful. My chest rises and falls heavily, trying to reclaim some sort of steady rhythm.

I have learned that this helps me when I'm overthinking my scars. I just have to get up and physically *run* from the negativity, and soon after I'm back to normal.

It's been two whole months since I last wore any bracelets. The only thing adorning my wrists is the occasional hair tie. With this success in mind and effective coping methods in place, I finally feel ready to do what I'm about to do.

I pull out my phone and log into Lulu's boutique. I open my cart and gaze at the beautiful dress I put there: A long mermaid style — slightly different from the one I wore and loved at the fitting, but in ways I never knew I'd love. The sweetheart neckline has a stunning lacey addition that gracefully goes up to my neck with a dainty design. It is still sleeveless, but the lace part covers my chest scar in a way that makes me feel confident and beautiful. I figure I can allow myself baby steps — arms bare, chest covered — that way I won't be overthinking both sets of scars on my actual day. I will be free to feel like a lovely bride.

I take a deep breath and hit the "buy" button.

—

Thank you! Your order has been processed!

—

I smile, almost squealing with delight. This happiness that came from finding my identity elsewhere … nothing can match it. Not any physical person or thing. The void inside me has been filled with something bigger than temporary pleasures, and It feels infinite. It feels like joy.

With so many wedding details coming together, I find myself *finally* getting excited for May.

As I pass by Kaya's house on my way home from the gym, I see the flowers we planted together are in full bloom. The purposefully drooping white blooms of Snowdrop flowers and the cheerful blue bunches of Early Scilla poke through the clean sheet of snow, giving Kaya that "pop of color" she wanted.

I've actually been waiting to hear from her all day. After months of praying, everyone at A&B is on the edge of their seat awaiting her much anticipated news. When I walk through my door, the message finally arrives:

From: Kaya

Sent: 12/19/19

Time: 2:04 pm

Surgery successful! This girl is cancer free!"

—————————

45

Grace

Five months later …

I fuss with the sash of my floor-length dress, trying to tie it so it flatters my bump. It's harder than I thought, so Rae's mother comes over to help me. Somehow, she ties it beautifully, in a way that makes me look like a model for a maternity magazine. I thank her with a smile and reach down to buckle my beige shoes, but I can't reach them either. I eye Ms. Brooks with an apologetic smile and she chuckles, coming over to help with them too.

"You're so beautiful, child. I've never seen someone carry their pregnancy so gracefully."

I don't feel like that's true, but I just wink at her, "It's all in the name."

The door to the bathroom slowly creaks open and both of our heads turn. Out walks Rae in the most gorgeous white mermaid gown. It looks like it was made for her.

"Oh …" Ms. Brooks places a hand to her heart and her face submits to a tearful smile, "There's my baby girl."

Rae smiles, "Stop it, mom, no crying."

A tear falls down her face anyway, "You're just so stunning."

They envelope each other in a tight squeeze.

"Hold it, missy!" Rosie says, emerging from the bathroom with a tube of mascara.

Rae laughs, "No, Rosie, it's enough already!"

She comes anyway, "You asked me to do your makeup. Now do you trust me or not?"

Rae rolls her eyes and bends down for Rosie to swipe it over her lashes a few more times.

"There," she says, "Perfect!"

Rae looks in the mirror and her lips part. She brings her fingertips to her face.

"Wow," she breathes.

I go over next to her and smile at us both in the mirror, "You *do* look gorgeous."

She smiles, "I don't think I've looked this good in my life."

"It's your wedding day!" Rosie says, "That's how you should feel."

Rosie went with a look that's unquestionably "Rae" — natural with just the slightest bit of glitz for the occasion.

There's a knock on our door.

"Come in!" we sing.

In steps Rae's dad, decked out in his military attire per Rae's request.

"Oh," He says, eyes falling on her.

Rae steps forward, looking down at her dress and then up at her dad, "What do you think?"

He shakes his head, looking her up and down with a smile, "I think you're the most beautiful bride I've seen since your mother."

Livia steps into the room with her beige bridesmaid dress, "Does that mean I've been removed from that position?"

Rae laughs as her dad kisses Livia on the head, "You both are the best things I've ever done," Then he looks at his wife, "My three treasures."

He opens his arms wide and they all go in for a group hug. It warms my heart to see. I can only hope I make a family like this for *my* baby girl.

They all separate and Mr. Brooks looks at Rae, "You ready to do this?"

She takes a deep, catchy breath, "Is it that time?"

He nods, "We're ready to line up."

She closes her eyes and breathes out. With a nod, she says, "Okay, I'm ready."

As we all line up, I can feel how special this is going to be. Having been let in on Rae's final goal for her and Adam as an engaged couple — to be abstinent until this very day — I can't imagine how elated they must feel for having truly lived up to their goal. Today is the day it all becomes worth it. Not only are they becoming one, but from here on out, there'll be no more guilt about sex. Everything is approved of and even *encouraged* by God to promote their oneness.

The processional music starts up — *"Long Ships"*, by Enya, and we all begin walking. As I make my way up the lush, grassy aisle, I feel slightly self-conscious about my bump, but then I catch sight of Liam and he blows me a kiss.

I smile through a blush, reaching up to straighten my glasses. When we're all lined up, Rae makes her gorgeous debut, and I make sure to sneak a glance over at Adam. Sure enough, his eyes are red-rimmed and overjoyed to see her. My heart melts all over again.

The ceremony is over in the blink of an eye. Thank goodness I remembered to do all the things I'm supposed to do. Straighten her dress, take her bouquet, hand her the ring. She and Adam share a tastefully romantic kiss, and just like that, they are Mr. and Mrs. Adam Compton.

The guests cheer as they run back down the aisle to "*This Will Be*", by Natalie Cole.

The DJ announces that the couple will be taking photos and asks everyone to proceed to the reception — a grassy area not too far from here, where we spent all morning decorating with sparkly lights and colorful lanterns.

As we all make our way over, I feel a light tap on my shoulder. I turn to see a blonde girl with light blue eyes. She smiles at me.

"Hadley," I say, "you made it."

"I did!" She says, "Thanks for the invite."

Our friendship hadn't grown the way I thought it would, but she still came to my baby shower and blessed me with a bunch of little girl clothes.

I pull a tendril of her neatly curled hair and it bounces, "Your hair! What'd you do with it?"

"Chopped it all off," She smiles, "You like it?"

"It's adorable," I say, nodding at her shoulder-length curls, "very happy and bubbly."

"I love it," she agrees, "I thought to myself, why not go a little Marilyn Monroe, right? You only live once."

I laugh, "It suits you."

A server comes by with a tray of sparkling juice. We both take a glass.

She inches closer and brings her voice to a whisper, "Hey, did you hear what happened with Jayden?"

I raise a brow, "No?"

I'd done a good job of trying to forget about him though.

"Well, he moved. To freaking *Madrid*."

"*What?*" I say, "What for?"

She shrugs, "I don't know. Some job thing I guess. Good riddance, right? One less face we gotta worry about."

"Amen," I say, clinking my glass to hers.

Suddenly a strong hand wraps around my waist from behind and I smile as Liam appears by my side.

"Hey, beautiful. Can I steal you for a sec?"

Hadley looks between the two of us, waggles her eyebrows and steps away.

"Who was that?" Liam says, guiding us off to the side.

"Um," I glance back at Hadley, "It's a long story."

"Grace!" I hear from a few feet away.

My mother is weaving her way through the guests, hand-in-hand with her new beau. I got to meet Stan for the first time two months ago.

"About time she brought you around," I had said to the well-groomed man. He was older, but good looking for his age. The only thing that gave it away were prominent smile lines around his eyes and his dark salt-and-pepper hair. He was good-natured and polite — a gentleman to my mother, and that's really all I could ask for in a potential stepdad.

"Hey mom," I say, giving her a squeeze, "Sup, Stan." We fist bump.

"I don't think you've met Liam yet, have you?" I say to him. My mom had, and *loved* him. *"He's way better than that Jayden boy,"* she'd said.

Liam holds out a hand and Stan shakes it, "I haven't, but it's a pleasure."

"Same here," Liam smiles.

My mom looks back to me, "So where are Rae and her man headed after this?"

"Italy," I smile, "Adam's been saving up."

"Wow," mom says, "What a dream!"

"Grrraaaccceee!" I turn and see Aunt Kim running for me.

She bear-hugs me and then eyes my belly, "Oh my gracious, Great-Aunt Kim can't *wait* to meet *you!*"

I smile widely, "Liam, this is my aunt. Well, second cousin, but whatever. She's Aunt Kim to me."

She turns to Liam and looks him over, "Oh my my, you are *handsome* aren't you? I've heard lots about you, Liam — I have high expectations, you hear?"

Liam just laughs, "Yes ma'am."

After about ten minutes of chatter, mom and Aunt Kim get into a heated discussion about medicine. With them occupied, I turn my attention back to Liam.

"Did you want to tell me something?"

He smiles, rummaging in his pocket, "Well actually, there's something I wanna *give* you."

"Is that Grace I see?" A familiar voice says.

I give Liam a sympathetic look and turn to see Kaya.

"Hey!" I say, giving her a side hug, "How are you?"

She does a little dance — "Happy to be here!"

"Laaaddddiieeess and Gentlemannn!" The DJ calls, "I present to you: Mr. and Mrs. Commmpton!"

We turn our attention to the front of the reception area and Rae is absolutely glowing as she enters with her new husband. Kaya and I cheer.

"And now, we will do the traditional bouquet toss!" He announces, "If I could have all the single ladies come up to the front pleeeaase."

I peek over at Liam and he laughs at me, nodding for me to go up there even though I am no longer single.

Hadley, Aunt Kim, Kaya, and I, with a sprinkling of girls from Rae's family gather together on the main floor.

With a flourish, Rae spins around and tosses the bouquet. If I had to try for it, I wouldn't have gotten it. I can't do many quick movements these days — but something about her spin was calculated perfectly to land right into my hands. No effort required. With an open mouth, I stare at the sunflowers in my hands. Everyone around me cheers.

I take my prize over to Liam as the men do the garter toss.

"I'm so sorry," I say to him, "*What* did you have to give me?"

He shakes his head with a knowing smile, "Not here. You just enjoy yourself for now and we'll talk after."

I frown, "Are you sure?"

"Yes," He says, nodding to the dance floor, "Now go join your girls over there."

Rosie and Rae are getting down to a song I've never heard before, but it has an awesome beat. I may be pregnant, but hell if I'm not gonna dance at my best friend's wedding.

***

By the end of the night, I'm absolutely breathless. The singing, the dancing, and the cleanup after the happy couple left had me shoeless in thirty minutes, and now totally beat. I slowly make my way to a chair and sit as Liam helps pick up the last few things. The extra weight of my belly is no joke on my stamina.

When Liam is done, he walks over to me and holds out a hand, "My queen."

I smile, taking his hand to hoist myself up.

"Are you ready to go?" He says.

I nod sleepily.

He walks me to the truck. His family had let us borrow it for carrying wedding decorations, but the Brooks family said they could get it all home afterwards.

He opens my door for me and helps me in, giving my hand a kiss before going over to the driver's side.

"So what'd you have to give me?" I yawn.

"You'll see," He says, taking my hand in his.

Instead of making the turn that'd take us to my house, he makes one I'm unfamiliar with. I say nothing of it, but the farther out we go, the more awake I become.

Where is he taking me?

We're on a dirt road now, headed for a meadowy area when he makes a right turn into the grass and parks the truck.

"Where are we?" I say, looking around. There's nothing but grassy fields for miles.

He smiles at me, "Stay here a minute."

It feels like forever that he's rummaging around in the back, but soon enough he comes to get me, "Okay, you can get out now."

I raise a questioning eyebrow at him as I take his hand. My bare feet hit the soft grass and I lift my dress with my hands. I circle around to the back of the truck and my eyes widen. I lift my hands to my mouth.

The bed of the truck is piled with blankets and he has lined the rim with sparkly lights. I can feel him watching me, so I look at him and smile, "Is this for us?"

He chuckles, "Well it's not for me and bigfoot."

Smiling, I wrap my arms around him, "This is gorgeous!"

He kisses my neck, "Climb on in."

He has to help me, but eventually I get up there. I collapse onto the softness of the blankets, sighing with deep contentment.

"Alright," He says, "Ready for your present?"

I turn towards him, all smiles, and nod like a child.

"Close your eyes," He says.

I do, holding out my hands.

He puts something small and cold in it, and I open my eyes to see.

"Before you get too excited," He says, "It's not an engagement ring. I'll do a much better job with that. This is more of a ... well ... a *Grace* ring.

I stare down at the beautiful piece of jewelry in my hand. It has a simple rose gold band with a smooth pink stone in the middle. I am instantly enamored with it.

"Did you make this?" I say, slipping it on my ring finger. It's a perfect fit.

"Of course," He said, "That stone in there is Rose Quartz. You said you weren't that into diamonds ... so instead I picked out one that reminds me of you — an alternative birthstone to diamonds."

I spread out my fingers, admiring it with a smile, "Hence, a 'Grace' ring."

"Exactly," He pokes me, "Aren't you gonna ask me what it means?"

I chuckle, "Of course I am. What does Rose Quartz symbolize, Mr. Cross?"

He smiles, "Some say peace and harmony, some say compassion and empathy, all of which are words I'd choose to describe you. But another reason I picked it is because it is known as "The Love Stone" ... and, well, I love *you.* So."

I lock eyes with him, my breath hitching slightly. It's the first time he's ever said it. He keeps his gaze on mine until a grin overtakes my face.

"Really?" I say.

He nods.

I can't help it anymore. I lean over to kiss him — a deep longing kiss — and when we pull away, I say it fast.

"I love you, Liam Cross."

"What?" He says, "I don't think I heard that clearly."

I giggle, whispering now, "I love you, Liam Cross."

He rubs at his ears, "Man, I'm gonna have to get my hearing checked."

I laugh, shouting this time, "I *love* you, Liam Cross!"

"Theeeerrre it is," He grins.

We laugh, falling back onto the pillows and staring into the sky.

For the first time, I realize what a beautiful view we have. There's not a cloud in the sky shielding the blanket of sparkling darkness above. Galaxies of stars are visible, it seems, way out here.

At this moment, with nothing but joy in my heart, I think back to how much my life has changed in the past eight months. I could never have guessed my life would end up here, wrapped in this man's arms, feeling truly loved for the first time in ages. It makes me think of something Liam said to me,

"God's plans are not my plans".

I also recall the first scripture I ever read — the one that started it all —

He counts the number of the stars; He calls them all by name. Great is our Lord and mighty in power; His understanding is infinite.

Scripture Highlight Reel

If you read this book all the way through, congratulations! You just had over 46 encounters with scripture in a real life, applicable setting. You were intentional about spending time with God, and that is always time well spent. Enjoy this highlight reel of all the scriptures you officially have in your repertoire!

- **Psalm 147:4-5** - *"He counts the number of the stars; He calls them all by name. Great is our Lord and mighty in power; His understanding is infinite."* NKJV
- **John 14:13-14** - *"And I will do whatever you ask in my name, so that the Father may be glorified in the Son".* NIV
- **Deuteronomy 31:8** - *"The Lord Himself goes before you and will be with you. He will never leave nor forsake you. Do not be afraid. Do not be discouraged."* NIV
- **Joshua 1:9** - *"Have I not commanded you? Be strong and courageous. Do not be afraid; do not be discouraged, for the Lord your God will be with you wherever you go."* NIV
- **Matthew 11:28-30** - *"Come to me, all you who are weary and burdened, and I will give you rest."* NIV

- **Psalm 139:13-16** - *"For you created my inmost being; you knit me together in my mother's womb. I praise you because I am fearfully and wonderfully made; your works are wonderful, I know that full well. My frame was not hidden from you when I was made in the secret place, when I was woven together in the depths of the earth. Your eyes saw my unformed body; all the days ordained for me were written in your book before one of them came to be."* NIV.
- **Psalm 32:5** - *"Then I acknowledged my sin to you and did not cover up my iniquity. I said, "I will confess my transgressions to the Lord." And you forgave the guilt of my sin."* NIV
- **1st Peter 3:3-4** - *"Your beauty should not come from outward adornment, such as elaborate hairstyles and the wearing of gold jewelry or fine clothes. Rather, it should be that of your inner self, the unfading beauty of a gentle and quiet spirit, which is of great worth in God's sight."* NIV
- **Luke 16:15** - *"He said to them, "You are the ones who justify yourselves in the eyes of others, but God knows your hearts. What people value highly is detestable in God's sight."* NIV
- **Galatians 5:19-23** - *"The acts of the flesh are obvious: sexual immorality, impurity and debauchery; idolatry and witchcraft, hatred, discord, jealousy, fits of rage, selfish ambition, dissensions, factions and envy; drunkenness, orgies, and the like. But the fruit of the Spirit is love, joy, peace, forbearance, kindness, goodness, faithfulness, gentleness and self-control. Against such things there is no law."* NIV
- **John 14:15-17** - *"If you love me, you will keep my commandments. And I will ask the Father, and he will give you another*

Helper, to be with you forever, even
the Spirit of truth, whom the world cannot receive, because it neither sees him nor knows him. You know him, for he dwells with you and will be in you." ESV

- **Matthew 4:4** - *"Man shall not live on bread alone, but on every word that comes from the mouth of God."* NIV
- **Deuteronomy 6:16** - *"Do not put the Lord your God to the test."* NIV
- **Luke 4:8** - *"Worship the Lord your God, and serve him only."* NIV
- **Philippians 4:13** - *" can do all things through Christ who gives me strength."* NKJV
- **James 4:7-8** - *"He gives us more grace. That is why scripture says: "God opposes the proud but shows favor to the humble. Submit yourselves, then, to God. Resist the devil, and he will flee from you. Come near to God and he will come near to you. Wash your hands, you sinners, and*
purify your hearts, you double-minded." NIV
- **Hebrews 4:12** - *"The word of God is alive and active."* NIV
- **Matthew 18:15** - *"If your brother sins against you, go and tell him his fault, between you and him alone. If he listens to you, you have gained your brother."* ESV
- **Jeremiah 1:5** - *"Before I formed you in the womb I knew you, before you were born I set you apart."* NIV
- **Proverbs 31:8** - *"Open your mouth for the speechless, in the cause of all who are appointed to die."* NKJV

- **1st John 1:9** - *"If we confess our sins, he is faithful and just to forgive us our sins, and to cleanse us from all unrighteousness."* NIV
- **Matthew 4:1-11** – this passage is written in Chapter 15 of *Edified.*
- **Identity In Christ List**: These 26 scriptures are written in Chapter 32 of *Edified.*

Acknowledgements

A huge thank-you to my amazing husband — the one who suggested writing a Christian Fiction novel in the first place, *and* who helped me find the perfect name for "Edified". Thank you for brainstorming with me and affirming me as often as I need it. You're exactly the muse I needed to finish this goal of mine.

Mom, I owe my love for writing to you! Forever grateful for our deep discussions about the books we are writing and laughing because we both understand 'writer problems'.

Mariah, thank you for always inspiring me, reminding me of what's important, and believing in me!

One big thank you to my faithful partner in writing, Kaitrin, for all your insight throughout the creation of Edified! Your encouraging comments on my unpolished manuscript turned my doubts about the novel into securities. You helped me see that it was something special and motivated me to see it through.

A big thank you to my amazing production team: My editor, Fatima, for your enthusiasm, and my cover designer, Taylor, for helping me create the book cover I've always dreamed of.

Thank you, Abby, for the amazing bachelorette trip that inspired a spontaneous road trip for our two protagonists <3 They needed it, and so did I.

When I began writing Edified, I had not yet joined Chi Alpha, but I slowly came to realize that the campus ministry felt so familiar to me because it was a lot like the little bible study group I had created called Above and Beyond (A&B). My decision to join Chi Alpha felt very spirit-led, and that feeling was confirmed when I met two girls in particular: Kindall and Felisha. Thank you both for countless nights spent wrapped up in blankets, eating cookies, and bringing our cares to the Lord. Girls who pray together stay together!

Lastly, but most importantly, thank you to the One who led this whole process. Many coffee-dates with you and pre-writing prayer sessions really made this book happen, and I will always be thankful that I can use my writing to connect with You! Thank you for teaching me what it means to find my identity in You, and what it means to be patient and persistent… May Your name be glorified in this work.

Edified Playlist

1. "Moral of the Story" - Ashe (Chapter 1 – Grace and Jayden)
2. "Irreplaceable" - Beyonce (Chapter 3 – Car Ride to Yoga)
3. "Girl" - Marren Morris (Chapter 6 – Home from the Dress Fitting)
4. "Need You Now" - Plumb (Chapter 7 – Officially Late)
5. "Broken Halos" - Christ Stapleton (Chapter 12 – Kaya's Story)
6. "Wouldn't It Be Nice" - The Beach Boys (Chapter 17 – Kitchen Cleaning)
7. "Jar of Hearts" - Christina Perri (Chapter 17 – A Surprise Visit)
8. "Margaritaville" - Jimmy Buffet (Chapter 23 – Stuck in Traffic)
9. "Messages from Her" - Sabrina Claudio (Chapter 25 – Grace's *Rainy Days* Playlist)
10. "Take a Bow" - Rihanna (Chapter 31 – The Final Goodbye)
11. "Soak up the Sun" - Sheryl Crow (Chapter 41 – Road Trip!)
12. "Fire Burning" - Sean Kingston (Chapter 42 – Burn Everything)

13. "The Only Exception" - Paramore (Chapter 45 - Stargazing.)

CPSIA information can be obtained
at www.ICGtesting.com
Printed in the USA
JSHW021231200623
43456JS00002B/100

9 781736 890301